KNOWLEDGE
TOWNS

Higher Education and the City
Costas Spirou, Series Editor

KNOWLEDGE TOWNS

*Colleges and Universities
as Talent Magnets*

DAVID J. STALEY *and*
DOMINIC D. J. ENDICOTT

JOHNS HOPKINS UNIVERSITY PRESS | *Baltimore*

© 2023 Johns Hopkins University Press
All rights reserved. Published 2023
Printed in the United States of America on acid-free paper
2 4 6 8 9 7 5 3 1

Johns Hopkins University Press
2715 North Charles Street
Baltimore, Maryland 21218
www.press.jhu.edu

Library of Congress Cataloging-in-Publication Data is available.

ISBN 978-1-4214-4627-1 (hardcover)
ISBN 978-1-4214-4628-8 (ebook)

A catalog record for this book is available from the British Library.

*Special discounts are available for bulk purchases of this book. For more information,
please contact Special Sales at specialsales@jh.edu.*

For Alexa Marie Reck
DJS

To my wife, Tamsen
DDJE

CONTENTS

ACKNOWLEDGMENTS

David J. Staley

The publication of this book is a testament to the efficacy of remote work. Although we have written this book together, Dominic and I have never met face-to-face before. In July 2020, I received a message over LinkedIn from a venture capitalist in New Hampshire who had read my previous book, *Alternative Universities*, and wanted to meet over Zoom to discuss areas of interest. Over the course of the next two years, Dominic and I have been meeting almost weekly; the conceptualization of this book was carried out over this virtual platform. Google Docs provided a useful forum for writing and revising each other's work. While much of the world grew weary with "Zoom fatigue," I found our meetings to be creative and productive, and I looked forward to each meeting knowing that it would mind-expanding. At various points over the last two years, we have promised ourselves that once it seemed safe to travel again, we would find time for lunch. To celebrate the launch of this book, perhaps now is the time for that lunch together.

I wish to thank Paul Carlson and Mark Zeller, both of whom are working on economic development in rural northwest Ohio and who were early sounding boards for the ideas explored here. Both Paul and Mark grasp the significance of colleges and universities as economic and innovation anchor institutions for their region.

I was fortunate to have been invited by John Jung, Louis Zacharilla, and Robert Bell to deliver the keynote address at the 2020 Intelligent Community Forum (online) Summit on the theme of small colleges as talent magnets. I was starting to use Dominic's concept of a "talent magnet" as a way to think about how colleges in small towns might reinvent themselves, and the ICF keynote afforded me the opportunity to test out many of the ideas elaborated on in this book. They also invited me to write a version of my address, published on the ICF website.

Melissa Morris-Olsen, director of the Center for Higher Education Leadership and Innovative Practice (CHELIP) at Bay Path University, has supported this project in ways she may not fully realize. Melissa invited me to become an honorary faculty fellow at CHELIP, providing me a platform to write a monthly blog on innovation in higher education. In addition, Melissa invited me to present a webinar on the theme of universities as talent magnets.

Dominic D. J. Endicott
I would like to thank Greg Britton for challenging us to turn what was envisioned as an article into a full-length book. I would also like to thank my coauthor, David Staley, for supporting me in the journey of writing my first-ever book. I believe his book, *Alternative Universities*, is the most creative project in truly thinking about the possible evolution of the university, and my initial approach to him was to explore how some of his models could be turned into reality. I never would have thought I could be a writer, but our sessions together and our joint work on this project have given me the confidence to write. I look forward to a lunch with the publication of the book.

The core themes in the book have built on real-life examples, including the emerging knowledge town transformations of Waterville, Maine, through the leadership of President David A. Greene of Colby College, and of Rochester, Minnesota, under the guidance of Stephen Lehmkuhle as inaugural chancellor for the University of Minnesota–Rochester.

We have been inspired by movements such as the Congress for the New Urbanism and the media advocacy organization Strong Towns, which seek to provide an alternative narrative to the model of sprawl that has dominated the past 100 years of development.

There are thousands of leaders of all types in towns, neighborhoods, and cities across America who work to make places better. If not for the daily toil of those who run and work in utilities, schools, ambulances, fire brigades, police, and countless other services, life in many places would be much more difficult. Organizations such as Main Street America have tapped into the drive of many thousands of people who have volunteered to reimagine and improve a downtown core or a run-down neighborhood. Our belief is that the energy of millions of Americans is ready to be unleashed as we set new priorities around what we want our places to be.

The idea of applying the concept of "talent magnets" to place-based strategies came from a lecture entitled "How Towns and Cities Can Become Talent Magnets, and Stay That Way," which I was asked to develop in October 2020 by St. Mary Development Corporation for a conference called The Business of Aging. I had been doing a lot of work on the longevity economy and realized that place was the prime determinant of good aging, and that good places were great for all ages. The term "talent magnets" has been used in the world of human resource management to refer to individuals that attract and nurture the talent of others, and it felt to me that it could be a way of defining what would be an ideal place. Thanks to Catherine Campbell and Tim Bete at St. Mary for providing me with the initial venue and audience to test out these ideas.

St. Mary and Ohio State University, where David Staley is a professor, are only about one hour apart from each other by car. Ohio, where both institutions are located, has often been a hinge state, and I would hope that it could be a fertile ground for some of the ideas in this book in the same way as my adopted home of New England; the British Isles, where I was born; and Catalonia in the Kingdom of Spain, where I grew up.

KNOWLEDGE
TOWNS

INTRODUCTION

The Knowledge Town

AMERICA IS AT THE DAWN of a wave of internal migration that will spawn an explosion of new types of colleges and universities, reaching deep into our country. Just as every town expects a church, bank branch, post office, coffeehouse, or brewpub, we will see a decentralized network of academies acting as cornerstones for the post-pandemic rebuilding of our society and economy. The combined effect of migration, place-based reinvention, and the decentralization of the college experience will pivot the United States toward the first cloud-based economy at continental scale. If we can avoid unnecessary wars or internal conflict and instead put our energy into this societal transition, we will experience a surge in well-being and sustainable economic growth.

The shift to remote work has liberated knowledge workers from the office. The length of the COVID-19 pandemic has vastly accelerated and expanded the prevalence of remote work. Mass adoption of remote work has made it more feasible for many to move to cheaper and better places. As many as 23 million Americans are planning to move permanently, per one survey by Upwork in October 2020.[1] This implies an economic reshuffle of $1.5 trillion in spending, or 6.5% of the

American economy.[2] The shift could be even larger. Perhaps as many as 100 million Americans live in expensive locations, typically along the coasts or close to major American cities,[3] and many could gain a substantial improvement in quality of life by moving to cheaper and better locations.

This groundswell will usher in a renaissance of small locations. Over 30,000 locations in the United States could bid to attract internal economic migrants.[4] As the opportunity for talent migration becomes evident, there will be intense competition among villages, towns, rural areas, and small cities to win over the capacity, energy, and capital of new settlers. This book aims to define the new competition for talent and provide practical approaches for those who want to win the race.

In an American economy increasingly defined by intangible value and knowledge, a place that wants to attract talent will require a thriving academic environment. There is thus a new opportunity for town and gown to partner in place-based regeneration. Regeneration strategies for both places and academic institutions will also be necessary to avoid economic and social decline. The pandemic has accelerated existing trends that put at risk the viability of many colleges and universities while challenging the prospects of many villages, towns, and cities. Colleges and universities will need to challenge aspects of their current model, consult the past, and imagine the future. A good place to start is by reviewing a set of choices for universities covered in the 2019 book *Alternative Universities: Speculative Design for Innovation in Higher Education*.[5]

As town and gown come together to develop a forward-looking strategy, they need to consider the history of each unique place and its institutions, its natural geography, and all of its assets and liabilities. They should also evaluate all possible drivers of attraction. Is the town walkable and bikeable, is the air breathable, are its services good, does it promote community exchange, does it enable innovation and commerce, does it provide cheap and high-quality housing, is it appealing across all generations? We could describe a place that can effectively address these questions as a "talent magnet."

Collaboration between town and gown is not new; it has been a key element in the history of our country. This alliance will be even more important in building the future United States. We will see a new fusion between place, academia, society, and economic growth. We will see the emergence of a highly proactive and socially oriented university or college, defined by Michael M. Crow and William B. Dabars as a "knowledge enterprise."[6] Institutions that fail to adapt will likely decline or disappear, much as have slow-to-adapt business enterprises.

The talent magnet and the knowledge enterprise are the twin sides of a new concept we seek to introduce with this book: the knowledge town. A knowledge town rhymes with a traditional "college town" concept, but takes it to a whole other level. The combined effect of a talent magnet strategy executed by towns and cities and a knowledge enterprise strategy executed by colleges and universities is to reinvent a place while positioning it to thrive in the twenty-first century.

Remote Work Changes Social and Economic Geography

COVID-19 has accelerated the shift of work to the cloud and the intangible or knowledge economy. This trend preceded the pandemic. According to one estimate, "For S&P 500 companies in 2018, tangibles, like real estate and equipment, comprise just 16% of company value, while intangibles, such as IP rights and reputation, are 84%."[7] The cloud is the gateway to this knowledge economy. Indeed, the cloud-mediated knowledge economy is as central to our lives today as farming, manufacturing, or services once were.[8]

COVID-19 has, moreover, accelerated by 5 or 10 years the transition of the US and global economy toward digital services, and broadly toward running core aspects of our economy over the Internet and the cloud. We have now passed an irreversible tipping point, as covered in a 2020 report on post-COVID impact by consulting firm McKinsey.[9] Digital transformation has become essential for almost every business on the planet.

The nature of work has also changed fundamentally due to COVID. Over the course of the pandemic, out of 100 million US knowledge-based workers, about 45% have worked remotely.[10] Firms have experienced good productivity in the new world of remote work, and knowledge workers have enjoyed their newfound flexibility.[11] Thus, some form of remote work now appears irreversible. Over half the knowledge workers surveyed in January 2021 by consulting firm PricewaterhouseCoopers (PwC) wanted to work at home at least three days per week and 29% wanted to work at home five days a week.[12] If this survey is representative, it implies that as many as 29 million American knowledge workers aim to work permanently at home. Leading firms such as Facebook or Twitter have made work from anywhere permanent for many employees.[13] Where tech leads, mainstream businesses will generally follow. Not all firms will allow fully remote work, but the majority will accept or even encourage hybrid models that make it feasible for families to relocate to within two to three commuting hours from central offices.

Knowledge workers and their families, many living in expensive locations due to prior work requirements, can now consider relocating to a wide range of less expensive places, often small towns, secondary cities, and rural areas, without a significant loss in income. For example, Albany, New York, is semicommutable to Manhattan but offers a large improvement in affordability, with average house prices in 2021 at $219,000 compared to $660,000 in New York City.[14] A fully remote family could buy a house in Tulsa, Oklahoma, in 2021 for an average price of $134,000.[15]

For each knowledge worker (and his or her family) that migrates, another two to three service jobs will eventually move with them, so the potential magnitude of job and population migration is larger.[16] Service roles (baristas, grocery workers, teachers, health care workers) have historically been chained to office-based occupations because the service had to be delivered close to where knowledge workers worked or lived. Since knowledge jobs have clustered around expensive cities, this has until now forced many service workers to either live in expensive locations, commute a long way to work, or both, resulting in low standards of living.

Where will these knowledge and service workers move to? Work-based restrictions and family constraints will be important factors, but the choice of destination will also be heavily influenced by the attractiveness of their destination.

Zoom Towns and Colleges

The pandemic saw the rise of so-called Zoom towns: usually secondary cities or rural areas that offer outdoor recreation amenities and a better quality of life. Many businesses were forced to pivot to remote work during the pandemic; as long as a place has robust enough connectivity, knowledge workers can work from anywhere, and thus these workers have been attracted to Zoom towns. Because such towns are frequently located in areas outside of major cities, the cost of living is much lower, so knowledge work salaries from big companies go much further than they could in the urban locations in which company offices are often located. "A new study from the Pew Research Center," reports the BBC,

> found that . . . one in 20 US adults have moved in response to Covid-19, with those younger than 30 most likely to have made the change. Many are urbanites from major coastal cities, like New York and San Francisco, who were spurred by the growing disconnect between stagnant wages and rising living costs as well as the prospect of bigger spaces and access to nature in the American interior. Now that influential companies like Facebook and Twitter have set the tone for long-term remote work even after the Pandemic ends, this young talent has been emboldened to seek out new horizons.[17]

A Gallup poll taken at the end of 2020 indicated that 48% of Americans would move to a small town or rural area if given the chance, which was up from 39% in 2018.

Some regions are acting on this newfound demand. Northwest Arkansas, for example, has started a "Life Works Here" initiative. The plan is to entice 100 new residents to relocate to the region, each of whom will receive $10,000 if they stay for at least a year. New residents might also receive a free bicycle, to traverse the plentiful bike paths in the region, or free annual membership to an arts or cultural organization. To promote these incentives, the Northwest Arkansas Council, which is in charge of the talent attraction campaign, brags: "With one of the best costs of living, plentiful outdoor lifestyle perks, nationally ranked arts, culture and cuisine scenes, and per capita income that's 14% higher than the national average, the Northwest Arkansas region offers a unique opportunity to create balance for those eager to move from congested and expensive larger cities and suburbs."[18] Similarly, "Ascend West Virginia" offers relocators "$12,000 to find a home among our hills and throw in a year of free outdoor recreation," including ziplining, rafting, and skiing. "Our free outdoor gear rentals will make lunch breaks a blast. Remote work from the mountains. It really is that simple," they boast.[19]

Ascend is initially focused on three West Virginia towns: Morgantown, Lewisburg, and Shepherdstown. The Morgantown program makes specific reference to the location of West Virginia University as part of its appeal to remote workers. One incentive, Ascend asserts, is that those who relocate to Morgantown "have the chance to earn remote work certifications through WVU along with access to the university's entrepreneurship ecosystem."[20]

Purdue University has likewise worked to lure knowledge workers to West Lafayette, Indiana. "Work From Purdue" is billed as "a first-of-its-kind remote working community on campus. Ideal for engineers, entrepreneurs, builders, creatives and innovators who have the flexibility to work anywhere and want to live and work among the brightest minds on the university's campus."[21] The program features professional and entrepreneurial programming through Purdue Foundry, a campus incubator; discounts on select continued education programs; a 50% discount for access to a coworking space; housing discounts; access to campus facilities; and a moving stipend of up to $5,000.[22] "Universities have long been selling points for community leaders seeking to widen their regions' appeal to possible new residents," reports the Chronicle of Higher Education, "an effort that may well be supercharged by the pandemic."[23] Indeed, it is our contention that the placement of a college or university—or a knowledge enterprise, as we will detail below—is a critical piece of any region's effort to attract remote knowledge workers.

A Strong Higher Ed Offer Will Be a Key Factor in Choosing a Location

A key relocation factor for many knowledge workers and their families will be proximity to an academic culture. Knowledge workers need to continuously upgrade their skills, so they will naturally benefit from local colleges that can teach these skills. With traditional higher education increasingly unaffordable, many families will also opt for lower-cost undergraduate solutions closer to home. For example, a family might choose a local community college for their children's associate's degree while they remain at home, before sending them away to complete the final two years away from home. Academic institutions also cluster the kind of talent that knowledge workers will enjoy learning from and socializing with. Even as many elements can be delivered online, an important aspect of learning will remain rooted in the physical world. Ultimately, we believe that teachers and students will remain predominantly place bound.

Knowledge work and academic infrastructure will not just be for desk-based jobs. Cloud tools will also become embedded into blue-collar areas such as agriculture, mining, or manufacturing. For example, farmers will need to reskill in precision farming, rewilding, or meat replacement, will want to periodically go back to school, and will prefer to live in a milieu in which new ideas in these fields are shared in coffeehouses, brewpubs, or at church.

As a result, the need for hyperlocal knowledge enterprises will become pervasive across the country. These may look very different from current forms of higher education. The move to the cloud and to remote work has also impacted the fundamentals of what it takes to operate an academic institution. Courses delivered via YouTube or EdX for free are competing with expensive college educations currently delivered over Zoom, ushering in a wave of "creative destruction."[24] Existing colleges that lack the balance sheet and income, and that fail to adapt, are expected to falter or shut down.[25]

But even as some institutions shut down, we will simultaneously see a wide variety of new knowledge enterprises, such as platform universities (organized along the lines of two-sided markets such as Airbnb) or microcolleges.[26] We could imagine a scenario in which a platform university could incubate a series of local microcolleges, some of which could grow to become larger colleges or universities, others could become full-fledged businesses, and others maintain their mission as local educational hubs.

The "micro" phenomenon could in some ways be comparable to the evolution of other hyperlocal enterprises. In the brewery industry, for example, the number of large breweries collapsed through consolidation from over 700 in the 1940s to below 100 by 1980.[27] Starting in the 1970s, we saw an explosion of microbreweries with much lower fixed costs and more innovative practices; these businesses now number over 8,000.[28] While perhaps colleges may find it offensive to be compared to breweries, the impact of innovative practices and reduction in fixed costs could nevertheless be similar.

The 2021 PwC Remote Work Survey also found that business enterprises planned to substantially downsize their city center offices and expand local offices as they rapidly adapt to the post-pandemic, distributed work reality.[29] After a long period of office work consolidation in central areas, we are seeing the pendulum swing hard in the opposite direction. Why should this be any different in academia?

The Connection between Places and Knowledge Enterprises

In seeking to determine the right models for today's environment, we need to consider how places and knowledge enterprises have historically interacted. Towns and cities have been built around access to transport, proximity to water or mineral resources, or for military purposes. But places have also been built around ideas and movements. Early English settlements in the Americas were led by Puritans seeking a place to practice their religion freely. This phenomenon was replicated by the Latter-Day Saints' long search for a place to worship, ending in their settling of Utah.

Colleges and universities require little in capital or population density for their formation. Many great colleges have been built inside large cities, of course. But there has also been a strong current of college foundation in villages and towns, often far away from population centers. Oxford and Cambridge in England were both started in what were tiny villages at the time. The first American university, Harvard, was similarly founded at some distance from the city of Boston, which at the time had a population of 15,000. Harvard's first class, graduating in 1642, had all of nine students.[30] The rural settlement pattern was repeated with what today are large east coast universities, such as Yale, Princeton, Rutgers, or Dartmouth. Many small liberal arts colleges, such as Williams, Amherst, Swarthmore, or Bowdoin on the East Coast; Grinnell, Oberlin, and Carleton in the Midwest; and Pomona and Scripps on the West Coast were founded in what were at the time rural areas. Since 1862, over 100 land-grant universities have been started in the United States, with a mix of urban and rural placements. Many universities were explicitly built as part of the ongoing westward expansion.

Reflecting this mixed pattern, today there is an even distribution of urban, suburban, and rural settings among the over 4,000 degree-granting institutions in the United States. The American dispersion of academic institutions is quite distinct from the European university model, reflecting different demographic constraints and challenges. In 1800, American population density was 5 people per square mile, whereas European density averaged 60 people per square mile.[31] In 1800 many of today's large American cities were so small that they barely registered, whereas the major European cities were well established. In Europe, the typical university model was for children to stay at home, whereas the American model was premised on leaving home under an assumption of lifelong mobility.

The American societal and economic model, with its many flaws, has clearly succeeded in terms of growth. In 1800, the American economy was perhaps 5–10% the size of Europe's, whereas today the regions are at rough parity. This brings us to a critical question: What is the relationship between location density, knowledge, and economic growth? Does economic growth require large, dense cities, or can it flourish in more dispersed environments?

Population Density, Knowledge, and Economic Growth

The prevailing view among many thought leaders has been that cities enjoy substantial economies of scale and thus that the trend is for the growing dominance globally of ever-larger cities. For example, leading global management consulting firm McKinsey has long advocated the dominant role of large cities, predicting that they would drive the bulk of future economic growth.[32] From this vantage point, knowledge enterprises such as universities should also increasingly be colocated with dense urban centers.

Talent indeed benefits from clustering, what we could term "knowledge economies of scale." Being in clusters such as New York City or Silicon Valley makes it easier to switch jobs, collaborate with partners, sell into clients, gain incidental know-how on the next big thing. Geoffrey West of the Santa Fe Institute makes a compelling case about the benefits of scale in his book *Scale: The Universal Laws of Life, Growth and Death in Organisms, Cities and Companies*.[33]

However, even prior to the pandemic, in the United States and elsewhere we have seen countervailing evidence of the benefits of a distributed knowledge model. One of the most famous investors, Warren Buffett, is far from the center of finance in Omaha, Nebraska. In 2018, a large wealth management firm, Bernstein, moved its headquarters from New York City to Nashville, suggesting that it no longer saw a big benefit from being close to Wall Street. There is growing evidence that innovative start-ups can be created in far-flung locations, such as Romania (where UiPath, one of the hottest IPOs in 2021, was founded) or Missouri (where Zapier, sold in 2021 for $4 billion, has been based since its foundation). Leading venture firm Bessemer Venture Partners argued in its *2020 Predictions on the Cloud* that massively valuable companies can be created in almost any global location.[34]

The American Demographic Anomaly

America's demographics are fundamentally different from those of other advanced global regions. It is far less densely populated, and it is also far less urban. Even after two centuries of strong population growth, American density per capita at 90 people per square mile is still much lower than Europe's 285 people per square mile and Asia's 384 people per square mile. The United States' density is comparable to that of Latin America (84 people per square mile) or Africa (117 people per square mile), but with much higher income per capita.[35]

The United States is also far less urban than much of the world, although in this case the divergence has been more recent. Following the US Civil War, the country rapidly urbanized. By 1950 New York City was the largest city in the world and the United States had 4 cities among the top 20. The top 10 US cities in 1850 represented 6% of US population of 23 million, but by 1950 the top 10 US cities accounted for 14% of its population of 150 million.[36]

After 1950, there was a shift toward the suburbs. Construction of the US highway system, the car-centered society, and the massive financing of suburban growth spelled the relative decline of cities. By 2020 the top 10 cities represented only 8% of today's 330 million Americans. In contrast, the prevailing global norm has been urbanization. According to the United Nations, in 1930 global urbanization was at 30%, but by 2018 it had passed 55%. As a result of global urbanization and American deurbanization, by 2020, of the top 150 cities in the world, only 4 were in the United States, with New York City still the largest US city but ranked at number 28 globally. The suburbanization of the United States has endured. Despite anecdotal evidence that younger Americans were flocking to the cities, the urban share of US population has not increased in the past 20 years, rural share has declined slightly, and suburban share has continued to expand.[37] With remote and flexible work, we believe we will see a further erosion of city dominance and a new wave of rural and suburban growth.

The New American Decentralization

The United States has adapted fast to the intangible and cloud economy. Even with the tremendous shocks of COVID-19, US stock-market capitalization by 2020 represented over 55% of global value, up from 32% in 1990.[38] The strongest growth in the United States has been in tech, which is the sector moving fastest into a remote-work and distributed model. Tech firms highly value the benefits of operating in clusters such as Silicon Valley, Boston, or New York City, but these locations also drive high real estate costs, salaries, and employee churn. Many tech firms thus far look to gain substantial economic benefit from decentralization. Where tech goes, the mainstream of the economy typically follows. Tech is today by far the biggest sector in market capitalization. As technology continues to disrupt every other sector, it forces incumbents in those spaces to either adapt or wane.

If knowledge enterprises and the broader knowledge economy do not require high density, and if the trend is toward increasing decentralization, this potentially means that any place in the United States with a critical mass of population, infrastructure, and charm could build a rich and sustainable growth model by attracting top remote talent. We estimate there are over 36,000 potential locations in the United States that could accommodate high-income, remote work and thus evolve to become talent magnets.[39]

If our hypothesis on the decentralization of work is validated, it could have an impact on every aspect of the US economy. For example, US residential real estate is worth over $30 trillion.[40] This value is concentrated into a small number of locations, anchored by the substantial benefits to the highest-paid and richest Americans living and working near these locations. Prior to the pandemic, the top 10 US cities represented collectively over $11 trillion in real estate value, or 34% of all US real estate value, even though they account for 8% of our population and less than .1% of our landmass.[41] Could this real estate value be reallocated, and where to? In this equation, what is the role of town and gown collaboration?

A massive migration of knowledge and service workers into up to 36,000 locations across the United States is an opportunity for both towns and institutions of higher education. However, the same forces creating this opportunity put at risk the economic and social foundations of many towns and institutions. We thus have a crisis: a time of great risk but also a time of unparalleled opportunity.

Talent Magnets

Our species has shown the ability and inclination to make a home almost anywhere on the planet. We have innate preferences, such as a need for community, shelter, food, and energy, and a love for being close to water and vistas.[42] But our engineering prowess means that we can adapt most surroundings to suit our needs or preferences. We are also a restless species, often seeking the greener grass. Thus, in principle, any place has the potential to become a talent magnet. There are perhaps as many as 4 million unique settlements across the globe. Each of these locations has, at least at one point in its history, attracted settlement and created community and has thus been, if only briefly, a talent magnet.

The challenge of talent magnets is that they often become their own worst enemies. Settlers exhaust the local resources, from megafauna in the Pleistocene or woods in Europe prior to the Industrial Revolution, to fisheries, aquifers, and topsoil today.[43] Urban settings also risk rapidly becoming polluted, overcrowded, prone to disease. As new settlers move in, land also becomes scarce, and its price rises, eventually creating an affordability problem for new migrants or for existing residents with lower incomes.

Many places resolve the affordability problem through densification, by clustering tightly, and by going increasingly more vertical. Other places solve this problem through horizontal spread, via suburban sprawl. Each strategy has limitations. Vertical concentration creates risks of disease, environmental degradation, and inequality.[44] Horizontal sprawl creates issues with traffic, pollution, excessive commutes.[45] Vertical or horizontal extremes create loneliness, as many people can become cut off from the regular social exchange of more traditional villages or neighborhoods. These are also fragile solutions: a high-rise is impractical, for example, when the elevator ceases to work as a result of power cuts. Suburbs are similarly of little use if we lose access to cheap petroleum. As we mechanize and automate our vertical or horizontal worlds, we encourage humans to become ever more dependent and physically and mentally fragile.

Talent magnets must be adaptive: it is evidently very different to become an attractive place for 10,000 people, 100,000, 1 million, or 10 million, and each place has its own unique geographical, historical, and cultural constraints. Talent magnets, to remain attractive, must solve the environmental degradation challenges. They must create solutions for affordability. They must encourage community building to share risks and combat loneliness. The best places make the most of their surrounding natural environments and historical underpinnings. They should also encourage lives of purpose and resourcefulness among their populations. In today's knowledge-fueled global system, places must also excel at supporting ongoing skill formation across their populations. This need will only accelerate as we move into a world of artificial intelligence, global connectivity, and cloud-based work.

Many places outside of the largest urban centers are discovering that in order to survive and thrive, like their partners in higher education, they are going to have to do something many of them do not want to do: reinvent themselves.

The remainder of this book is organized as follows:

- In chapter 1 we define twelve key principles behind a talent magnet, illustrating each principle with a scenario that represents a potential path by an individual, a group, or an institution that embodies each principle. These principles seek to encapsulate the rules for small and large societies to succeed given the constraints and opportunities that operate today.

- In chapter 2 we delve into the knowledge enterprise, and we explore how each of the twelve principles of talent magnets can successfully be applied by an academic institution that seeks to evolve to a stronger and more compelling impact on the social, economic, and environmental context of its community.

- In chapter 3 we develop a series of archetypes for town and gown collaboration—in effect, the simultaneous codevelopment of talent magnets and knowledge enterprises. We begin with a virtual blank sheet of paper, a place that has neither a college nor much of a town, and end with exploring how an entire state or region could seek to evolve.

- In chapter 4 we consider how different personas or institutions could take on the principles developed throughout the book and apply them to their own context. We again begin small, considering the potential actions of ordinary citizens, and end with the potential moves of some of the most powerful institutions and cities in the land.

- In the conclusion we wrap up our ideas and propose some potential next steps for readers.

1

Modern Society and a New Definition of Talent Magnets

THE ECONOMIC AND SOCIETAL MODEL in place since the end of World War II, what we might call the motor society, is giving way to a new model. Those places that adapt fastest to the new rules will prosper. Failure to adapt will likely lead to disappointment and decline. In the business world, a new firm model and playbook is emerging. One venture capital firm, Wing VC, has coined the name "Modern Enterprise" for the winning approach, which they define as an "agile workplace, built on data and powered by AI (Artificial Intelligence)."[1] By extension, we can think of the concept of a modern society, similarly defined by agility, use of data, and the application of artificial intelligence. In addition, we might also think of a society designed to deliver purpose, community, biodiversity, and well-being. The modern society concept can operate at the level of a community or hamlet, a village or neighborhood, a town, a city, a region, or a country.

As with Hemingway's remarks on bankruptcy, the change in the playing field has happened gradually, then suddenly. The gradual phase was the buildup over decades of unsustainable trends such as excess debt, inequality, obesity, excess resource use, and high pollution, collectively creating pressure for change. A key enabler of transformation was the maturation of the core information technology infra-structure: cellular, broadband, computers, smartphones, software, and cloud technology. The sudden phase was the wrenching shift in 2020 brought about by COVID-19, the global response to the pandemic, and the acceleration by five or more years in the rate of remote work and in the level of digital adoption.[2]

In the postwar model, roads and highways were designed for car speed, not human travel. Zoning design separated activities that had historically belonged together and segregated communities by race, age, and income. Regulatory and accreditation schemes limited work and educational possibilities. Cities spent heavily to attract companies in the hope that they would bring jobs. Knowledge workers were largely chained to the office and the daily commute. Pollution and resource use were neither well measured nor effectively managed. As this model has reached its end stage, families have increasingly been required or encouraged to buy expensive housing, education, and health care, with ever-declining value for the money. What were previously viewed as idealized talent magnets, such as the Motor City model of Detroit or the prevailing suburban town or city, are no longer attractive.

In modern societies, knowledge work becomes flexible, remote, and measurable. Families can thus more easily move to the location that best suits them. Degrees and diplomas can be earned from anywhere, and their value can more easily be measured.

In this context, forward-looking towns and cities invest in attracting workers and families, knowing that jobs will follow. They learn that they must provide clean air, walkable and bikeable neighborhoods, a balanced urban and rural ethos, housing that delivers high value at low cost, and a diverse population mix. They harness the tools of the digital economy, delivered as a public utility. This is analogous to the successful adoption of public water, electric, and gas systems of earlier eras.

A critical factor in ushering in modern societies has been the mass unplanned experiment with remote work during 2020 and 2021, with growing indications that remote work will become a mass phenomenon well into the future.[3] The pandemic came at a time when there was sufficient infrastructure to support a "good enough" work experience from home.

What is the new playbook for places that want to become talent magnets in the modern society? We can consider 12 new rules of place-based success, mirroring the 12 elements of a knowledge enterprise that we define in chapter 2:

1. Act local but harness the cloud.
2. Encourage lives of purpose, not of possessions.
3. Clear the air and slow down the streets.
4. Harness the economic potential of the community.
5. Recruit purpose-driven migrants.
6. Support the bionic worker.
7. Engage lifelong learning.
8. Build an innovation cluster.
9. Unleash the commercial dynamo.
10. Rewild your population and land.
11. Turn housing into a service.
12. Rediscover the lost art of placemaking.

These are detailed further below. In each case, we first define the rule and then develop a scenario that illustrates how the rule could be applied.

Rule 1. Act Local but Harness the Cloud

Places must deliver intensely local initiatives. At a local level, the impersonal nature of the net makes way to real-world community, mutual care, and positive externalities of place. Local strategies are best when incremental and when they are premised on the unique history, geography, infrastructure, nature, and culture of each place. In the motor society introduced by Henry Ford, we homogenized use of land, the nature of schools, the restaurant experience, and homes, often with a lowest-common-denominator approach. This delivered a form of efficiency but robbed us of agency, adaptability, and soul. Returning to localism requires collaboration among all citizens who have a stake in a certain place, certainly those living there but also those with familial, collegiate, work, or other connections. A central theme of local strategies is that they are regenerative. "Regenerative" means that they do not exhaust but rather replenish the resources they use. In agriculture, mass farming is exhaustive, requiring ever greater inputs of machines, fertilizers, and pesticides per unit of output. Regenerative farming replenishes the soil by blending various combinations of crops and animals to deliver higher profit per acre, reduce the need for industrial inputs, and increase carbon capture.[4] It is a great example of a triple win: economic, social, and environmental sustainability. By analogy, regenerative streets deliver combinations of housing, bike paths, walkable areas, transit, and cars, to bring higher city profit per acre and reduce expense in parking spaces, highways, and social care; and reduce carbon emissions.

But localism alone can lead to myopia and irrelevance. Places must also understand and plug into the global cloud-based economy, learning to exploit its potential. The knowledge economy is now the dominant paradigm in the world of work. A key indicator is that whereas in 1970 the value of stocks was 80% driven by "hard assets," in 2021 over 85% of global market capitalization was based on intangible assets. With advances in fiber-based and wireless communications, it is increasingly feasible to tap into the knowledge economy from anywhere. Investment in creating an environment that is attractive to knowledge workers generates a strong economic windfall, since these professionals will tend to drive innovation, spending, and new jobs wherever they settle.

Scenario

A remote developer team settles into a small, isolated, town, attracted by quality of life, low-cost housing, outdoor activities, clean air, and good fiber or satellite access. Over time, team members form families and deepen roots while working for a succession of global clients.

Remote working continues to expand as global corporations are forced to adapt to the demands of their most productive employees and to competition for talent from "remote-first" companies.[5]

Local institutions such as colleges, museums, cafés, and coworking and maker spaces help locals and new residents develop a broad range of skills, offering everything from new skills (low-code access to artificial intelligence programming) to ancient tradecrafts (coppicing trees and building log cabins). Flexible work allows settlers and their families to spawn small-scale farms, brewpubs, pod schools, manufacturing plants, and construction companies, while maintaining high incomes from their knowledge jobs. Some start-ups formed in the region are acquired at good prices by global technology companies or private equity firms, recycling wealth into the community and seeding an angel investing network.

The town attracts ever more "remotes," including friends of the early "remote settlers" and others pulled in by word of mouth or by new work opportunities. Service jobs begin to expand as new settlers generate the need for more schoolteachers, doctors, grocers, butchers, fishmongers, cheesemongers, baristas, sommeliers, plasterers, carpenters, and electricians.

There is a risk with growth that this town becomes another overpriced Boulder, Colorado or another sprawling exurb. But the thoughtful leaders in this town design and implement a "balanced growth/green strategy," reducing vehicle miles traveled, gradually densifying, and maintaining a low cost, clear air advantage.[6]

The central core of the town moves from homes averaging two stories to homes averaging four stories, in many cases doubling or tripling the number of homes without using new space and while maintaining the affordability that initially attracted settlement. Car capacity on streets and in carparks is reduced by two-thirds and is replaced by a mix of transit, protected bike-paths, and walking paths, so that eventually most trips below three miles are people powered and carless.

The additional density, combined with enlightened zoning, massively explodes the number and variety of local stores, cafés, theatres, and bars. As the dense core becomes ever more attractive to live in and pulls in further demand, the town continues to expand upward incrementally, along what urban designer and author David Sims calls the "Linear Barcelona" strategy of incremental densification.[7]

The city planning committee anticipates the risk of sprawl. Early in the town expansion, it acquires and repurposes much of the surrounding land for a variety of regenerative economic uses, including ecotourism, outdoor activities, rewilding, and regenerative farming and fishing, as well as future expansion of the downtown core and the preservation of critical communication links via rail, road, or water.

The combination of a thriving downtown and an enriching periphery becomes an ever more compelling magnet for visitors, many of whom decide to settle permanently. When the vertical limit of six stories is reached in the downtown core, the city decides among competing strategies for expansion. One option is to develop a parcel of land adjacent to the core into a new "gently dense" neighborhood while maintaining the walkable/bikeable ethos of the town core.[8] Another is to build a green connection (combining trains, bike paths, slow-mobility roads, and other tunnels) and develop a new satellite within five miles of the initial core. The city decides to pursue both, supported by a local bank that recycles local deposits into high return-on-investment expansion projects.

The income of the city grows, and its balance sheet becomes substantial: the land that it acquired cheaply is now much more valuable, some of the start-ups it helped incubate have paid off, and it collects a diverse range of taxes and fees from a growing set of economic activities. This allows it to continue to anticipate future green growth, while ensuring affordability and healthy living. An ever-growing mix of "townies" and "globals" become involved in designing and building the future city. A digital twin model of the town and a wide range of future scenarios are available for all to consult via mobile, laptop, or VR glasses. Anyone can build a future scenario, with intuitive "no code" software. Scenarios can be voted on by all residents, from the master plan to the choice of facing and material in the homes. This democratic process determines the "purpose" of the town as it continues to evolve. The digital twin also includes a financial model, available to investors and builders. Local developers are encouraged to take part in new building, working within form-based codes that reflect the town purpose. The transparency of the town development model attracts financing from outside, supplementing local financing.

Rule 2. Encourage Lives of Purpose, Not of Possessions

Acquiring and showing off possessions generates serotonin, among the most powerful mood controllers in the animal kingdom. But the hit is evanescent, and this behavior often triggers an escalation as peers seek to match or outbid. This results in often inefficient investments in houses, cars, boats, vacations, high-status degrees for our children, and so on. Marketing cleverly hijacks our serotonin reward systems, encouraging us to make foolish decisions. The fallout is debt, fragility, and misery. Status competition has become more intense with the prevalence of social networks. Drugs (both prescribed and illegal) are often used to compensate for the negative effects.

An alternative approach to gaining serotonin is via purpose-led paths, through community, and from increasing physical activity.[9] Purpose-led lives are focused on achievement and can result in wealth but are anchored around serving a higher goal and the needs of others. Whereas possession-based paths are exhaustive (with more possessions creating the want of further possessions and a race to infinity), purpose-driven paths are regenerative (when purpose or meaning is achieved, it reduces the further need for possessions to maintain or grow it, since giving to others is its own reward).

It is easier to rekindle the embers of purpose-led lives at a local level, and in the localism of modern societies there is a new chance to direct energies to this effect. Each individual seeking purpose must address the following question: What is the biggest load I can bear, one which best channels my skills and interests into serving the broader needs of my society?

Places must also have purpose: a sense of where people come from, of where they are evolving to, a reason for being. All places have a foundation myth, a story of how they came to be. All have a natural context and inherit the infrastructure, vernacular, culture of times past. Places can easily lose their purpose, impacted by economic, environmental, or social decline, or by the homogenizing bleakness of suburban sprawl. Leaders must periodically ask: What is the most useful role of our place, one that best channels its history, nature, and culture into serving the broad needs of its surrounding society?

Strong purpose leads to beauty. Among the highest expressions of beauty are the Roman cities, roads, and aqueducts; the churches and cathedrals built across European cities; the magnificent train stations of Victorian London; or the planned layout of the city of Edo, which later became Tokyo.

Scenario

A business executive, recently downsized, moves back to his or her hometown with his or her spouse. The couple sells their expensive home and downscale to a modest house, dramatically reducing monthly spending and thus monthly income needs. The executive builds a portfolio of activities, including coaching local teams, guiding local start-ups, and doing some consulting for global clients to maintain a required income. The spouse starts a business from home, helping families manage complex life events. The couple builds a new network of friends based on common interests and shared purpose.

As the couple develops roots in their new town, they step up their involvement and investment. The former executive channels decades of skills and contacts into conceiving, launching, or supporting a wide range of purpose-driven endeavors: helping the town as it seeks to develop a clean growth strategy, seed-investing in mission-oriented start-ups, investing in a new manufacturing plant to take advantage of reshoring and 3D printing capabilities.

The spouse's business has growing demand. Their town is undergoing a rapid transformation as its ethos becomes attractive to many looking to live a simpler and more meaningful life. But conceiving and executing a life change is not easy, and many will need support in streamlining their possessions, restructuring their budgets, selling their old houses and buying new ones, moving and adapting to a new community. Meanwhile, life itself keeps throwing up new challenges: aging relatives that need help as they suffer physical and cognitive decline, young adults seeking to build their lives in an economy plagued by debt and inflated costs of health care, housing and education, the next generation just being born. In helping others to solve these life problems, the business gains steady profit and growth while remaining strongly anchored in purpose.

A purpose-driven group, comprising both "townies" and "globals," begins to get together to conceive, prioritize, fund, and execute on an ever-larger set of purpose-driven challenges. They turn unused land into a community garden, encouraging young and old to work with the soil and experience the calming effects of planting and gardening. They carve out walking and biking paths in land acquired by the group and donated to the town and convince the town planners to fund protected bike paths from several key locations to enable safe travel into nature. They launch and lead fundraising for a maker space that will teach critical building skills and trades to locals of all ages and stages, helping to provide new job options and alleviating the growing shortage of blue-collar skills. They lead a town strategy for a major upgrade in connectivity infrastructure, resulting in high-speed Internet across the town that uses an open access model. They conceive, finance, and create a new microcollege oriented around skill acquisition, innovation, and new start-up formation in high growth areas of the knowledge economy. To this end they partner with a regional university interested in building a small presence in town. They leverage town buildings, including the library, city hall, a museum, and a donated space to house this college.

As this group gains confidence and success, it begins to work closely with town management to conceive of a bolder, long-term strategy of place. There are many critical challenges for the town, some perennial, and some because of its growing attractiveness. Archaic zoning restrictions mean that housing supply cannot keep pace with growing demand, causing house prices to rise and making the town increasingly unaffordable for most; traditional growth would lead to an explosion in car trips because the town has historically prioritized car travel over people travel; a growing population creates new demands on schooling, health care, and social care that the city is not prepared for; it is hard for town businesses to staff, because housing is unaffordable for workers; many in town want to live in smaller and more efficient homes than those available, but there is strong pressure from some to "preserve" the current density; many in town quite like housing appreciation, since it helps increase the value of their assets, even if it limits the long-term success of the place.

The path is clear. The "purpose-driven growth" group needs to find one or more projects that are significant enough to point to a new growth paradigm, without overwhelming the town with too radical a vision. They look for guidance in other places and decide to focus on two specific initiatives: a vernacular workforce housing initiative and a market plaza initiative.

The workforce housing strategy is inspired by Martha's Vineyard's "Island Housing Trust," which designs, finances, and builds housing aimed at meeting the needs of workforce and low-income residents while preserving the unique ethos and vernacular of place. The town builds a range of flexible and low-cost housing close to its center, using density to keep the cost down. It uses the opportunity to create additional commercial and public space adjacent to the projects. This housing vastly expands the workforce population that can live in town, helping alleviate the labor needs of local businesses and reducing traffic by maximizing proximity to work and walkability.

The market plaza initiative is inspired by a long tradition including Italian piazzas, Covent Garden in London, Faneuil Hall in Boston, and the Grove Arcade in Asheville, North Carolina. Drawing inspiration from each, they design a pedestrian-only plaza with a multiuse central building designed in the town vernacular, providing a mix of housing, interior public space, and retail storefronts. The outer layer of the plaza is similarly built up, providing additional housing and commercial capacity. The plaza is linked to parking areas by protected bike paths, encouraging human-based locomotion, along the lines of Venice, Italy.

These two projects achieve both a direct and a long-term objective. They resolve the need for a significant expansion in housing, they provide additional capacity for local commerce while substantially expanding demand for local products and services, and they minimize additional car use by seeking to radically reduce the number of required car trips. They preserve and enhance the character of the town, while demonstrating the potential from "gently dense" expansion, laying the groundwork for the next turn of the flywheel.

Rule 3. Clear the Air and Slow Down the Streets

Dirty air leads millions of people to age and die prematurely, reduces the IQ and wellness potential of unborn children, and increases violence levels.[10] Recent work suggests that dirty air also reduces farming outputs by up to 30%–60%.[11] Car-centered street design drives air pollution and reduces walking and biking. The median trip length in the United States is around three to five miles, yet cars dominate most local trips. In contrast, in Holland over 60% of trips below three miles are completed via walking or biking.

Heavy traffic levels and high vehicles speeds, with unprotected or nonexistent biking and walking paths, make walking and biking very risky. With the extended range of electric bikes and scooters, it is now theoretically feasible for people of all ages to replace car-based travel for over 50% of their trips, but only if such travel is safe. Commercial activity increases as streets are slowed down and become walkable and bikeable. Community interaction increases as well, improving wellbeing and reducing costs of social care. Experience in European cities such as Copenhagen, Amsterdam, Paris, and Seville shows massive pent-up demand for shifting from car-centered to people-centered transit. Places that evolve to clean-air/slow-streets models become highly attractive to settlers. The combined effect of improved health, inward talent attraction, increased commerce, and increased community is to massively improve the economic potential of a place.

Shifting to a clean-air/slow-streets model is hard, especially in areas where public transit is unviable as a complement to walking and biking, such as, for example, in many rural and suburban locations and some pockets within dense urban centers. We become accustomed to a car-based model, and many will complain if capacity is reduced. However, many cities have recently made a shift, and there is a growing body of evidence on how a shift can be managed and how to address potential objections to change.

A climate change group, C40, provides a primer for city leaders on how to ensure a successful transition, building on the recent success in Barcelona, Spain.[12] Their prescription includes (1) secure a mandate and act fast so that the rewards happen within a single political cycle; (2) focus on benefits to walkers/cyclists (versus downsides to drivers) and be flexible on the details; (3) use all city infrastructure options to improve the walking and cycling experience; (4) interconnect walkable and bikeable paths with one another and to public transit; (5) replicate proven strategies from other cities, for example easy bike rental; (6) and communicate frequently and widely about the many benefits of this program. This approach will be familiar to anyone involved in a major "change management" effort in business and government.[13]

COVID-19 has provided both the opportunity and the requirement to expand "open streets." The opportunity came from the temporary shutdowns around the globe, which briefly reduced the presence of cars on streets. The requirement came from the growing public awareness of the social and health benefits of a switch to a human-centered street. The Open Streets Google spreadsheet tabulates over 200 cities around the world that slowed down their streets to cars during the COVID-19 epidemic.[14] Sadly, many cities failed to take full advantage of a once-in-a-century opportunity to make a radical transition, but those that did have benefited from the leadership.

Paris has accelerated its plans to migrate toward a bike- and walk-friendly city in response to COVID-19, with the creation of 650 kilometers of car-free capacity.[15] This strategy is complemented by a broader national strategy, which provides funding for biking across 150 locations in France.[16] If France reaches Dutch levels of bike adoption, it can save 26,000 lives per year, gain on average a half-year increase in life expectancy, and gain a potential GDP increase of 3%, or $72 billion per year.[17] The US equivalent would be a gain of 123,000 lives per year and $600 billion per year in direct economic impact. The indirect impact from talent attraction and higher economic output is likely to be substantially higher.

Europe has the benefit of both global leaders, such as Holland and Denmark, and a rapidly growing set of iconic cities, including London, Milan, Barcelona, and Berlin, that are fast migrating toward a human-centered transit model. Its cities developed before the car, and they have preserved public transit much better than the United States. How could an American town or city, starting much further behind, pursue an evolution toward a European-style walkable and bikeable city?

Scenario

The town group charged with evolving to a walkable city meets to plot out their strategy. They recognize the likely resistance as well as the potential from successful efforts elsewhere. Building on prior success in incrementally expansive strategies, they pursue a sequence of moves.

The first moves are tactical: they institute a series of walkable days, allowing the town to experience the benefits of periods of lower traffic; they place temporary cement bollards to expand protected bike lane capacity; they expand restaurant capacity and tactically close off a small number of streets. Polling citizens can be very useful: one city saw 90% approval from citizens for adding extensive biking.[18]

The second turn of the flywheel requires some fixed-cost investments: key routes, such as those connecting to transit, the downtown core, or parks, are prioritized, as well as paths that maximize biking and walking to school. Street-calming investments, such as bumps, chicanes, signs, radars, and speed cameras, can also be deployed. Some of this investment could be funded by housing initiatives such as covered in rule 2. In essence, the city transfers the zoning profit potential from gentle densification into investment in walkable infrastructure.

Evidence suggests that use of bike paths expands with proper infrastructure. One US study showed that even pop-up lanes drove immediate increases in bicycle use of between 11% and 48%.[19] Paris saw a 45% increase in biking in 2020 as a result of its comprehensive biking investment.[20] Cities must seek to maximize biking usage, and publicize this success, to build citizen demand for further expansion.

The next turn of the flywheel would be to further extend the network of segregated and protected bike lanes. It might also include a range of infrastructure investments: pedestrianized streets and widened sidewalks, expansions in bike rental, secure bike parking, traffic-light signaling that prioritizes pedestrians and cyclists, and intersections designed to maximize safety for pedestrians and cyclists rather than car speed. These are matched with a series of campaigns to drive awareness and usage: "car-free street" and "open-street" days, cycling and road safety lessons, bike and walk-to-work days, and employer-supported cycle to work programs.

The most advanced biking strategies have been characterized with persistent, annual expansion in infrastructure. Copenhagen, for example, having accomplished a world-class level of active travel in the city core, is now building a network of "biking superhighways" of 784 kilometers. Designed to enable daily biking commutes, these super-highways link 23 municipalities to the capital city.[21]

Whereas the pioneers in human-centered transit, Holland and Denmark, had to work over decades to achieve their results, there is growing evidence that places can opt for a "big bang" approach. Barcelona has pioneered the reinvention of streetscapes through the superblocks framework.[22] The grid-based car-centered network built in the nineteenth century is being transformed into a series of citizen-oriented superblocks (each comprising 9 blocks in a 3 × 3 block grid). In a superblock, traffic is slowed to one lane and there is no through traffic, thus limiting car driving to users within the block. This promotes the rekindling of social, multigenerational connections. This strategy has recently been extended to cover around half the current Barcelona city grid, covering around 1 million people.[23]

Rule 4. Harness the Economic Potential of Community

Strong communities gain externality benefits through networks of informal friendship and caregiving and the resilience they engender. The value of these benefits is not easily captured in our accounting methods and thus is not factored into many planning decisions. Building a high-traffic lane can reduce the number of social connections and daily contacts by 50% to 75%.[24] Traffic destroys or dampens informal networks, increases loneliness and depression, and thus feeds the need for compensatory and expensive social care systems. Suburban sprawl and physical separation worsen these conditions. As we slow down our streets, promote human-powered movement, and provide greater density and coherence to the downtown core, we can rekindle the fabric of social connections at the neighborhood and city level, gaining both wellness and economic growth.

It is difficult to imagine what community-led economic growth looks like when our infrastructure and zoning has for decades led to the opposite. The COVID-19 lockdown has, despite its substantial harm to many small businesses, provided some clues on how rapidly we can regain a community-based, bottom-up, reciprocal model. In places where busy streets were slowed down to allow for outdoor restaurants and activity, we have seen renewed social interaction and engagement. A wave of social-justice activity has rippled across many of the world's democracies as ordinary citizens of all types have come together to protest.

From these beginnings, we can see the potential to evolve from simple toward ever more sophisticated community-led growth models. We can look to lessons from historic place-based settlement and growth for clues on how this evolution might look.

Scenario

The foundation of community economic revival is the nuclear and extended family and the related ties of kinship and friendship.[25] Family and friends provide many mutual, multigenerational services, in many cases engendering equal benefit to the provider and the recipient and allowing the group to have greater resilience in the face of adversity.

Beyond friends and family, the second cycle of community-driven potential comes as volunteers offer to help those with challenges. During COVID-19, interest in volunteering has increased in some places by over 20%, as people struggling for meaning in an upside down world have found it through helping others.[26] Other-oriented actions, with no need for reciprocity, form a regenerative foundation. One study by the Mayo Clinic suggested six key benefits for volunteers from completing their mission: it (1) reduces the risk of depression; (2) provides a sense of purpose and teaches valuable skills; (3) helps one stay physically and mentally active; (4) reduces stress levels; (5) helps one live longer; and (6) helps one make new friends and stay connected.

Individual volunteering can evolve into group-level activities. In European settler cultures in nineteenth- and twentieth-century North America, barn building was a commonplace community activity, as it was beyond the capabilities of a single family to raise such a large structure. After extensive preparation, the community would come together to raise the barn framework over the course of one or two days. Barn raising became a foundation for a settlement to create bonds of reciprocity and mutual interest. Communities such as the Amish have continued this practice until the present day, and there is renewed interest in mainstream culture in rediscovering these practices, both literally and as a metaphor for community-led development.[27]

A third stage of community-led engagement is the formation of civic organizations, groups with a mission to improve one or more aspects of life that are typically oriented around the community itself. Alexis de Tocqueville, in *Democracy in America*, noted the tremendous social capital created by the many civil societies that had sprung up across the land. Today, these range from craft- or hobby-oriented groups to volunteer public safety organizations, debating societies, and genealogic gatherings. Colleges and universities typically begin as a special type of civic organization, as attested by their legacy of nonprofit status even as some have become fabulously wealthy.

In his 2000 book *Bowling Alone*, Robert Putnam warns us of the risks to the loss of social capital in contemporary life through the disappearance of many group-level associations and activities.[28] But the instinct for such groupings remains strong. The Hoover Institute estimates there are over 1 million nonprofit associations in the United States, generating a collective annual income of $320 billion and employing 11% of the American workforce.[29] There are signs that despite the many chronic pressures on society pre-COVID and the acceleration of these pressures through the pandemic, new informal and formal civic networks are emerging apace.[30]

Family, friend, and volunteer caregiving and support are often uncompensated and thus are not captured by our statistical systems. However, the pathways for reciprocal exchange create trust, and this forms the basis for future market-based exchanges. This pattern is archaic: the culture of gift giving predates commercial exchanges, and there are indications that the networks of gifts and tributes laid the foundations for economic commerce.[31]

How should a town or neighborhood rekindle the embers of community-led activity? THNK.ORG proposes the following elements to the formation of a strong community, whether based in a place or connected over distance: (1) create a collective intention; (2) establish a distinctive identity; (3) create working practices, delivering a range of concrete services or actions; (4) establish a safe space; (5) create personal connections; (6) organize "soul feeding" activities; and (7) provide distributed roles for each member.[32]

How does economic growth then emerge? We can think about several emergent economic benefits from the growth in community engagement. The costs of paid care provision and social care will be reduced because more of this care will be provided by community networks. Costs associated with mental health and other forms of health care also decline as both sides of a caring transaction gain benefits. Businesses benefit both from the economic networks built upon the rails of reciprocity and from the increased productivity of employees involved in volunteering and other community activities, with estimates of up to

$5K a year in incremental benefits for each employee that commits to volunteering.[33]

Knowledge enterprises are particularly well poised to thrive in such an environment. Teaching and learning, if done well, can raise our collective game. What if with a few lessons, I can teach someone a skill that they can use for the next 40 years? How does teaching help me achieve my own purpose and transcendence, in the knowledge that its impact will outlive me? We all have something to teach and much to learn.

A new energy thus infuses into the community, with trust leading to the formation of new businesses, with purpose-driven people within a supportive environment taking greater risks to build something better, with an emergent cacophony of new ideas bubbling forth as one person mimics another but adds his or her own unique twist.

The ground is thus prepared for attracting a wave of inward migrants who wish to bring their own energy and community into the mix.

Rule 5. Recruit Purpose-Driven Migrants

Making a place more attractive should be combined with active recruitment. Potential migrants have already moved or are making decisions right now about where to move to, and places cannot afford to have every element of their strategy completed before they bid for this talent pool. In fact, they must seek to attract migrants with skills relevant to their long-term modern society strategy.

Villages, towns, and cities that want to tap into talent need to develop and implement a talent-attraction plan, determining what mix of talent can contribute best to the future evolution of their location while creating a strong future narrative and implementing sufficient change on the ground to establish credibility. They should also initiate tactical moves to gain traction, including recruitment campaigns targeting the general population and focused initiatives along the lines of Tulsa Remote.

Tulsa Remote is a program designed to attract high potential talent.[34] Launched in 2019, in Tulsa, Oklahoma, it selected 100 out of 10,000 applicants, each funded with $10,000 to spend one year in the city. The program was highly successful, with 70 of the 100 migrants remaining in the city, 35 buying a home, and a strong integration of the migrants into the community. The program has been expanded in its second year to 250 migrants, and it has helped to put Tulsa in contention as a finalist for a Tesla factory. A key driver of success has been the prioritization of migrants with a strong sense of purpose and willingness to contribute to Tulsa. Similar strategies have been replicated in Alabama, Georgia, West Virginia, and Vermont.[35] Talent attraction is arguably the most powerful lever for a community to thrive in the modern society, but we generally lack a theory and practice on how to do it well.

In the knowledge economy, three subrules on talent matter the most. First: the greater the marketable talent, the more the individual can choose how and where they want to live. Second: marketable talent is distributed as a power law or Pareto distribution, with the most talented being massively more productive than the average person. Third: marketable talent has the potential to massively multiply.

We can see this effect in the story of Jeff Bezos, Amazon, and Seattle. A quirk of fate (the presence of a large book distributor) led Amazon to be founded in Seattle. Jeff Bezos demonstrated a unique set of skills and drive, leading him to form a company that is today worth more than $1 trillion. Over the ensuing decades this led to over 75,000 direct Amazon employees in the Seattle region, in addition to contractors and others. Economists suggest that the "multiplier effect" in job creation could mean that between two and five jobs are created for every knowledge economy job.[36] This means that the indirect job growth count of Bezos in the Seattle region could be 250,000 or more.

Despite this success, the Seattle region has failed to match job creation with an equivalent level of new housing, causing a housing affordability problem. According to the Federal Reserve Bank of St. Louis, the average price for a house in the Seattle metro area has gone up by a factor of almost four since 1994, the year Amazon was founded. This compares to 2.5x growth for the average American house.[37] Seattle and many other knowledge economy hubs have become ever less affordable for the average family. A modern society strategy needs to match talent attraction with maintaining supply of housing to enable broad rather than narrow prosperity.

The Amazon case is an extreme example of a multiplier effect. But there are thousands of fast-growing companies that have each created 500, 1,000 or 2,000 new jobs in the past decades. High-growth firms, many focused on the knowledge economy, have historically clustered their employees in the location of foundation. The need to be close to financing, client, partner, and talent networks have led to these firms in turn clustering in a small number of locations, such as the Bay Area, Boston, New York, Seattle, and London. Many of these locations have restricted housing supply, thus becoming unaffordable to most. This condition creates a pressure cooker for a new paradigm.

With work moving to the cloud and an ever-growing ease for companies to get financing, sell to clients, work with partners, and hire employees without strong geographic restrictions, there is a vast amount of top talent that is free to move anywhere. The places that can recognize the needs of this talent and attract them to their communities can generate a cascade of jobs, economic growth, and vitality if they learn how to harness it well, especially if they ensure they can match the supply of talent with an equivalent supply of housing. They also need to be cognizant of the potential contribution of a wide diversity of talent in terms of gender, race, age, learning and working style, physical and practical skills, musical and artistic ability, community-building strengths, and inspirational capabilities. Talent strategies need to be diverse and interwoven.

Talent attraction thus needs to be long term, cognizant of the rapidly shifting reality of the cloud economy, comprehensive, and inclusive. A potential sequencing is laid out below, beginning with harnessing the full potential of current citizens.

Many of us are not operating at our full potential. Full potential here is defined as answering the following question: What is the biggest load that you can bear, one that challenges you but whose barriers you can overcome, one that best harnesses your talents and interests and best serves the need of your community and society? By addressing this question, we enter a path of purpose and meaning, helping ourselves and an expanding circle of family, friends, neighbors, and fellow citizens while simultaneously becoming a stronger participant in driving economic, environmental, and social growth in our surrounding communities.

There are myriad reasons why we may think we cannot be on a path of purpose. Poor health, debt, family responsibilities, a subsistence-level life, poor education, and an unforgiving geography could be viewed as limitations, and they certainly may limit us from achieving some goals. But these barriers in fact define purpose. If your biggest challenge is to fight a disease or help a family member, then that is your path of purpose. If you can overcome one challenge, you will then be in position to take on the next. As you overcome progressively bigger challenges, you may be placed to take your impact beyond your immediate circle and toward society. This is the "Hero's Journey," an archetypal path to pursuing a life of meaning, best captured by Joseph Campbell.

Helping the maximum number of citizens get on paths of purpose becomes a key foundation to then attract migrants. Civic organizations can become powerful allies, since many are founded upon a moral purpose, as can businesses, since they benefit economically and otherwise by having more purposeful employees. Purpose-led citizens will be critical "receptors" for the incoming group of migrants. They will be oriented more around helping others than themselves, and they will be more open to the skills and experiences of newcomers and less protective of property values that create affordability gaps for others.

Targeting a diverse group of migrants with a wide range of skills and temperaments will be critical, especially in the initial wave of talent attraction. Aaron Bolzle, the pioneer behind Tulsa Remote, worked especially hard to ensure first that the initial cohort of remote migrants would represent the most diverse range of skills and types, and second, that both the migrants and the current citizens were oriented around reciprocal exchange.[38] The migrants were in part selected based on their willingness to contribute to the future of Tulsa. Those tasked with welcoming these migrants were also chosen based on their willingness to support newcomers.

There are formidable barriers for any person or family to move. There is friction in finding a home, in moving, in setting up new services. There is fear of loneliness, of not fitting in. States have gradually increased licensing requirements and taxes, which make it hard to earn a living if, for example, one spouse has a service job. There are strong reasons to stay in place, including friends, family, and familiarity. Overall, moving is an expensive and risky proposition, even if remote work eliminates at least one of the risk factors. Cities need to map these barriers and design programs that reduce the friction of migration. These could include an offer of temporary housing subsidization, the creation of welcoming groups, support in helping family members to find local work, and help accessing schools, medical services, and utilities.

As the talent attraction program gains momentum, we can become more systematic and ambitious. For example, we could build a database of people with a connection to the region. This could include a diaspora map of those who have left, those who may have come to study and then departed, and those who have spent summers or even just visited.

As we will cover in rules 11 and 12, there is a high risk that talent attraction creates future problems if it is not matched with an adequate housing strategy. "Locals" are often concerned about the risk of "gentrification" as newcomers move into a new neighborhood or city and invest in local businesses and housing.[39] A key concern is that these newcomers will drive house prices up, making it unaffordable for local families to continue to live there. This is a very real concern, and during the COVID pandemic, we have seen a surge in house prices, with average price inflation of 15%–25%.[40] In essence, the "gentrification" issue has become a mass-market phenomenon, simultaneously impacting most of the country.

The response is not to somehow prevent people from moving. Housing price inflation (notwithstanding that during 2021 it is in part driven by loose monetary policy) is a very strong positive signal that a town is desirable. It makes investing in new homes more economically attractive and should be viewed as a major opportunity: to use a wave of new housing to evolve your town or city into a trifecta of economic, environmental, and social sustainability.

Rule 6. Support the Bionic Worker

Automation and artificial intelligence threaten careers, and the rate of job replacement is quickening. COVID-19 has accelerated the elimination of many roles, first shutting down big parts of the economy, then creating the opportunity (the enforced shutdown) and motivation (pressure on retail profits, increased risk perception of employing humans rather than robots) for rapid automation of many jobs.

The risk to current employment is substantial. The World Economic Forum estimates that 15% of jobs across 35 countries surveyed in 2020 were immediately at risk from COVID-related shutdowns, and a similar magnitude of work was at risk of replacement by automation. McKinsey estimates the global workforce at 3.5 billion people. Various analysts suggest that close to 10%, or 350 million jobs, are at risk of automation during the coming decade.[41]

But there is enormous potential from the merger of human and machine talent. Digital tools are becoming increasingly easier to master, through advances in low-code and no-code software and robotic process automation. Digital tools can rapidly detect shifts in job needs locally and globally. Learning paths can be designed to accelerate digital learning and to adapt to the style and preference of each user.

Human and machine collaboration is so pervasive that it rapidly becomes background activity. As an example of adaptation, a senior citizen who used to play bridge online three times a week pre-COVID now plays bridge six times a week via an online platform. She and her partner, both over 80 years of age, have progressively sharpened their bridge skills and routinely win over much younger players. What used to be a socially and generationally segregated experience due to local constraints has become much more diverse. Adaptation in "play" often suggests models of adaptation in "work." The adoption by most knowledge workers of video-based interactions has created a new culture and source of knowledge capture. New human-machine collaboration is accelerating at breakneck speed.

An example of how humans and machines can work together is the explosion of "low-code/no-code" tools. These allow tasks today done by programmers to be accomplished by people with more basic digital skills. The number of programmers globally is estimated by research firm Evans at 27 million in 2020, growing to 45 million by 2030.[42] In contrast, the total number of digital workers is estimated by *Forbes* at 1 billion in 2020, a number that could easily double by 2030, providing a much larger base of potential bionic workers.[43] Every advance in no-code tools opens access to business opportunity in the cloud to more people, who can leverage their creative skills, critical thinking, and analytical talent without having to master coding.

The impact of the remote work migration will also create a wave of new work in the services economy. Assuming that over time 10 million American knowledge workers relocate to other towns and cities, with a multiplier effect on service jobs of 3x, implies that 30 million new service jobs will be created in these new locations.

The integration of coding into work will happen across virtually all job categories. Take retail, a sector with a baseline number of 16 million American workers, many with low-paying jobs.[44] A Capgemini study on the future of retail jobs suggests that many traditional front-office activities (merchandising, static displays, physical signage, trial rooms) could migrate to digitally assisted methods (augmented displays, virtual trial rooms, sensor-based navigation, touchless payment).[45] Similarly, back-office activities in warehousing or vendor management could be automated but create new jobs in predictive analytics, Internet of things, and other domains. Knowledge worker migration from larger cities to a network of small towns will likely continue to feed the opportunity for digital commerce, including new start-ups riding on platforms such as Shopify. Many knowledge workers will experience up to a 100% increase in disposable income through the combination of lower costs of housing, commuting, and taxes, and we could expect that they will cycle back spending into new retail experiences.

Towns have an opportunity to tap into this interest by supporting "high street" and "neighborhood" retail. This can begin with tactical moves such as market stalls or mobile van-based retail. In line with some of the "gentle density" moves defined in rule 2, they can encourage retail expansion as additional home capacity is created. In many neighborhoods in America, retail is prohibited by zoning codes, many of which also require single-family homes by law. A change of zoning to allow retail and adjustments in neighborhood density restrictions would also result in an explosion of hyperlocal retail and the reemergence of neighborhood retail clusters.

Towns can also support the formation of home-based retail. Etsy and other maker platforms help over 4 million people to develop and run an online business from home.[46] Forward-looking towns can support this kind of business through maker spaces, financing, and regulatory simplification (eliminating unnecessary licensing, for example). The more successful home-based businesses could migrate into pop-up stores or market stalls and eventually become new permanent retailers.

The example of retail suggests that places can act as catalysts for their workforce to adapt to the new work reality. What could a sequence of moves look like?

Scenario

Many of the policies in place today limit jobs and commercial activity. For example, traffic-clogged streets restrict commerce, limiting job formation in stores, cafés, gyms, and other local retail establishments; zoning limits activity in residential zones, restricting the creation of jobs from neighborhood stores; productive downtown buildings are overtaxed, disincentivizing job formation; zoning limits house and street regeneration, thus harming construction jobs; overbuilt sprawl crowds out economic activity and hollows out the vital center; cities subsidize firms moving in, at the expense of workers and overall taxes. All these policies need to be reversed.

Equally important are approaches to proactively drive growth: provide access to software tools, training, coworking spaces, human coaches, and apprenticeships, especially in areas where new inward migration could drive growth; build suitable housing (low-cost, age-friendly, convenient) to attract families; make streets child- and senior-friendly (and thus four-generational); create vibrant downtowns and neighborhoods; partner with citizens and institutions to support skill acquisition in new local and cloud job opportunities; create a spirit of settlement and opportunity, to attract inward migration; create an economic model to measure quality of healthy living and lifetime value; develop an exciting storyline laying out the purpose and destiny of your city.

Civic leaders should take stock of how friendly their city truly is toward work and develop a plan to set right those aspects that today are wrong. They make some early, visible, no-brainer moves (tactical and highly visible moves to slow down streets, open up sidewalk space for cafés and restaurants and the promotion of market stalls). In parallel, they develop a roadmap to include a sequence of progressively more comprehensive moves.

Rule 7. Engage Lifelong Learning

With online college courses competing with free courses on Coursera or EdX, the value of traditional academic programs is under challenge. Meanwhile, the rapid shifts in work, combined with lengthening working lives, create pressure for us to acquire new skills at every stage in life. Partnering with local academic institutions is an important element in developing a modern society. Academia must reinvent itself along with its host city or town, a point we will elaborate in chapter 2.

The education system is a cornerstone of the knowledge economy. It is estimated by Holon IQ that education drives global annual spending of over $5 trillion in 2020 and is projected to pass $7 trillion by 2025.[47] But the influence of this sector is far more pervasive, as it provides socialization, civic engagement, and preparation for all to participate in society and the economy.

When the education system falters, its absence is sorely missed. The World Economic Forum estimates that during the pandemic over 1 billion children have missed on average half a year of education, likely reducing their average lifetime income by 3%, for a total long-term cost of $10 trillion.[48]

With accelerating technological, industrial, environmental, and social change putting pressure on continuous learning, education will necessarily become embedded into every age and stage of our lives. As Lynda Gratton and Andrew Scott explain in their book *100-Year Life*, we will need to evolve from a three-stage life (schooling, work, retirement) to a multistage life in which learning, working, and living are interwoven across our entire lives.[49]

An example of reimagining the later years is Lasell University in Boston, Massachusetts. While serving a traditional college student demographic, Lasell has combined that with a much older student population. Lasell Village offers people as old as 90 years of age the potential to live and study alongside the younger generation of students.[50] This model allows older, richer students to subsidize younger students and all generations to benefit from interacting in the context of learning.

A foundation of a place-based lifelong-learning strategy is at the intersection of two of these models: the platform university and the microcollege. The emergence of large-scale online learning platforms, including massive open online courses (MOOCs) such as Coursera; online program managers (OPMs) such as 2U; massive hybrid universities (such as Southern New Hampshire University, or SNHU); and digital customer academies such as UiPath Academy, suggest the emergence of a wide range of potential platforms. At the other end of the scale, a microcollege could start with as few as 20 students and 2 teachers.[51]

Combining a microcollege with one or more platforms and access to a modest amount of physical space allows the cost to start a new "academy" to be negligible. Meanwhile, the accreditation rules that have historically limited who could provide education are being displaced by outcomes-based and skill-based learning. Two of the five most valuable companies in the world, Google and Apple, no longer require a degree, and this pattern will only accelerate.[52] If one of the goals of learning is to increase lifetime income, it may be better for people to put their work-oriented effort into getting into Lambda Academy (where one only pays tuition if he or she makes a minimum income postgraduation) or take free coursework at UiPath (arguably the best "university" in the world at which to learn robotic process automation). Clearly there are many other reasons to go to traditional colleges or universities. However, as free learning paths become more pervasive, and college education ever more expensive, there is a substantial opening for alternative higher-ed models to thrive.

Similar innovation is happening at the K–12 level, for example through rapid growth in home schooling and pod schools. A study by the US Census Bureau indicates that the share of households providing home schooling grew from about 3% before COVID-19 to 12% in 2020 (note that in this analysis the Census Bureau excluded households where children were attending their regular school via remote tools).[53] The explosion in home schooling cuts across every race and geography. The fastest growth recorded by the Census Bureau came in the African American population.

In chapter 5 we delve into various scenarios and approaches for how places can integrate the knowledge enterprise into their strategic planning. Below, we offer one path of evolution.

Scenario

A small, somewhat abandoned, mill town in New Hampshire starts to feel the influx of remote working migrants from southern New England. It is close enough to major highways for a one- or two-day-a-week commute into Boston. It benefits from cheaper housing, cleaner air, historic mill buildings, and access to outdoor recreation in lakes, mountains, rivers, and the ocean. The school population grows for the first time in decades. Many in town need to learn new skills, ranging from knowledge work skills to meet the needs of cloud-based employers, to blue-collar skills to support growth in house construction, repair, and maintenance.

The town owns considerable property and makes it and other re-sources available to support the formation or expansion of knowledge enterprises. It also helps new start-ups in this area access grants and philanthropy. A maker space in one of the old mills becomes a center for people to learn tradeable blue-collar skills. Several pod schools emerge to enable alternative teaching models. The state has shifted its spending allocation to provide parents with more control over how educational spending is allocated. This provides parent-controlled but state-funded support for these new models. The massive growth in charter schools, from none in 1990 to over 8,000 across the United States by 2020, is an indicator of the potential for new models of K–12 education.

The town sees an opportunity to test several microcolleges. Both academics and experienced professionals have moved into town, so there is a critical mass of potential teachers. The town partners with a regional university to formulate and set up a low-cost campus, special-izing in new industrial models. This leverages the availability of unused mills, renewed interest in reshoring manufacturing, and advances in manufacturing software and additive manufacturing technology. Ac-cess to cheap wood from nearby forests leads to a specialization in bio-char, a process allowing highly efficient carbon capture.[54]

A second microcollege exploits the potential for rediscovering old construction techniques and blending them with new available tech-nologies. The region is experiencing a doubling in housing demand, and there is a lack of skills. It is also critical that new housing is designed to accommodate smaller families, an aging population, and an emerg-ing boomlet in babies. This microcollege extends to also cover urban design, in particular the adaptation of Dutch and Danish models in the United States. It develops partnerships with knowledge enterprises in Holland and Denmark and with IKEA, an innovative Swedish company that has taken its expertise in retail and home goods into home manufacturing.

A third microcollege spins out from the biochar experiment. This sector is maturing, and the region has substantial capacity, so a biochar institute is formed to become a key center for skills development, research and development (R&D), and certification in this space.[55] The institute is physically located in the town, but from the beginning operates in a blended model, teaching students across the globe.

Over time, the town starts to envision itself as an incubator of microcolleges. People looking to learn and those with something to teach start to migrate to the town, much as they did in the Middle Ages in places such as Bologna, Paris, or Oxford. The town develops its own platform for microcollege incubation, supporting a plethora of experiments, much like a venture capitalist would. It also supports other small towns that aim to go through a similar transition.

Some projects fail, but at minimal loss since they did not require much investment to get going. Some projects succeed and begin to gain critical mass. Successful projects add new disciplines and attract more capital, students, and faculty.

One generation later, the mill town has evolved into a thriving "college town." The combination of natural resources, the charm of the mills, sufficient proximity to major cities, good rail and road networks, and an explosion of possibility attracts all types: empty nesters looking for a "gently dense" urban experience, environmental pioneers, scholastic entrepreneurs, new services providers tapping into the combination of increased demand and desire for new experiences.

The risk for this town is that it could have failed to anticipate its success and one generation later it becomes yet another overpriced town, with the drawbridge metaphorically pulled up. But the city anticipated this possibility and laid out a green growth strategy designed to maintain housing affordability, reduce carbon use, and maintain sustainable growth. The bones of the old infrastructure and comfort with three- to four-story buildings allowed a tripling in size while reducing roads and parking. The income generated from economic activity was ploughed into a network of bikeable and walkable paths.

A generation later 80% of children bicycle to school, making this town a magnet for parents everywhere. Eighty percent of over-70s also bicycle, in many cases with the latest electric bikes and tricycles. A link has been built to the main rail network. Car ownership has declined from the American average of 797 per 1,000 people to a Dutch level of 545 car owners per 1,000 people, and car usage has fallen as well.

The town is so attractive that it risks being flooded by migrants, as much as it continues to expand supply via its green growth strategy. This risks its goal of meeting the affordability gap.

Working with 50 other small towns in the region, and with financing from several global foundations, the town creates a sort of Marshall Plan to support the replication of what it took one generation to achieve, to happen in a decade. Its knowledge enterprise ecosystem works to support the formation of microcolleges in each location, suited to the highest priority problems and business opportunities of the time. Veterans from the initial wave are sent to seed projects across the new network of towns, rail, biking, and animal infrastructure built to connect locations to one another.

One generation later, the ethos has been replicated across the entire region. Each town has its own distinct twist, but all are part of a regional economy that is thriving economically, socially, and environmentally.

Rule 8. Build an Innovation Cluster

Remote work drives decentralization of innovation. As talent hitherto living in expensive innovation hubs such as San Francisco or Boston moves to places with superior value for the money, there is an opportunity to reboot local innovation clusters by combining this incoming talent with sources of local competitive advantage and creating companies that target large and underserved global markets. Placemaking strategies should tap local and global finance. They should promote a broad range of entrepreneurial activity: profit and nonprofit, local and global, in start-ups, in existing firms, and in local institutions. They should also plan for success and ensure that they adapt their housing and support systems as the innovation economy becomes more significant.

Scenario

Boulder, Colorado, has emerged as an innovation cluster. Harnessing natural beauty and many outdoor options, its leaders encouraged early on the establishment of a highly ranked university (University of Colorado Boulder). Later, Boulder attracted high-tech and biotech firms while preserving a significant amount of green space and limiting the American suburban experiment. Venture capitalists and entrepreneurs have been attracted to the quality of life. Today Boulder has a higher per-capita rate of venture capital than Silicon Valley.

Unfortunately, Boulder has become a victim of its own success. The price of housing has grown by 3.5 times between 1995 and 2020, compared to a US average of 2.5 times. By failing to adequately meet demand in the core city, Boulder has contributed to sprawl in its surrounding region.[56] The city used zoning to restrict population growth, becoming increasingly less affordable and less diverse. If, instead, it had accommodated a process of green growth, combining "gently dense" natural growth with promoting a mode shift to walking, biking, or transit, it could have accommodated a more balanced model of economic, social, and environmental growth.

The failure of Boulder and many other leading cities to use the pull of innovation to create a balanced housing market creates an opportunity for hundreds of other cities and regions. The pathway to replicate the "Boulder thesis" has been captured by venture capitalist Brad Feld in several books, including *Startup Communities*.[57] Unlike historical approaches to innovation focused on expensive and long-term investments such as traditional university or research campuses, Feld's approach is premised on creating a bottom-up culture of entrepreneurs. Per Feld, there are four key elements in this prescription[58]:

"Entrepreneurs must lead the start-up community." This can begin with something as simple as regular dinners and other group events.

These create opportunities for innovators to get together, gain energy from others, and gather support in what is always a very risky endeavor. As people with drive and skills come together, there will be a natural bubbling up of ideas, partnerships, spinouts, and other innovative practices. As these contacts turn into start-ups and these in turn become scale-ups and some are acquired, this can lead to wealth formation. Successful exits rapidly lead to a second wave of innovation, as some who have sold decide to start new companies and others to become angel investors in new firms.

"Leaders must have a long-term commitment." Building an innovation ecosystem is a generational project, and those who have the wealth, experience, or position to take a leadership role should commit to staying involved for several decades. They must be patient. Innovation cannot be manufactured on demand but rather needs to emerge. But there are strategies that tend to complement and inspire innovation. Many of the rules in this chapter and the overall thesis of the book are about creating an environment with a quality of life and cognitive engagement such that innovation becomes a natural outgrowth.

"The start-up community should be inclusive of anyone who wants to participate in it." It is easy to become restrictive in defining what are the "right" kind of innovators, based on their field of expertise or prior background. But there is growing evidence that innovation can happen anywhere and be accomplished by anyone. Many of the best ideas are combinations of separate domains, such as the application of gaming technology in the design of buildings and cities. Groups that have not traditionally been able to access entrepreneurial funding, including women and people of color, are bringing their own experiences and interests to further broaden the impact of the innovation economy.

"The startup community must have continual activities that engage the entire entrepreneurial stack." Cross-pollination should go beyond founders and investors and extend deep into the population. Key intermediaries, such as local government, banks, insurance providers, and others should be involved. Innovation should be encouraged at every level, including helping the formation of "lifestyle" or "mom-and-pop" businesses such as farm-to-table restaurants, small retail stores, organic farms, or environmental products.

As an innovation ecosystem starts to gain maturity, it is important for place-based leaders to think about it differently than a "factory" or a "hospital" or a "regeneration district." In Feld's words, "Startup communities . . . behave using the characteristics of complex adaptive systems. Humans really have trouble understanding how to work with complex systems. We have trouble with positive feedback loops, we have trouble understanding exponential curves both up and down."[59]

Understanding complexity is as important in creating effective innovation ecosystems as it is in successful placemaking. The failure to understand complex adaptive systems is behind the long-term catastrophe of the motor society model. Leaders at the time had become enamored with the power of technology and forgotten the ancestral lessons in placemaking. In *The Master and His Emissary*, Ian Gilchrist argues that this technocratic instinct reflects a growing dominance of "left-brain" thinking in our society, leading us to seek to impose a deterministic and limited view of the world and eschewing the tremendous but harder-to-capture strength of our more holistic "right brain."[60] Thriving modern societies will need to do the hard work of diagnosing these types of imbalances and developing approaches that integrate the superpowers of both left and right brain.

For a place to generate innovation, it is thus important that we first change our mindset, learn new skills, and recover forgotten lessons. This includes learning to understand how new habits are adopted, how they are transmitted from person to person, how network effects are generated, how to achieve local economies of scale, how emergent processes work, and how our brains work.

We can learn from other such systems, including the history of other towns and cities, many of which grew for centuries as complex adaptive models, with limited central planning. London, England, is a very good example of a city that experienced tremendous growth in a largely unplanned way. In 1666, a fire famously burned a large part of the old city of London. Five master plans were laid out for London's regeneration, but eventually the decision was to allow a bottom-up process.[61] The creative and open process of building London was closely interwoven with the emergence of a highly innovative commercial and trading class.

A powerful rule for an innovation cluster is to seek to solve local problems or to harness unique local resources, in each case where there is a global opportunity. A great example of this is the Netherlands: being at or below sea level, the Dutch have become pioneers in managing rising seas, eventually exporting their know-how around the world.[62] A city with polluted riverways could focus on reducing pollution, including initially learning from other places with prior success and over time seeking to become a center of excellence in this space.

Innovation can be enhanced by the presence of colleges or universities. The early move by Boulder to accommodate a branch of the University of Colorado was a foundation of its innovation economy. Places without such a university will need to combine new university models (as covered in rule 7) with the encouragement of entrepreneurial activity. To seed such a process, the talent attraction strategy (covered in rule 5) should include securing high-multiplier academic and innovation talent.

Rule 9. Unleash the Commercial Dynamo

Beyond the fast-growth innovation economy, there is a core economy associated with logistics, services, manufacturing, food production, health care, construction, banking, insurance, and many other sectors. There is a "natural" level of commercial potential in many places that is waiting to be unleashed. Often, this engine is held back by a combination of restrictive practices, physical and legal roadblocks, a lack of entrepreneurial culture, unsupportive tax policies, and bad prioritization. These include zoning restrictions that bar commercial activity in "residential" areas, onerous licensing requirements, city subsidization of sprawl at the expense of dense urban settings, and tax policy creating high marginal taxes for emerging entrepreneurs.[63] By understanding these restrictions, building consensus around their costs and benefits, strategically removing key barriers, and supporting high multiplier actions, places can unleash waves of growth.

Detroit's rise and fall illustrates both the enormous economic potential of place and the risks associated with growth that fails to balance economic, social, and environmental sustainability.

In 1903, the year when Ford started making cars, Detroit was a second-tier city with a population of 286,000 people.[64] Detroit had a very good geographical position for accessing raw materials, markets, and financing and benefited from a thriving innovation culture that pivoted fast into the automobile sector. By 1915, 13 of the top 15 car brands were based in Detroit, and as the massive ecosystem unlocked by the car grew, so did its population. By 1950 Detroit was the fifth largest city in the United States, with a population of 2 million people.

However, from this peak, the city began a long decline, even as the car became an ever more central aspect of American life. Over the ensuing decades Detroit's manufacturing plants lost share, first to nearby and more flexible suburbs, then to its new competitor, Japan, and later to more nimble cities in the US South. As this happened, its core economic engine went into a long pattern of decline, and Detroit was unable to find a replacement. Race riots in 1968, followed by white flight to the suburbs, accelerated the hollowing out of the downtown core. Detroit's population shrank from 1.8 million in 1950 to around 600,000 in 2016.[65] The city hit rock-bottom when it declared bankruptcy in 2013.[66]

Historian Thomas Sugrue, in his book *Origins of the Urban Crisis*, argues that the foundation for the decline in Detroit was the inability of black workers to advance in income and for black families to move into predominantly white neighborhoods.[67] Nobel Prize–winning economist Paul Krugman and others have argued that the city might have recovered from the loss of its industries but that it was the extensiveness of sprawl that sapped its core economics.[68] This sprawl was initially enabled by the network of highways connecting Detroit to suburban locations and the displacement by cars of what was once a vast street-car network. Sprawl then accelerated as the center of the city became increasingly less attractive relative to the suburbs.

Since 2013 Detroit has staged a solid, if still fragile, recovery. Dan Gilbert, founder of Quicken Loans, has invested over $5.6 billion in the city and led the comeback.[69] An economic index of the city created by the Chicago Federal Reserve and indexed at 100 in 1997 shows the city hitting a low point of 85 in 2010, climbing back to 100 by 2015, and reaching 110 in 2019.[70] House prices have doubled between 1985 and 2020, compared to a 2.5x average for America but a major improvement from the low point of 2013.

A precipitous fall is not preordained. Krugman compares the fate of Detroit with that of Pittsburgh, a city with a similar history. Pittsburgh, despite also experiencing deindustrialization and population declines, has been able to adapt and become a vibrant innovation economy, including leadership in high-growth segments such as robotics.[71]

Our Towns, a book by James and Deborah Fallows, describes how cities such as Holland, Michigan, Eastport, Maine, and Greenville, South Carolina, found strategies to adapt to adversity and rebuild their economic and social engines.[72] Holland, for example, overcame its harsh winters through a gradual strategy of snow melt using the heat from wastewater. This system now covers much of the downtown, encouraging year-round gathering and commerce. Eastport innovated through the actions of a group of women entrepreneurs, which became a kind of venture studio to create a wide range of businesses. Greenville has benefited from becoming a center of high-performing STEM (science, technology, engineering, and math) and art schools for its surrounding region. The Fallows's book illustrates the potential for commercial regeneration to transcend rural and urban, red state and blue state.

Every place has a unique set of conditions, and there is no single approach to generating or regenerating a pattern of sustainable economic, social, and environmental growth (what could be termed a triple win). Infrastructure projects or significant involvement by a major private player, such as was the case in starting the Detroit recovery, can be helpful. But the change must come from within, from the collective of the place.

John Kanja and Mark Kramer, in their article "Collective Impact," propose five key drivers of success for communities as they seek to come together to solve a key social challenge: (1) a common agenda or purpose, (2) a shared measurement system, (3) mutually reinforcing activities, (4) continuous and sustained communication, and (5) backbone support organizations.[73] We can play out how they would apply into a triple-win regeneration strategy.

Scenario

A group of citizens comes together to plot out an ambitious triple-win growth strategy. They represent an urban district that has fallen on hard times, with a legacy of social, environmental, and economic misfires. The group is designed to be broadly diverse, by gender, orientation, age, ethnicity, religion, neurodiversity, skills, wealth, and interests.

It first works to articulate a common purpose. Building on an industrial past, a troubling history of racial adversity, and emerging tensions across religious, age-based, and wealth-based differences, the group seeks to become an exemplar of what a multidiverse regenerative strategy could look like. They delve into the literature and gain growing conviction around the idea that diversity could go beyond a slogan into a competitive advantage. Paul Gompers and Silpa Kovvali show that a more diverse mix of investors and entrepreneurs increases the return for venture capital.[74] The group builds on this idea and seeks to recruit an advisory board composed of successful entrepreneurs of all kinds. They go out of the way to promote the most diverse set of skills, including full representation by sociodemographic variables such as race, gender, or age. The group also recruits across the entire business spectrum, mom-and-pop stores, world-scale start-ups, philanthropies, concerts, museums, gray or recently deregulated spaces such as crypto or cannabis, and entrepreneurs inside large corporations. A second layer of purpose emerges: the desire to solve a triple-play challenge. The group aims to achieve Copenhagen levels of walkability within 10 years rather than 40. The rationale is that the changes required to achieve this will simultaneously require zoning reform, new housing, street reform, new tax structures, new licensing for cars and other vehicles, new transit models, changes in schooling, and many other changes and, in so doing, unlock social improvement and economic growth.

The combined group now develops a narrative of place, a story of the past, the present, and a desired future. Participants are asked to write a story of their past and present and to define an idealized future of place, of their personal relationship with the place, and how they want to contribute to this desired evolution of self and place. The group leaders create a combined narrative, aggregating hundreds of individual commitments, openly and with input from the community, using a moderated wiki tool. Those with suggestions for improvement are required to commit to contribute, reducing the levels of frivolous or unrealistic suggestions.

From this effort, the regeneration process moves into a series of subgroups, organized around common subgoals, areas of interest, and skills. These groups have names such as "Slow Streets," "Open Cafés," "Rewilders," "Learning Lab," "Repurpose Buildings," "Pods," "Blue-Collar Academy," "Microcolleges," "City Gardens," "Brew Pubs," "Café Culture," "Zoning Reform," "Building Financing Society," "Artists in Residence," "Music Bands," "Tactical Urbanism," "Resilient Beaches," and "Open Network."

Each group is encouraged to think big and to define a key set of intermediary milestones. Groups with a compelling strategy and team are seed-funded with a sequence of small, progress-based stipends. After an initial period, they are then asked to seek future funding from private interests, including raising it from a venture capital firm with funding from key local institutions and families. The goal is to focus work on economic viability and to reduce dependence on grant funding.

These groups are designed to promote a high level of diversity, to avoid "group think," and to maximize resources. They are encouraged to both cooperate and compete with one another. Cooperation is critical because there is substantial overlap in group objectives and there are benefits from skill swapping. Competition is also important, driving energy toward success and helping to fuse together people that might otherwise have little in common into a team.

Many of these efforts require long-term commitment and consistency. To this end, there is an effort to rapidly develop ways for the most committed and effective team members and groups to become self-sustaining and generate living income. For example, the "Repurpose Buildings" group first works with "Blue-Collar Academy" to learn practical renovation skills and then with the "Building Society" to tap local investors to buy several houses to renovate. This generates both living wages for building work and capital growth from successful housing projects that can be then turned into a new wave of investment and regeneration.

As the most successful groups gain traction inside the district, some want to expand their remit and their sources of financing. In some cases, what began as an association could spin off a private company. The dedicated venture capital firm is designed to bridge this gap, supporting emerging firms with a mix of equity, debt, and other financial tools. Groups that expand beyond the district to other places may in the future be in position to access later-stage financing to build a national or international firm. In this case, the district of origin will be a key beneficiary, since the founding team will likely stay in place, and as the firm becomes larger, it will continue to recruit locally.

The cycle of regeneration will also include failed efforts or ones that reach modest success before losing momentum. The leaders of the process monitor the performance and potential of each group, ensure that waning projects can be brought home with the least damage, and encourage the emergence and incubation of new ideas.

Over time the district regeneration contributes to a shift in culture toward a sense that anyone, at any stage, can be part of an "authoring of place." The projects become more ambitious, more people migrate into the district, and external capital begins to move in to support real estate, local businesses, and start-ups. There is a very real risk of the "gentrification trap," whereby the district becomes so successful and overpriced that it begins to exclude some groups.

Anticipating this risk, as the district gains momentum, the planning group extends a hand to work with other districts or nearby cities to encourage copying and adaptation. It is in the interest of the original district to spread the mission: lifting nearby places will reduce the pressure of "gentrification," elevate the growth rate of the surrounding economy, provide natural expansion for projects and companies in the original district, and allow some team members to set new challenges for themselves.

As a district becomes successful beyond its local catchment area, it may begin to operate in other regions or internationally. Some of the projects may have unlocked large global opportunities, and there is a vast supply of districts and cities in the United States alone requiring a regeneration strategy.

The backbone organization behind the initial district strategy began as a very light and small group. As it gains success and extends its mission, it also starts to replicate across other districts and cities. It is wary of the risks of bureaucracy and uses an autonomous cell approach for seeding and expansion. No group is ever larger than the "two-pizza" rule, a concept popularized by Amazon that defines the supposed ideal size of a project team.[75] If size matters, they may evolve into a different structure, such as a company, an academy, or a nonprofit.

Rule 10. Rewild Your Population and Land

The balancing of enclosure and nature runs deep in our psyches. We prize our homes but delight in gardens. We will pay up to twice as much for a house with views of mountains or bodies of water.[76] We consume nature but marvel at plants and animals. We restore our health by bathing in woods, seas, and lakes. The most attractive cities have combined growth while retaining natural elements, exemplified by London's parks and gardens or Boston's Emerald Necklace.[77] In the motor society, this natural balance was discarded, and today we are paying for this mistake, socially, in our bodies, but also in harming economic growth. Rewilding can be viewed as a strategy to restore the balance of town and green. It is also a strong economic engine: the draw of well-managed green habitats can combine with more profitable use of land from biodiverse farming.

Knepp farm in Sussex, England, has pioneered a shift from traditional intense UK farming to a new model based on rewilding. Ancestral animal species have been reintroduced and are lightly managed, allowing natural cycles of breeding and the emergence of animal herd structures and intraspecies collaboration. In the absence of natural predators, regular culling produces high-quality meat at low cost. Additional revenue comes from ecotourism.

In the US grain belt a movement for regenerative agriculture is afoot. At the time of the European settlement, the amount of topsoil was as high as 14–16 inches.[78] Mechanization of agriculture, while driving increasingly improved productivity, has been systematically depleting the soil. One 2021 study of the corn belt, using satellite imagery, estimated a loss of between 24% and 42% of topsoil.[79] Soil erosion has broad consequences: weak soil requires industrial application of fertilizers and pesticides, contributing to environmental pollution in the waterways downstream of farms, rivers, and lakes and to overall transfer of carbon from topsoil into the atmosphere. Farmers become dependent on industrial inputs, with subscale farms struggling to make money, thus contributing to the concentration of land and farming into ever larger groups, even more committed to mechanized approaches.

According to Regenerative International,

Regenerative Agriculture is a holistic land management practice that leverages the power of photosynthesis in plants to close the carbon cycle, and build soil health, crop resilience and nutrient density. Regenerative agriculture improves soil health, primarily through the practices that increase soil organic matter. This not only aids in increasing soil biota diversity and health but increases biodiversity both above and below the soil surface, while increasing both water holding capacity and sequestering carbon at greater depths, thus drawing down climate-damaging levels of atmospheric CO_2.[80]

A 2018 study by Claire LaCanne and Jonathan Lundrgen, on the potential of regenerative farming on corn, the largest American crop, estimated that these practices would increase profit margins by 78% and reduce pest levels by a factor of 10 while recapturing significant levels of carbon and driving improved water retention.[81] Walter Jehne, an Australian scientist, estimates that shifting to regenerative practices in farming and forestry at a mass scale could reduce 20 billion tons of carbon per year, enough to reverse planetary carbon buildup while simultaneously making farms more profitable and reducing reliance on large-scale farms.[82]

Despite the potential of rewilding and regenerative agriculture, a transition is far from easy. Mechanized approaches are efficient in the use of labor and require little adaptation to the underlying terrain. In contrast, regenerative agriculture requires testing a wide range of cover crops, combining husbandry and cultivation and adaptation to changing weather conditions and the overall evolution in soil health.

Gabe Brown, pioneering farmer and author of *Dirt to Soil*, writes that it took him least four years and considerable experimentation to shift from industrial to regenerative agriculture.[83] Nonetheless, he was able to return arid dirt into increasingly richer and healthier soil and to consistently increase farm profits. What is now required is a large-scale process of knowledge transfer, skills development, funding, and R&D to extend the experience of a few pioneers into a large-scale movement.

Scenario

A rural college town on a river that flows into the Great Lakes sits in an agricultural region suffering the social, environmental, and economic effects of mechanized agriculture. With exhausted soil, its farming tradition is under pressure. Polluted waterways create health risks. The lack of opportunity drives a talent drain of its most promising citizens, including many graduates from the local college. The college has long been in a precarious financial position, and COVID-19 has put it in jeopardy of a shutdown.

A diverse group of "town and gown" pioneers sets up a cell of "re-wilders," supported by an existing group that has achieved considerable rewilding success in a neighboring state. The group develops an ambitious strategy to shift 50% of farming in the region to regenerative models within five years. Their global objective is to prove Jehne's thesis in a big enough environment and with sufficient insight that the practices can be rapidly translated across the United States and globally.

Building on successful city regeneration efforts, the group spins off a series of subgroups covering a range of activities. These include "Re-wilding Corridor," "Corn Regeneration," "River Regeneration," "Eco-Tourism," "Center for Regenerative Agriculture," "Regenerative Supply Chain," "Regenerative Financing Society," "Tactical Urbanism," "Academic Reboot," and "15-Minute City."

Each group recruits a founding team and develops a strategy based on self-authoring exercises among its members. As the group strategies gain traction and credibility, the emerging place-based thesis is to transform the entire city and college into a global center of excellence in applying regenerative farming, fishery, forestry, and husbandry practices.

The college, facing financial difficulties, pivots into a new structure, separating the asset base from the education layer. The college focuses on regeneration, integrating disciplines such as economics, English, mathematics, robotics, chemistry, and physics and adding specialized practices such as soil management, reforestation, and water management. The asset management team develops a platform university model. Global academic centers with interest in regeneration are encouraged to set up microcolleges and to learn and experiment in the US Midwest. Global investors and corporations with a commitment to net-zero carbon are tapped for carbon credit purchases, grants, and venture funding. The town pitches the economic potential for early movers in what could become a multitrillion-dollar global market.

Environmental cleanup of the waterways, combined with a rapid shift to a bikeable and walkable city, positions the city to become an attractive place for visitors, remote knowledge workers, and outdoors enthusiasts, a kind of "riverine" Boulder. The talent drain ceases, and many of the college students stay in the city postgraduation to work in the new projects and companies that emerge. Empty nesters move in, attracted by the campus environment, quality of life, and housing flexibility resulting from the densification process.

As the city and region gain confidence, expertise, capital, and a supporting infrastructure, they increase their level of ambition. The college infrastructure team now hosts a range of universities and microcolleges and has been invited to replicate the model in other failing colleges.

This eventually leads to an even more ambitious strategy. The region, now including several other towns along the river and on the adjacent lake, gets together to build a "rewilding corridor" that will run for over 50 miles. This corridor is designed to transform the entire agricultural, riverine, and lake environment to a preindustrial level of cleanness, to promote large scale species migration, and to provide a parallel network of human-powered pathways for a wide range of interests. This initiative is in part modeled on the American Prairie Reserve in Montana.[84]

Rule 11. Turn Housing into a Service

Housing is a massive asset class (over $30 trillion in value in the United States), and the largest expense category for most families. Homes are central to family dynamics, to our sense of self, and to our financial stability. Houses are also a key dividing line between wealthy and poor, a major source of financial stress for many, an asset class with poor and declining productivity, increasingly at odds with the needs of our society, and a sector with weak adoption of software models. By analogy, the second largest expense, the car, has innovated much faster, is rapidly digitizing, and is evolving toward a service model. There is an opportunity to reconceive the role of housing into a service, adopting many of the learning of other services transitions in software and other domains. Examples of housing as a service include college campuses, high-end hotel and resort experiences, condominiums with service layers, and senior-living homes. However, these tend to serve niches of wealth or age, and these markets are highly fragmented.

There are several start-ups in this space, pointing the way into new models: Stablegold Hospitality offers low-cost, extended stay in economically disadvantaged areas; Veev has developed an integrated process to cut construction costs in half and time to build by a factor of four; Ascent Real Estate is providing affordable housing by investing in gentrifying neighborhoods and using long-term deed restrictions; Icon is a 3D construction printing company; Boklok is a Swedish spin-off of Ikea and Skanska focused on low-cost prefab housing; and Venn is an Israeli company focused on neighborhood management.[85]

Zoning is at the root of poor housing outcomes. Jacob Krimmell and Joseph Gyourko have done extensive work on the impact of zoning regulation on housing costs, concluding in a 2021 study that highly regulated areas could drive a "zoning tax" of over $100K per quarter acre in the most expensive cities.[86] With a history of discriminatory zoning practices and strong evidence of disparate impact of zoning on the least advantaged, there is a growing willingness of citizens to push their leaders to substantially adapt zoning from single-family housing to duplex and other higher-density options. Strong Towns, a grass-roots organization dedicated to shifting US housing and urban strategies toward incremental and regenerative strategies, suggests that 2021 could be the year of transition, pointing to dramatic relaxation in zoning restrictions in states such as California, Connecticut, New Hampshire, and Utah.[87]

The combination of innovative models, new technologies, and zoning relaxation could spur a once-in-a-generation wave of opportunities for towns to remake themselves.

Scenario

Laconia, a New Hampshire mill town with 16,000 people, sits at the confluence of several lakes, including the state's largest, Winnipesaukee.

Despite being a tourist draw due to its unique location, the downtown core has suffered from poor zoning and old housing stock. The lake region is suffering from pollution, with runoff, invasive species, and nutrient loading. House prices have averaged $250K, roughly the US average but considerably lower than in the neighboring state of Massachusetts. Laconia is 90 minutes from Boston, and a future train line could connect the region to the New England hub.[88] In 2021 there is a proposed law to allow single-family homes with sewer and water access to be converted into duplexes and fourplexes.[89] With remote workers moving into the city and region, Laconia sees an opportunity to regenerate the town with new housing solutions.

The town forms several autonomous groups, including "Housing as a Service", "Blue Collar Skills," "Lake Regeneration," "Open Streets," "Talent Recruitment," and "Microcolleges." The teams work to develop self-authoring plans, which coalesce around a strategy to turn Laconia into a next-generation lake town. It takes inspiration from the lake towns of Switzerland, places such as Lucerne, Geneva, or Zurich—some of the most desirable towns in the world.

The "Talent Recruitment" team develops a plan to attract a sociodemographically diverse group of 500 to 1,000 people to the community along the lines of Tulsa Remote. The "Microcolleges" team works with the local Lakes Region Community College to develop a plan to create three microcolleges, one focused on lake regeneration and fisheries, one on urban regeneration and new housing models, and one on housing skill development.

The urban regeneration team works with the city, key landowners, banks, and townspeople to develop a plan. Laconia has excess parking downtown, and most trips today are by car. The initial focus of the plan is to gradually convert the downtown area into a medium-density walkable neighborhood, reusing much of the parking space for buildings or green areas. Buildings are designed for flexibility and mixed use, within the historical vernacular of the town. For example, a four-story building in the local vernacular might include a grocery store, café, and coworking space on the ground floor, a wide mix of different-sized apartments in the middle floors, and a rooftop restaurant overlooking the lake.

Given the need for flexible living arrangements for local workers, outdoor types, remotes, regenerators, and snowbirds, several buildings are designed to meet their respective needs. One building is set along the lakefront as a base for outdoors enthusiasts who want to access kayaking, biking, and hiking and includes a specialized rental and retail store, a café, and a training school, as well as options for short and medium stays. Another building is optimized for remotes, including coworking space, conference rooms, concierge services, and blended home/office configurations. Snowbirds with nearby lake houses can downsize to smaller waterfront units, with boating and other services on demand. Local worker housing is embedded in all buildings rather than segregated into separate dwellings. This reduces the required commute to work and integrates locals with out-of-towners.

Recognizing the role of housing as an asset, a wide range of options are provided by the corporation that manages housing. Some customers will reinvest the proceeds from selling a home on the lake or in an expensive town in one or more apartments that can create passive rental income and surge capacity for family visits. Those with limited assets will automatically accumulate ownership in their building as renters, with the ability to either increase their asset (for example by investing extra cash) or withdraw (by selling into the housing equity pool). These mechanisms allow much greater diversification than the binary buy or rent options available historically.

A network of protected bike paths is built, starting in the old train station and extending radially to enable safe human-powered transit from the broadest number of destinations. Using some of the lessons from rule 3, there is a sustained infrastructure and communications strategy to shift trips below three kilometers away from cars and trucks. There is considerable resistance, given that the status quo is considered by many a fundamental right and that many of the roads are controlled by the state transport authorities. In building the bike paths, the city prototypes a snow-melt strategy along the Holland,

Michigan, model that ensures the network is available year-round and uses the path building to lay out fiber infrastructure to better meet the needs of cloud working.

The combined effect of building and new transit turns the downtown core into a high people traffic location year-round. Summer activity is followed by leaf-peepers in the fall, and ice-fishing in the deep winter. Demand for food, local shopping, and other services is first met by pop-up vans and stalls and by outdoor expansion of the existing restaurants. Over time Laconia becomes a foodie destination akin to successful seaport towns such as Portland, Maine, or Portsmouth, New Hampshire, which have similarly combined their natural placement and historic downtown to great effect. Many foodies will start to do "the circuit," combining the best of the ocean and the best of the lake.

The central axis for expansion becomes the "housing-as-a-service" innovation. The corporation that manages housing is owned by the town and serves the long-term needs of the community. It acquires land and buildings as they come on the market; it develops and builds a variety of housing options; and it generates a range of profits from daily, weekly, or monthly services and from episodic capital transactions. As its asset base builds, it diversifies into enabling home options for townspeople, everything from starter-home financing through ethical reverse mortgaging or other options for later life. Recognizing the critical need for community at the earlier and later stages of life, it embeds senior living into its building strategy. Embedding becomes very powerful: older people are surrounded by younger people, and both generations provide and receive voluntary care on a reciprocal model. By reducing the risk of being killed by cars and providing protected bike paths, both these vulnerable populations experience much more outdoors life and gain greater agency than the prevailing models today.

The housing corporation works closely with other town utilities, including electricity, waste, and fiber broadband, to ensure that the city provides the highest caliber of services. It leverages its growing capital and land-base to actively support lake environmental cleanup; as a major landowner, it is a direct beneficiary of such improvements.

Anticipating the risk of excess demand for housing, it continuously monitors the balance of supply and demand and seeks to build to maintain a stable ratio. By combining various financial streams, it is less sensitive to periodic swings in the cost of building and the price of housing. It gains increasing depth in managing zoning, construction, housing, and services management, thus becoming ever more efficient.

The success of the Laconia Housing Corporation attracts the attention of other places and financial backers. Mindful of needing to stay focused but with a broader mission, the corporation helps to seed similar ventures across neighboring towns and cities. Each town corporation is encouraged to develop its own strategy and to use autonomous cells. The corporation is also interested in building connecting human-transit networks with neighboring places. Tapping into the diverse needs of snowmobilers, e-bikers, cross-country skiers, walkers, birdwatchers, hikers, and runners, it builds multilane networks connecting to adjacent towns, with separation by category and adjusting for seasonality.

This network begins to grow on its own as new places ask to be connected and are encouraged to develop their own place-based strategy. As the network gains size and scale, a new wave of visitors, part-timers, and full-timers move into the town and region. The flexible housing model becomes even more useful.

New models of living and working emerge. For example, some remote workers rotate through multiple locations, walking from town to town, with their belongings packed and unpacked by staff. The transition often happens over a weekend, and on Monday they are back at work, but from a new place. They spend time that used to be dedicated to commuting in exploring the new location, making new acquaintances, taking courses at the local microcollege. If they own a home, this can also be rented out to others by the corporation, essentially subsidizing their roaming lifestyle. Employers are very supportive of this lifestyle, since they know that these employees are fitter, happier, and thus more productive than ever before.

Rule 12. Rediscover the Lost Art of Placemaking

Behind the success of many cities was a long-term vision and commitment and tradecraft in placemaking. The aggressive push during the motor society period to build highways, raze city neighborhoods, and build suburbs has left tremendous physical and psychological scars and explicitly rejected traditional placemaking norms. Movements such as the Congress for the New Urbanism and successful placemaking strategies in pockets across the United States suggest that there is a groundswell of interest in rekindling placemaking.[90] With the opportunity for 30,000 or more villages, towns, and cities in the United States to bid for talent on the move, the need for and value of placemaking knowledge will become a top priority. This includes aggregate-level skills, such as neighborhood master planning; specific skills, such as engineering safe coexistence of biking, walking, and cars; and new data skills, such as extracting information and drawing insights on livability metrics from factors such as air pollution or walkability.

What are some key elements of a place? Social Life Project provides some insights and many inspiring photographs covering some of the most popular places in the world in "11 Transformative Agendas to Restore Social Life in Your Community." These include

1. "Bringing Back the Public Square"
2. "Using Markets to Bring Social Life Back Everywhere"
3. "Starting with Sidewalks is the Key to Creating the Streets We Want"
4. "Turning Buildings Inside Out: Architecture of Place"
5. "Creating New Community Hubs"
6. "Capitalizing on the Appeal of Waterfronts"
7. "Expanding Cultural Destinations to Spark Imagination"
8. "Strengthening Assets that Express a City's Character"
9. "Highlighting a Community's Identity by Creating Great Amenities"
10. "Creating Social Life for All"
11. "Having Fun."[91]

Although each showcased transformation has a unique twist, the common theme is around bringing crowds together; integrating nature and culture; making places accessible to all; designing for creativity, exchange, and happiness; and shifting from car-centered to people-centered movement.

If these are the kinds of urban settings we desire, the question is, How do we organize to deliver such outcomes? One of the best guides for place-based leaders is a book by architect David Sims, *Soft City*, which is based on his extensive experience in urban planning in Scandinavia.[92] Sims's book, with photographs and illustrations that make his concepts come alive, is organized around nine key ideas, which resonate with many of the themes of the modern society thesis. The nine concepts advanced by Sims are:

1. "Diversity of Built Form"
2. "Diversity of Outdoor Spaces"
3. "Flexibility"
4. "Human Scale"
5. "Walkability"
6. "Sense of Control and Identity"
7. "Pleasant Microclimate"
8. "Smaller Carbon Footprint"
9. "Greater Biodiversity"

The theme that ties all of this together is the notion of "gentle density," building ways that bring people together while providing them with ways to easily withdraw into private spaces. Some of the most desirable cities in the world, places such as Paris or Barcelona, have densities in the range of 40K–50K people per square mile, whereas American cities are in the range of 10K–20K people per square mile.[93]

There is a perception by many in the United States that the kind of "gentle density" seen in Europe or Japan is somehow "un-American," that every American must grow and mow a large lawn and live in the largest home that he or she can afford. This perception is closely aligned with the idea that there is a fundamental right to drive a car anywhere, that the car is a source of freedom.

These assumptions are belied by the popularity of walkable places as tourist destinations, whether open spaces such as the Grand Canyon, denser American places such as Manhattan or the French Quarter of New Orleans, or the ultimate in European walkability, Disneyland. Despite this, given the incumbency of the motor society, the burden of proof is on demonstrating to sceptics that there is a better way. Rekindling the art of placemaking is as much about changing perceptions and assumptions as it is about facts on the ground.

The global environmental coalition C40 provides a guide toward place-based regeneration with a 2020 article titled "How to Build Back Better with a 15-Minute City," which includes a number of key principles: (1) establish a citywide 15-minute vision, overall and by neighborhood; (2) collect data and seek participatory input from people across the city to map out the presence or absence at neighborhood level of the amenities, businesses, job types, public spaces, and other elements that have been identified as core to your city's 15-minute city vision; (3) using this information, translate your citywide vision into a plan for each neighborhood, focusing first on those that are furthest away from the goal (lower-income neighborhoods), ensuring that their residents and local businesses are involved in designing measures for improvement; (4) improve biking and walking infrastructure, including reallocating street space to pedestrians and cyclists; (5) create complete neighborhoods by decentralizing core services and developing a social and functional mix; (6) implement planning measures to help neighborhoods thrive; and (7) encourage teleworking and service digitization to limit the need of travel.[94]

Through all these examples we see the threading of triple-win approaches: social, environmental, and economic growth cannot be in conflict but must be in a system of reinforcement. We must also recognize that we are building back into a much more distributed world rather than the pre-COVID paradigm focused on the dominance of megacities. How then could a state such as a New Hampshire think about placemaking at the state level?

Scenario

New Hampshire has long enjoyed its influential position in the American electoral cycle. It is somewhat anomalous in the fractured American polity as a "purple" state, combining its libertarian roots ("Live free or die") with an infusion of liberal values from southern New England. In the shadow of neighboring Massachusetts and surrounded by crunchy Vermonters on one side and down-east Mainers on the other, New Hampshire has sometimes struggled for a stronger sense of identity. COVID has sparked a wave of interest in the state, and it was among the top three destinations in the country for inward migration in 2020.[95]

The state executives and legislature see that New Hampshire has an opportunity to lead the country in a different way. What if there were a mechanism to combine the interests of left and right, to combine economic growth with social and environmental improvement? These interests have often been felt to be in conflict, but the emerging learning about regenerative growth models is pointing to a real opportunity to do well and do good.

Towns and cities across the state have been experimenting with new models of placemaking. In the north of the state, where the winter limits commercial activity, Berlin has developed a proposal for a downtown snow-melt strategy, along the lines of Holland, Michigan. Even though the first proposal was denied funding, its title ("Renewing Berlin with Renewable Energy") indicates the mindset. The coastal jewel of Portsmouth has been investing for the past decade in becoming a high-tech and culinary destination. New Hampshire hosts 24 colleges and universities, ranging from Ivy League institutions such as Dartmouth to disruptive innovators such as Southern New Hampshire University, 7 community colleges, and 6 state university campuses. The state has become one of the hottest real estate markets in the country as remote workers have moved from higher-cost and higher-tax states in the Northeast, and some second-homers have flipped to make New Hampshire their home state. Key industrial cities such as

Manchester and Concord are positioning for a growth wave anchored around the New England innovation economy.[96]

We could imagine an overarching strategy based on the modern society rules. It is conceived as a top-down initiative, with support across all branches of government and politicians and city leaders from left and right. The high-level aspiration is as a green-connected state, with a network of thriving small and medium-sized towns and cities pursuing a new kind of "industrial revolution" along the lines of what happened in the nineteenth century but now oriented around a triple-win model of sustainable growth.

But for this ambitious plan to succeed, it will need to work at the grassroots and town and city level. The small backbone group tasked with sparking a green-growth revolution adopts a cell-based approach. New Hampshire has 230 towns, from the largest city of Manchester, with 112,000 people, to the famous early-voting hamlet of Dixville Notch, with 11 inhabitants. The team focuses on 70 towns with 5,000 people or more.

Each town has a task leader who works with interested participants to develop "two-pizza" groups. Small towns might typically have one or two groups, whereas larger cities would likely end up with 6–10 groups each. In total, 200 cells are formed. Each is funded with an initial grant of $10K.

Groups cluster around the themes in the 12 rules: "local/global," "purpose," "slow streets/clean air," "community-led growth," "talent attraction," "bionic workers," "lifelong learning," "innovation," "growth engine," "rewilding," "housing as a service," and "placemaking," which in turn create more specialized spin-offs, such as "biochar," "Dutch bike networks," "riparian lives," "lake regeneration," "urban villages," "microcolleges," "blue-collar skills," "platform university," "financing transformation," and "New Hampshire train spine." In total, there are 50 unique group types.

Teams are encouraged to go through a self-authoring exercise for themselves and their place and to plan for a sequential process, beginning with small tests and evolving toward an ever more ambitious agenda. The general ethos of the top-level initiative is covered in the "soft city" or "15-minute city" design paradigm, but each group is encouraged to develop its own interpretation. Cells are encouraged to work with key stakeholders in their respective towns, to focus on gaining fast traction and local credibility and to build a "triple-win" case of social, environmental, and economic sustainability. A new set of execution-oriented grants are made, of varying levels based on the quality, traction, and ambition of each proposal.

The first wave of projects is tactical in nature: rapid changes to transform urban landscapes on the "open street" model; a first round of talent attraction programs; test runs of a microcollege; rewilding experiments; market stalls and market days; skills-formation events; community engagement and volunteering. Almost every town has existing institutions or programs whose missions fit with one of more of these placemaking initiatives. This kind of collaboration allows teams to operate at a faster pace and helps to integrate local stakeholders into each placemaking strategy.

There is a strong effort to manage communication and learning, across all the teams, and with the wider public. It is critical to get some early wins and to actively communicate the progress and the potential. There will likely be concerns around car restrictions, gentrification, new inward migrants, expansion in school populations, and risk of traffic growth. Data capture and rapid learning of failures and successes is equally important.

The second wave of projects will be more ambitious in nature, taking longer, consuming more capital, and requiring cells to seek external sources of funding and to provide credible return-on-investment results. They might include new biking infrastructure, a first wave of "gently dense building," a full launch of a "microcollege," a fully funded "lake cleanup" project, a "regenerative farm," a "biochar" project, and a thriving downtown plaza.

As these projects progress, towns and cities will differentiate, with some moving faster than others and some initiatives evolving into areas of specialization. The backbone team will shift over time toward a role of thesis refinement, orchestration, capital allocation, knowledge transfer, scaling, and platform development. It will encourage the sunsetting of weaker projects and teams and the formation of new areas or spin-offs from existing initiatives. It will tap into larger-scale funding to support the ambitions of the most effective teams. It will seek to coordinate and network cross-state initiatives such as the rail spine and a parallel high-fiber connectivity network, as well as human-centered and animal-centered pathways that could eventually allow animals and humans to cross the entire state, safely and without use of engines. The backbone team will also liaise with similar efforts in adjacent states, across the United States, and internationally.

As projects move into maturity within 5 to 10 years the results of the strategy become more visible. The population of half of the towns has grown by 20% or more, while simultaneously emissions have been cut by substantially eliminating car-based rides and replacing them with walking, biking, trains, and other transit options. Highly walkable and bikeable core downtowns across many of the larger and mid-size cities, many of them mill towns, have shown the opportunity for a postindustrial renaissance. Human-centered networks, connecting cities and towns, extend for hundreds of miles, contributing to a substantial increase in fitness, improvements in body mass index, and reductions in health-related costs. New Hampshire, traditionally a vacation destination for people from southern New England, becomes an outdoor attraction for visitors across the country, many of whom return home demanding the same quality-of-life improvements and some of whom decide to test living in New Hampshire through the many flexible options for housing as a service.

New Hampshire's knowledge enterprise network is thriving. A plethora of microcolleges are operating across many of the 70 target towns, and several have evolved to become full-size colleges and specialist institutions in new areas of social interest, such as urban development and regenerative farming, husbandry, forest management, and fisheries. The innovation economy is also thriving, and the region has become a leader in the new fast-growing venture capital area of "society tech" focused on triple-win areas such as healthy aging, lifelong work and learning, future cities, and circular economy. A new wave of companies with global ambitions are now based in New Hampshire, positioning the state for a wave of regenerative expansion during the 2030s.

Conclusion

Why is there a new set of rules, and what binds these ideas together? Our view is that we are coming to the end of an economic model, one that worked well for a while but has increasingly lost traction. The failure in this model is manifest in the debt bubble, growth in the levels of obesity, depression, and health inequality, a reversal in the life expectancy curve, and rapid growth in deaths of despair. COVID has only served to accelerate the end of this cycle, while simultaneously creating a new possibility through the unprecedented shift in work to a placeless location. Paradoxically, this shift creates a once-in-a-century reshuffle in the role of place, reducing the importance of the megacity and revitalizing the opportunity for every other place. For the United States, and for those towns and cities that are alive to this possibility, this is a sort of "mulligan," an opportunity to move fast, redo the mistakes of the past, and usher in a modern society that is robustly positioned for the future. The same fundamental thesis could apply anywhere in the world.

These 12 rules are tied together by three common elements: connectedness, economic opportunity, and iterability. One scourge of the prior model has been the silo-based approach, in which every key player stayed very focused in his or her area but often lacked the instinct and concern for the broader whole. In the modern society, while developing specialist skills and areas of interest, we need to regain a sense of group-level purpose around the ambition of the whole. This tends to happen most easily at the local level but can eventually aggregate into regional or even national alignment.

A second assumption of the past was that we could achieve economic efficiency or high-quality living but not both, whereas our premise is that for each of the rules the economic benefits are sufficient that they become self-financing and that the overall benefit of the complete application will be a strong surge in economic growth along with a reduction in the use of resources. This is analogous to how the Japanese debunked the American myth in the car industry that you could have quality or low cost but not both. They showed through Kaizen and other techniques that improved design could achieve lower costs and higher quality. In essence, they showed that there was a design issue. We have a similar situation today. The current weaknesses in our society are a design problem and can be solved with improved designs.

The third assumption was a deterministic big-bang approach inherited from the success of World War II and applied for too long into ever larger projects. In contrast, the new model is iterative, options based, success based, and scalable based on evidence. This is the model of the most impactful asset class during the postwar era, venture capital.

The extension of venture capital design into the broader economy is a core foundation of the modern society. Could we use the venture capital model to harness natural, human, and financial capital into the creation of thousands of talent magnets?

2

The Knowledge Enterprise
as an Alternative University

IN CREATING THE CONCEPT OF "KNOWLEDGE TOWNS," we are not simply proposing placing a traditional college within a town or city. That is, we envision a particular kind of institution of higher education, which we call a "knowledge enterprise." This could be an incumbent college or university, but in our formulation a knowledge enterprise takes a different institutional form. Indeed, it is an alternative university, one that at present does not exist.

Next-Generation Town-Gown Relations

Costas Spirou has devised a topology of what he terms "urban entre-preneurial activity," meaning the initiatives of universities in their surrounding communities. For years, many universities, especially those that reside in urban locations, were aloof and cut off from their surroundings. The same might be said of small colleges, even those in so-called college towns. While the college might have been an important source of demand for local services—bars, restaurants, and other businesses that cater to students—and while these colleges might be a source of local employment, they very rarely take an active role in economic development or creative placemaking.

The first, most basic level of urban entrepreneurialism is "real estate expansion centering in the acquisition or development of facilities for the purpose of providing fundamental services to students."[1] Judith Rodin at the University of Pennsylvania led a group of universities in the late 1990s/early 2000s who recognized their responsibilities to the neighborhoods and surrounding communities in which they were embedded, and which had fallen into disrepair. "We would strive to rebuild West Philadelphia's social and economic capacity by simultaneously and aggressively acting on five interrelated fronts," recounted Rodin. "We would make the neighborhood clean and safe with a variety of new interventions. We would stabilize the housing market. We would spur economic development by directing university contracts and purchases to local businesses, many of which we would help to initiate. We would encourage retail development by attracting new shops, restaurants, and cultural venues that were neighborhood friendly. We would improve the public schools. We were committed to a spirit of seeking true partnership."[2] In these cases, the university extends beyond its ivory tower into the community as a catalyst for economic growth and social improvement.

The second level of urban entrepreneurialism identified by Spirou involves "aggressive commercial undertakings which have the capacity to yield additional revenue. The income may derive from retail, hotels, restaurants, and related activities."[3] Smaller colleges in rural areas also have recently turned to economic development, although not necessarily on the model of the innovation district. James Martin, James E. Samels, and associates list characteristics of these "new American college towns," including the creation of a walkable downtown, investments in public infrastructure, cultural diversity, hospitals and access to health care, "campus curbside appeal," craft and microbreweries, a bookstore, and hotel and other mixed-use codevelopment.[4] Colgate University, for example, now owns and operates a historic inn with a tavern, a bookstore, and a movie theater in the village of Hamilton, New York. Colgate is also constructing affordably priced housing for university staff and other local workers and is looking to build a mixed-use development that would include coworking and incubator space. Colby College in Waterville, Maine, "is drawing on the fundraising campaign, cash reserves and debt financing to pump some $82 million into the redevelopment of five major projects on Main Street, about two miles from campus," reports the *New York Times*.

> The first to open was a 200-bed residential hall for students and faculty in 2018, Colby's only off-campus housing. Across the street, it spent more than $5 million renovating a long-vacant bank building, then dangled low rents to woo an outlet of a Portland-based pizza pub and a software company looking to train local workers. An artisanal chocolate shop with a cafe is on the way. And nearby, the college is building a 53-room hotel and restaurant, a visual and performing arts center, and an arts collaborative with studio spaces.[5]

While the "college town" in these cases pursue a new economic development and placemaking strategy, the "college" in the new college town model does not seem especially "new." That is, aside from codevelopment with the city on real estate projects and perhaps the extension of the bookstore to the community, it is largely the town that has changed; the college retains its traditional purpose, with the addition, perhaps, of a codevelopment initiative on the periphery of its mission. In the model we are proposing here, town and gown *both* change together to attract talent.

Spirou's third category represents the highest level of urban entrepreneurial activity in which a university might engage. "The real estate expansion of land holdings within this urban space," writes Spirou, "allows [entrepreneurial universities] to strategically position themselves to develop strong partnerships with industry and advance science, technology, knowledge, and innovation with the aim of becoming catalysts for major urban revitalization and future economic growth."[6] More specifically, some large universities have spawned "innovation districts," business incubators that commercialize university research and intellectual property, and Spirou documents the impact of several of these across the country.

Richard Florida identified the role played by research universities in attracting talent. "The new view of the university as fueling the economy primarily through the attraction and creation of talent, as well as generating innovations, has important implications for public policy." Florida wrote in 2005,

> To date, federal, state, and local policy that encourages economic gain from universities has been organized as a giant *technology push* experiment. The logic is: If the university can just push more innovations out the door, these innovations will somehow magically turn into economic growth. But the economic effects of universities emanate in more subtle ways. Universities do not operate as simple engines of innovation. They are a crucial piece of the infrastructure of the creative economy, providing mechanisms for generating and harnessing talent. Once policymakers embrace this new view, they can begin to update or craft new policies that will improve the university's impact on the U.S. creative economy. We do not have to stop promoting university-industry research or transferring university breakthroughs to the private sector, but we must support the university's role in the broader creation of talent.[7]

Usually that refers to attracting students and faculty to a university. But a knowledge-enterprise-as-talent-magnet, as we are conceiving it, is in the business of attracting a wider range of talent than just students and faculty. This strategy succeeds not simply by the passive location of a college in a town or region: a knowledge enterprise is an active attractor of a range of talent. Florida was referring to R1 research universities in urban centers. Our argument is that smaller colleges and universities in rural areas or secondary cities can pursue a talent magnet strategy.

Our approach looks beyond economic development as it has been practiced or the narrow interest in catalyzing tech projects. Indeed, ours is a strategy for attracting talent—people—before companies.

Like Purdue or West Virginia University, colleges and universities can play a leading role in advancing a talent magnet strategy for their regions. This must extend beyond a stand-alone program on the periphery of campus. Attracting knowledge workers and other talent should move to the center of the academic enterprise. That is, the college as talent magnet becomes the mission, the purpose of the institution. In order to survive and thrive in the new political economy of higher education, many existing colleges and universities located in areas outside the urban centers of the knowledge economy will have to reinvent themselves as knowledge enterprises.

We borrow the name knowledge enterprise from Michael Crow and William Dabars. They use the term to identify what they call the "new American university," describing an entity that is "committed to discovery, creativity, and innovation, accessible to the demographically broadest possible student body, socioeconomically as well as intellectually, and directly responsive to the needs of the nation and society more broadly."[8] We have appropriated their term to distinguish a kind of academic organization that aligns directly to a region's talent magnet strategy. Thus, when we say "college" or "university," we are referring to incumbent academic organizations. To identify an organization as a knowledge enterprise means one that has other features as well, features that accelerate a talent magnet strategy. In our formulation, a knowledge enterprise *is* a talent magnet.

Furthermore, a knowledge enterprise is defined by more than its attachments to a local town or region. Many existing colleges and universities may reside or are situated in a town or region. Some might even be engaged in economic development, either by serving as a property owner in the city, as a source for demand from local business, or, more recently, as "innovation hubs," where the intellectual property of university research is commercialized as technological products. In these circumstances, universities are understood to be economic drivers.

A knowledge enterprise certainly engages in economic development, but this is only a portion of its overall mission. A knowledge enterprise may look like an incumbent college or university but is distinguished by its additional commitment to the 12 features of a talent magnet strategy:

1. The knowledge enterprise is the region's node connecting it to the larger knowledge economy.
2. It educates for and encourages "lives of purpose" not only among traditional-aged students but for residents of the town or region.
3. Rather than occupying a hermetically sealed corner of the town, a knowledge enterprise is physically expansive, extending outward across the town such that it becomes a "15-minute campus."
4. A knowledge enterprise functions as a central—perhaps the most important—"third place" for the community.
5. Using its expertise in enrollment management—in the recruitment of student talent—the knowledge enterprise works with the regional economic development team to drive a talent-attraction plan. The mentorship of students is extended outward: mentorship to knowledge workers becomes a vital service offered by the knowledge enterprise.
6. A knowledge enterprise is that institution that educates for the interface between machine and human intelligence, supporting the "bionic worker."
7. A knowledge enterprise provides lifelong learning services as a central part of its mission, not simply as a community enrichment. These take three forms: cultural programming, professional development, and "superager" services.
8. A knowledge enterprise is an innovation cluster, but not only focused on incubating the next big-tech company. It is a creativity cluster, incubating and implementing a full range of novel ideas.
9. Faculty are encouraged to be entrepreneurs, to take their ideas and develop new enterprises. Entrepreneurship joins research, teaching, service, and mentorship as faculty responsibilities. Additionally, the knowledge enterprise functions as a venture capitalist fund both for faculty ideas and for entrepreneurs in the larger region.
10. The culture of a knowledge enterprise is rewilded. Environmental consciousness is treated as a transcurricular value.

11. A knowledge enterprise is a "fourth place" for the community, a blending of home, work, and convivial places serving students and the knowledge workers in the larger community.
12. Urban development extends from the knowledge enterprise outward toward the town, upsetting the usual town-gown relationship.

A knowledge enterprise is not exclusively in the business of educating 18- to 22-year-old undergraduates—the main service provided by incumbent colleges—although that could certainly remain an important mission of the enterprise. That is, a knowledge enterprise could still offer degree programs in health sciences, information technology, and other "in demand" fields. They can continue to have sororities and other facets of student life. They can continue to host intercollegiate football and volleyball games. Such an academic organization already describes many colleges that reside in smaller towns and regions. And as such, these are not currently set up to serve as talent magnets as we conceive of them.

The customer base for a knowledge enterprise is expanded to include adults—and not only those seeking job retraining, although in a distributed knowledge ecosystem and economy, that may very well be an audience for the services of a knowledge enterprise. Those adults could be those 60 years of age and older, and the knowledge enterprise could include as part of its services to be an institution that serves "superagers," those who wish to rigorously exercise their brains after retirement. Like incumbent colleges and universities, a knowledge enterprise might engage in research and the production of knowledge. But primacy is placed upon that knowledge that is especially useful in addressing local issues, as when a city engages in a rewilding strategy or when redesigning to become a 15-minute city. An incumbent college or university might refashion its mission to include acting as an idea incubator, as a studio for creative production, and as a "third place" that helps generate social capital. A knowledge enterprise does not merely reside in its city or region: it physically extends such that the knowledge ecosystem of the region is largely synonymous with the knowledge enterprise. So central to a thriving town or region, the knowledge enterprise almost acts as an intellectual and epistemological "utility" for the town, a service as necessary for a livable place as emergency services, clean water, and competent government. Indeed, we might define the value of a knowledge enterprise as a "university as a service" (UaaS) for a place.

In the same way that towns and cities must transform their economic development model and creative placemaking strategies to become a talent magnet, existing colleges and universities who wish to lead a region's talent magnet strategy as a knowledge enterprise must redesign their institutions, must transform their college into a knowledge enterprise.

1. Act Local but Harness the Cloud

Access to broadband is an indispensable way to plug into the global cloud-based knowledge economy. Indeed, no jurisdiction can lure talent to a location without it. Many small towns and rural areas do not have access to high-speed broadband of the kind necessary to harness the cloud. Therefore, as part of a talent magnet strategy, the knowledge enterprise takes the lead in bringing broadband access to a place that otherwise might not have it. Many local colleges already have arrangements to provide broadband to their campus for the faculty and students of the institution. In a talent magnet strategy, the knowledge enterprise extends its broadband out into the community, in effect serving as a utility for the entire region.

Aside from this technical requirement, harnessing the cloud also means a reorientation of the educational practices of the knowledge enterprise. The philosopher Roberto Mangabeira Unger has observed that the industrial economy—what was at one time "the most advanced practice of production"—was not confined to a singular location. Part of what made industrialization the most advanced economic practice, Unger asserts, was that its production regime was broadly distributed across a number of sectors and across a wide geographic extent. "Earlier most advanced practices of production—mechanized manufacturing and industrial mass production—set their mark on every part of economic life despite their close connection with one sector: industry," he writes. "The knowledge economy should in principle be susceptible to even more widespread dissemination. . . . [yet] despite its appearance in many sectors it has remained in even the richest economies and the most educated societies an archipelago of islands alien to the main tenor of economic life around it."[9] This observation also holds for the geographic extent of the knowledge economy, which is concentrated in spatial archipelagos like Silicon Valley.[10]

Today, the most advanced practice of production is the knowledge economy, which Unger defines as "the practice of production that is closest to the mind, and especially to the part of our mental life that we call the imagination."[11] Yet this advanced practice is confined to a small minority of workers and is geographically limited. He refers to this condition as an "insular vanguard." Unger argues that we must strive to create the necessary infrastructure to extend the knowledge economy, to foster an "inclusive vanguard," as it were. "The central thesis of this book is that many of our most important material and moral interests depend on whether the knowledge economy—the now most advanced practice of production—will continue to be confined to insular vanguards, advanced fringes within each sector of the economy. The knowledge economy can turn into an inclusive rather than an insular vanguard."[12] One way that this might occur is for more places—especially unexpected places such as rural or smaller-town locations—to plug into the knowledge economy. "There must then," Unger asserts, "begin a dispute to which we are unaccustomed: not about the relative proportions of market and state but about the institutional arrangements by which we organize decentralized economic activity."[13] This could include its geographic extent, and thus our call for a talent magnet strategy: that the knowledge economy, carried out over the cloud, can extend to encompass a wider geographic area, not simply be confined to the Bay Area, Miami, or a few plugged-in urban areas.

This economic expansion cannot happen with just a snap of the fingers, of course. "The program of an inclusive form of the knowledge economy," Unger argues, "can advance only as part of a movement changing education, culture, and politics, as well as innovating in the institutions of the market order."[14] According to him, a knowledge enterprise transforms its educational mission to align with the strategy of an inclusive knowledge economy.

One definition of the knowledge economy is that innovation is a regular—rather than accidental—feature. "A third period in economic history begins," says Unger, "when innovation loses its punctuated character and the constraint of diminishing returns is relaxed or even reversed." Continual innovation is what he sees as the promise of the inclusive vanguardism of the knowledge economy: "Innovation, however, becomes more perpetual than episodic. It becomes internal to the process of production as well as reliant on science and technology imported from outside the production system. The constraint of diminishing marginal returns loosens because good firms begin to resemble good schools, and the development of production to resemble the development of knowledge."[15] Production in the knowledge economy resembles the university, and this is why the university as a knowledge enterprise becomes crucial for a talent magnet strategy: the local knowledge enterprise becomes the node that connects an otherwise isolated place to the larger inclusive knowledge economy.

If innovation is a central and endemic feature of the knowledge economy, then it turns out that play, conjecture, and imagination become critical cognitive abilities. "Another deep trait of the knowledge economy," observes Unger,

> is the close relation that is established between how we work and how the mind develops ideas and makes discoveries. Production has been the transformation of nature and the mobilization of energy in nature with the help of technologies that enhance our powers. Now it becomes more accurate to say that the growth of knowledge becomes the centerpiece of economic activity. New products or assets and new ways of making them are simply the materialization—in goods and services—of our conjectures and experiments.[16]

Conjectures and experiments—even play—become the basis of education in the knowledge economy, and thus these attributes enjoy an elevated position in the knowledge enterprise.[17]

Cultivation of the imagination, especially, becomes a key pedagogical outcome of the knowledge enterprise, if for no other reason than because "to the extent that it is disseminated and deepened, the knowledge economy places the imagination at the center of economic life."[18] Imagination is usually dismissed as something children or impractical dreamers and poets engage in, not a serious or economically productive exercise. Not so in an inclusive knowledge economy. "This is the aspect of the mind that we name imagination: the mind as anti-machine by contrast to the mind as machine," argues Unger. "The approximation of production to imagination is the heart of the knowledge economy, and ever more so as it spreads and deepens."[19] If production equals imagination, then educating for the cultivation of the imagination must be situated as a central purpose of the knowledge enterprise.

Inasmuch as incumbent universities are asked to provide job training and to engage in workforce development, a knowledge enterprise preparing students for an inclusive knowledge economy must substitute older pedagogical methods with those that emphasize the cultivation of higher-order abilities. "The educational requirements of mass production for ordinary workers are minimal. . . . They place few or no demands on the acquisition of higher-order capabilities," argues Unger.[20] "In its approach to technical education it must repudiate the model of technical training that the world learned from Germany: one emphasizing the job-specific and machine-specific skills needed to operate the ridged machine tools of the age of mass production and to navigate economies organized around the historical, rigidly separated trades and professions. It must put in the place of that model one giving pride of place to generic, flexible, high-order capabilities."[21] The act of cultivating the imagination of its students, in insisting that students conjecture and experiment and play, is one means by which the knowledge enterprise plugs into the knowledge economy.

"The education of protagonists of an inclusive form of the knowledge economy must exhibit four basic characteristics," concludes Unger. First, "the method of education must give priority to analytic and synthetic capabilities, and more generally to the powers associated with the imagination—the mind as anti-machine—over the mastery of information." Second, this education "prefers selective depth to encyclopedia superficiality." Third, "it affirms cooperation in teaching and learning over the juxtaposition of authoritarianism and individualism that has traditionally characterized the classroom. Teams of students and teachers within and among schools should be the primary instrument of teaching and learning." Finally, "every subject and method be presented from at least two contrasting points of view."[22] These four characteristics animate the curriculum of the knowledge enterprise, aligning it with the wider knowledge economy, helping to attract talent to a particular area.

2. Encourage Lives of Purpose, Not of Possessions

There is some evidence that suggests that there may be a shift underway in the nature and practice of capitalism. Rather than chasing a strategy of US-style capitalism—with its emphasis on maximizing shareholder value—or the state-sponsored capitalism emblematic of China's economy, Jean-Dominique Senard, the chief executive officer of the French company Michelin, practices a style he terms "responsible capitalism." In this formulation, companies seek profit, "but their purpose must also take into consideration the social and environmental impact of their activities." A similar variety of capitalism goes by the name "conscious capitalism." One of the core values of the conscious capitalism movement is that company purpose is of greater importance than profit. According to John Mackey, former CEO of Whole Foods and one of the founders of the conscious capitalism movement, "Companies need to shift their emphasis from profit maximization to purpose maximization."[23]

For Mackey, a company exists to fulfill some larger purpose; profit follows from the achievement of this higher purpose. "Every conscious business has a higher purpose, which addresses fundamental questions such as: Why do we exist? Why do we need to exist? What is the contribution we want to make? Why is the world better because we are here? Would we be missed if we disappeared?"[24] In order to be a conscious business, the first answer to "Why do we exist?" cannot be "To enhance shareholder value."

Mackey sees business as a profession, one driven by higher purpose as is the case with any profession. "Every major profession has a higher purpose as its reason for being. This is true of medicine, which is about healing. It is true for education, architecture, engineering, and the legal professions. Each is animated by service to a higher purpose, one that is aligned with the needs of society and that gives the profession legitimacy and value in the eyes of others. Each of these professions, of course, is also partly about making profit and earning a living. However, when any profession becomes primarily about making money, it starts to lose its true identity, and its interests start to diverge from what is good for society as a whole."[25] Beyond job training or workforce development, identification and pursuit of a higher purpose is suffused throughout the curriculum of the knowledge enterprise. Whatever the field, higher purpose is the prime pedagogical motivator.

And this is especially true of the business program. "There's no intrinsic reason why business should be different from any other human endeavor," Mackey asserts. "The same enduring ideals that animate art, science, education, and many nonprofit organizations can and should also animate business." Higher purpose, he believes, might be divided into four archetypes: (1) the good: service to others—improving health, education, communication, and quality of life; (2) the true: discovery and furthering human knowledge; (3) the beautiful: excellence and the creation of beauty; (4) the heroic: Courage to do what is right to change and improve the world.[26]

These ideals—not simply profit maximization—are the types of purpose to which all businesses should aspire. Thus, the business program of a knowledge enterprise has conscious capitalism—and the quest for a higher purpose—as its pedagogical and philosophical foundation.

In addition, the arts and humanities hold a central place in the curriculum of the knowledge enterprise. For the better part of four decades, but especially in the last decade, the arts and humanities have been diminished at many universities. There has been a recent spate of colleges that, facing budget shortfalls, are cutting humanities programs in the name of being "market responsive," claiming that students want majors that provide marketable skills that lead directly to postgraduation employment and clearly delineated career pathways.

The humanities are those disciplines that consider questions of meaning and purpose. Per Seattle Central College,

> The humanities are the stories, the ideas, and the words that help us make sense of our lives and our world. The humanities introduce us to people we have never met, places we have never visited, and ideas that may have never crossed our minds. By showing how others have lived and thought about life, the humanities help us decide what is important in our own lives and what we can do to make them better. By connecting us with other people, they point the way to answers about what is right or wrong, or what is true to our heritage and our history. The humanities help us address the challenges we face together in our families, our communities, and as a nation.[27]

To be clear, the humanities disciplines are not defined solely by their investigation of questions of purpose and meaning. But what other disciplines in the university deal so directly with these questions? As the National Endowment for the Humanities puts it, "The humanities help us answer big questions. What is the meaning, value, and purpose of human life? What is justice? What is equality? What is freedom? How might a just society function? How do individuals relate to the state and society? What are the moral consequences of human action? Why do both cruelty and good exist? How do people best work together?"[28] Humanities disciplines—such as philosophy, literature, ethics, history—are given a prominent place at a knowledge enterprise that follows a talent magnet strategy precisely because they directly address questions of purpose and meaning.

Opportunities to engage in service-learning opportunities are a central component of the knowledge enterprise. Many incumbent institutions have vigorous service-learning programs, of course, where "students learn educational standards through tackling real-life problems in their community." More specifically, a center at Michigan State University practices what it terms "Community Engaged Learning," which is "a teaching and learning strategy that integrates meaningful community partnerships with instruction and critical reflection to enrich the student learning experience, teach civic and social responsibility, and strengthen communities."[29] Service learning is more than skill building or job training; it is an approach to learning that emphasizes a commitment to something higher than the self, one model definition of a purpose-driven education. At a knowledge enterprise pursuing a talent magnet strategy, service or community-engaged learning is a rigorous program, with the expectation that students take at least one course in service to the community.

Indeed, such service-learning courses are open to the members of the community. Knowledge workers are invited to take these courses and engage these opportunities through a sabbatical from their current jobs. We tend to associate sabbaticals as a privilege of academics: time away from teaching and research to engage in other projects or just simply time to think. The knowledge enterprise offers sabbaticals to professionals to similarly recharge, for time away from their responsibilities, to think and reflect, and, especially, to engage in community-engaged learning. The Community Sabbatical Research Leave Program, located within the Humanities Institute at the University of Texas at Austin, is designed to permit leaders of local nonprofits to take time away from their duties to pursue a research question.[30] The knowledge enterprise takes the idea of a sabbatical for working professionals in a new direction: anyone in the region could apply for such a sabbatical not to work on some technical issue but to engage in what all good sabbaticals should, and especially to consider questions of meaning and purpose.

3. Clear the Air and Slow Down the Streets

Although she has not coined the term, Paris mayor Anne Hidalgo wants to phase out automobile traffic in her city and redesign the city such that anything that a resident might need can be reached within a 15-minute walk or bike ride. In what she calls "the 15-minute city," Hidalgo "wants to encourage more self-sufficient communities within each *arrondissement* of the French capital, with grocery shops, parks, cafes, sports facilities, health centres, schools and even workplaces just a walk or bike ride away."[31] The 15-minute city, according to a *Public Square* article by Andrés Duany and Robert Steuteville, "is defined by its ability to provide access to all human needs by walking or bicycling for a quarter hour or less."[32]

The scientist Carlos Moreno has identified four key features of such a city:

- Proximity: Things must be close.
- Diversity: Land uses must be mixed to provide a wide variety of urban amenities nearby.
- Density: There must be enough people to support a diversity of businesses in a compact land area. Note that Manhattan-level density is not needed, as many low-rise neighborhoods in San Francisco and other US cities prove.
- Ubiquity: These neighborhoods must be so common that they are available and affordable to anyone who wants to live in one.[33]

A city or town pursuing the talent magnet strategy of "slowing down the streets" thereby works toward becoming a 15-minute city. This requires strong leadership from the mayor and other city officials. But in addition, the local knowledge enterprise provides expertise—continuing the theme of localized research. Student projects and courses are built around the city as laboratory for transforming into a 15-minute city.

Urban planners already look to college campuses for their model for slowing down the streets. On most college campuses, students and faculty move from place to place by walking or by bike or scooter. In idealized campus design, automobiles are banished to the margins of campus. If only our cities were as walkable as a college campus, some urban planners dream.

Aside from providing expertise, contributing to a "clear the air and slow the streets" strategy might actually prove to be the most difficult thing for a knowledge enterprise to enact. What if we extended the walkable campus idea outward, beyond its confines behind ivy-covered walls? That is, what if the college itself were refashioned as a "15-minute college"? To do so, we would need to physically redesign the campus. Rather than a collection of buildings clustered together in one part of town—and thus reachable only by automobile—in this scenario the college expands outward, not unlike the way the constituent colleges that make up Oxford University are distributed throughout the city. While any individual college might be walkable—once it is reached by automobile—the campus itself would not necessarily be within a 15-minute walk or bicycle ride for anyone in the city.

One way a campus might spread outward across the city would be to establish a number of microcolleges. A microcollege would be an educational enterprise consisting of one faculty member and twenty students.[34] This arrangement would be similar to the one that governs Deep Springs College, which has only 3 faculty members and 27 students. The knowledge enterprise could be redesigned as a series of microcolleges. This would mean not only a physical reorganization but an epistemological reorganization as well. Instead of being organized by departments and disciplines—and the individual buildings that house these—microcolleges are organized around the particular pedagogical and epistemological philosophy of an individual professor. In a way, each one would be like scientific laboratories in our current university structure: a minienterprise overseen by a senior faculty member who leads a team of postdoctoral, graduate, and undergraduate researchers. Imagine such a laboratory-style organization for a host of disciplines: the artist's studio or the humanist's seminar serving as a microcollege. These microcolleges would be distributed throughout the town, so that an individual could be within a 15-minute walk or bike ride to this critical service. The knowledge enterprise becomes a fractal entity, one that exhibits self-similar units across scales. It would be fractal in that each microcollege resembles the larger whole. Paul Downton refers to such entities as "urban fractals," meaning that "any part of the urban system that contains sufficient characteristics of that system to represent the essence of that system in microcosm."[35] Downton sees such structures as forming the basis of sustainable cities.

These self-similar units of the knowledge enterprise need not take the specific form of a microcollege. That is, the unit need not be as small as a single professor and two dozen students. A microcollege could be designed as a knowledge enterprise in miniature. Thus these would be neither just a chemistry building or history department located somewhere in the city. Each node, each fractal unit, would consist of a cluster of college buildings, including housing, recreation facilities, and other buildings in service to the microcollege. (See the idea of a fourth space below.) The knowledge enterprise, in the form of the microcollege, is as important and necessary as a store, a doctor's office, or a place of worship.

When we describe the knowledge enterprise below as being porous and an open third place, it is in part because of its 15-minute physical layout.

4. Harness the Economic Potential of Community

Gary Becker famously formulated the idea of human capital, and since the 1980s, especially, one of the main—if not the main—goals of higher education has been human capital development, defined by Lexico as "the skills, knowledge, and experienced possessed by an individual or population, viewed in terms of their value or cost to an organization or country." Jamie Merisotis has updated this idea with his definition of talent, by which he means "not simply innate ability . . . but more broadly the combination of knowledge, skills, abilities, and other capacities that are honed through learning and experience in ways that not only improve individuals, but advance society in general."[36] A talent magnet strategy, obviously, concerns itself with attracting and retaining talent, of developing human capital. But a knowledge enterprise committed to a talent magnet strategy also seeks to develop social capital.

Social capital refers to "the network of relationships among people who live and work in a particular society, enabling that society to function effectively."[37] The pandemic caused not only an economic downturn—a diminishment of our economic metabolism—but also a curtailment of our social metabolism. One mission of a place-based knowledge enterprise is helping to maintain a healthy and vibrant social metabolism, meaning the rate, diversity, and quality of the exchanges in a community. Many colleges already engage in this kind of social capital development with their students, faculty, and alumni; a knowledge enterprise extends this mission outward to include the wider community. Instead of acting strictly as a technology commercialization incubator, the knowledge enterprise also serves as a region's "social capital incubator."

This incubator would be more than just the kind of outreach and engagement that many colleges already engage in. One of us (Staley) curated such a social capital incubator, called the Neighborhood Institute. It was a working group of faculty and students that studied the unique issues of the residential and commercial neighborhoods surrounding Ohio State University. But a key part of the working group was that university knowledge and expertise was paired with knowledge from the members of the surrounding community. That is, town and gown were in conversation with each other, with knowledge from the community valued as much as that from university experts. Traditional outreach and engagement tends to be unidirectional: expert knowledge professed outward to a community of nonexperts. The conversations sponsored by a social capital incubator might not only foster cooperation on solving local problems: the conversation could also involve community members performing music, reciting poetry, or recounting the history of the region. In so cultivating social capital through engaged dialogue, the knowledge enterprise acts as a platform for community-generated knowledge.

These kinds of interfaces for convivial gathering have been termed "third places" by Ray Oldenburg. If home is the "first place" and the office or other place of employment is a "second place," then a "third place" is a public environment that fosters networking, conversation, and community or perhaps simply fun, play, and relaxation. Scholars at the Brookings Institution claim that in a third place "social classes and backgrounds can be 'leveled-out' in ways that are unfortunately rare these days, with people feeling they are treated as social equals. Informal conversation is the main activity and most important linking function. One commentator refers to third places as the 'living room' of society."[38] Knowledge enterprises pursuing a talent magnet strategy therefore serve as the apex third place for a community.

Nancy Cantor has eloquently defended the idea of a university as a social capital incubator: "This vision of universities as civically-engaged anchors, by definition, expands campus boundaries by drawing upon multiple communities of experts from different sectors of our society—academic, corporate, non-profit, governmental, cultural, and community, to name just a few. It requires what I'd call a shared 'third space' where talented people from many backgrounds with diverse expertise and perspectives can collaborate." She emphasizes that this third space is a nexus of academic and local communities. Like the Neighborhood Institute, one goal of this third space is to

> co-produce vital knowledge and innovation. One might imagine it as a two-way street for teaching, learning, and discovery. It incorporates new voices, builds trust, and transforms the history of one-way engagement between universities and their communities. No longer can "we" position ourselves as the only legitimate experts, telling others how to fix their problems or using their communities as laboratories with little benefit to them. Together, instead, we can and do create a shared sense of community and communal responsibility.[39]

Keith Smyth observes that universities are especially well positioned to provide third spaces for their communities. Oldenburg's identification and demonstration of the importance of third places for building social capital "has been pivotal in encouraging sociologists, civic leaders and activists to look critically at how our public spaces for congregating (e.g. museums, cafes, pubs, parks, even barber shops) can provide a locus for democratic discussion and debate, community action, creative thought and expression, and importantly also for frivolity, friendship, and harmonious interaction." Indeed, the form of such university-sponsored third spaces might resemble that of the so-called Ragged University. "Based upon the philanthropic tradition of the Ragged Schools of the 1900's," reports Smyth, "the Ragged University provides opportunities (in libraries, pubs, and other public venues) for scholars, academics, artists and artisans to share their knowledge and experience with peers who have similar interests, a simple curiosity, or a hunger and thirst to learn." Echoing the exhortations of Cantor, Smyth proclaims that "universities need to challenge themselves to properly define their relationship to the communities within which they sit. In doing this, they need to move beyond broadly-worded aspirations and strategies relating to public engagement and civic responsibility, and instead commit to and help drive a culture of action and active partnership between their institution and their wider community."[40]

Some universities have already been deliberate and strategic about cultivating third spaces on their campuses. For example, in an *Inside Higher Ed* article, Professor KerryAnn O'Meara explains how the University of Maryland has carved out third spaces, especially for "women, underrepresented and professional-track faculty members, and those interested in academic leadership."[41] These spaces are deliberately constructed outside of departments, colleges, and other preexisting institutional forms. Sophie Benson, writing in *iO*, explains the concept further: "Lectures, seminars, one-to-one tutorials, workshops; there are plenty of ways to learn at university, each with its own significant value to students. But the time away from those more formal studies is equally as crucial for a fulfilling, successful educational experience. The 'in-between' moments when people can relax, recharge and connect with others are, according to the Gensler Experience Index, 'when people are most open to discovery and new experiences.'"[42] This is indeed an excellent way to develop social capital, but the Maryland example and others like it face inward, exclusively for members of the academic community. As part of a talent magnet strategy, the wider community also benefits from this "in-between space." If not the entire campus, then at least a significant portion of the knowledge enterprise should be inviting, porous, "in-between," and open to all.

Other forms of university physical infrastructure could be employed to build social capital. Think of the athletic facilities at many existing colleges. In addition to being used by the undergraduate students for intercollegiate athletics and for their own recreation, what if these facilities were opened up to the larger community, creating a sort of intramural sports program for the residents of the town? This would not be a free service but more like a gym membership and would be a way to accelerate the formation of social capital.

Some third places established in knowledge economy cities serve as refuges and a respite from the rigors of the day. According to Benson, 3DEN, for example, provides residents of New York with an "urban sanctuary" for "the in-between moments of the day." The company "offers nap pods, workspaces, lounge spaces, meditation rooms and charging stations among other spaces." And some universities are also establishing such rest stops as third places. Benson writes, "The University of Manchester, for example, was the first UK institution to introduce a nap pod, opening the 'Zzz Zone' in 2014. Others around the globe, including University of Miami and Stanford University, have followed suit, and University College Cork has stated that napping on campus is now 'officially encouraged.'"[43] These are spaces for university residents, but we may wonder: Who else might be permitted to nap during the day? Could the knowledge enterprise also provide places for naps, meditation, and reflection for any and all in the community?

"The university campus of today is the perfect Third Place," argues Ray Fleming. "Most campuses now have visually appealing, comfortable drop-in spaces where you can easily gather a group to work on a learning challenge. With good internet access (which really is at the base of Maslow's hierarchy these days with food and water), and with the same characteristics of the Third Place created by Starbucks—including the right amount of caffeine. And with the people to provide education, advice and coaching, alongside an appropriate balance of tutorial and lecture-style learning experiences."[44] In functioning as a third place for the wider community, the local knowledge enterprise drives social capital formation.

5. Recruit Purpose-Driven Migrants

Colleges have traditionally been in the business of attracting talent. At one level, this means attracting faculty talent. This also means attracting student talent, the job of enrollment management. Under a talent magnet strategy, the knowledge enterprise takes this expertise and works closely with the city's economic development team to design and implement a talent-attraction plan. In describing the remote worker attraction programs at Purdue and West Virginia universities, the *Chronicle of Higher Education* observes that "one reason universities may be well situated to be stewards of [these programs is that] they are versed in retention strategies, regularly deployed to make sure students stay on track to graduation."[45] But this is a service few colleges currently engage in. That is, bringing young (student) talent to a college is not even half of the strategy. Many colleges have student retention strategies, keeping students at the college for four (or more) years, seeing them through to graduation. A talent magnet strategy would also involve strategies for keeping talented people in the area after they graduate.

One of us (Staley) once taught at a small college in Southeast Ohio that drew students from the region but also from the East Coast. Some of these students wished to remain in the area after graduation: the college had many desirable qualities, such as being located on the Ohio River, nestled in the Appalachians, etc. But aside from the quality of life, these recent alumni had few economic opportunities that would have enticed them to remain. There were chemical plants across the river, but the college did not have programs in chemical engineering (although it did have a well-regarded program in petroleum engineering, but graduates of this program tended to find work elsewhere). Many of these alumni were entrepreneurial, seeking to launch new enterprises, but lacked the funding, support, or ability to create a market.

Imagine if the college had worked more closely with the city to develop a strategy whereby the college attracted talent and the city developed strategies to retain this talent. This might have involved the college rethinking the kind of student it recruited or the kind of talent it would train (that is, what programs might have been offered that would have aligned with opportunities in the region?). The city economic development office could have helped foster an environment that would have aided these budding entrepreneurs.

At a knowledge enterprise that follows a talent magnet strategy, faculty play an active role in recruiting and retaining talent. Faculty serve as active members of the recruiting team—indeed, this is made a significant part of their responsibilities, along with teaching, research, and service. Faculty are also active in student retention via their expanded roles as mentors. Daniel F. Chambliss and Christopher G. Takacs argue that successful colleges—those that provide high-quality education and, importantly, those that provide a memorable experience to students—have meaningful personal relationships at the core of the enterprise. "[The] pervasive influence of relationships suggests that a college—at least insofar as it offers real benefits— is less a collection of *programs* than a gathering of *people*."[46] The knowledge enterprise, when recruiting talent, thus emphasizes the people of the institution, not specific programs, as seems to be the case for many colleges at present. Look at the website of any randomly selected college. The home page will very likely emphasize athletics or specific programs; to find out anything about specific faculty, one needs to click several times. A knowledge enterprise committed to recruiting talent emphasizes the quality of the faculty of the institution. "Here is your psychology professor!" beams the home page of the college website. "Professor Smith will change your life." "Curriculum is nice," conclude Chambliss and Takacs, "but may not be fundamental for a good college. But good people, brought together in the right ways, we suspect are both necessary and perhaps even sufficient to create a good college."[47]

"Good people" refers especially to those faculty willing to serve as mentors to students. "The most valuable relationships students have with teachers are *mentorships*," Chambliss and Takacs assert. "These entail a significant personal and professional connection, lasting more than just one course or semester. They can't simply be assigned, but neither do they happen just by accident."[48] These are relationships beyond the professing of knowledge in a formal class setting: "The defining characteristic of a mentor is a concern for the student beyond the immediacies of a course. . . . At the simplest level, a personal connection with a teacher seems to encourage students, even those just trying to get by, to work harder in classes. . . . Some mentors draw students into close intellectual engagement."[49] Such mentorship would appear to correlate to improved academic performance, and positive perceptions of the entire college experience. Even the small act of inviting students to dinner at the faculty member's house—the simplest act of mentorship—has notable effects both on student performance and their connections to a college. "No matter what variables were introduced," report Chambliss and Takacs, "no matter what analyses were used, no matter which researchers did the analysis, the results stood firm: a single visit by a student to a professor's home clearly correlated with the student's satisfaction and willingness to 'choose again' to attend the college."[50] We might tentatively conclude that strong mentorships are a factor in effective retention.

Faculty roles would be altered: from being strictly a professor (one who professes knowledge) to also being a mentor: one who offers advice and guidance. This means much more than the constructivist "guide on the side" teaching philosophy: students are drawn to a college because they will not only be mentored but educated. Many of the formal classes at such a knowledge enterprise take the form of tutorials: one-on-one or one faculty meeting with two or three students at a time. This relational approach to knowledge is not transactional but transformative. Faculty serve as professional mentors, and the knowledge enterprise is a mentoring organization.[51]

Retention and completion seem to correlate to the development of a strong relationship with a mentor. One service that a knowledge enterprise might offer, therefore, is professional mentoring services. Mentoring as service would extend outside the college to encompass the entire region, especially to the purpose-driven migrants the town is seeking to recruit. Indeed, these knowledge workers are drawn to the region because of the access to the professional mentors from the knowledge enterprise. The availability of professional mentoring becomes a key part of the region's talent retention strategy.

6. Support the Bionic Worker

One of us (Staley) gave a talk at the Air Force Research Laboratory at Wright-Patterson Air Force Base and was treated to a tour of the facilities. I had an interesting encounter in one of the chemistry labs, where I was shown a machine that was automatically and autonomously measuring and mixing chemicals, the sort of task that might have been carried out by a junior scientist (or even a volunteer undergraduate). But I was particularly struck by the observation of one of the chemists, who said that in bringing such machines into their lab, the chemists were "teaching tools to be team players." In this lab, at least, the future was already happening: humans are partnering with autonomous intelligence.

While there have certainly been those who argue that we face a jobless future, with all human work automated away and made redundant by the combination of robotics and artificial intelligence, a more likely scenario is unfolding in that chemistry laboratory: that humans and machines will become "teammates." That means knowledge workers will need to learn how to team with artificial intelligence.

As of yet, no knowledge enterprise exists that educates "bionic workers." That is, there is no existing academic institution where students go to learn how to team with machines. Developing that interface will become a key purpose of future knowledge enterprises. An interface is defined as "a point where two systems, subjects, organizations, etc. meet and interact," and, with regard to computing, "a device or program enabling a user to communicate with a computer." In this formulation, the knowledge enterprise becomes that device for communicating with artificial intelligence. Developing such an interface becomes a service the knowledge enterprise provides to both traditional undergraduates and to the bionic workers attracted to a place.

This interface education will involve more than simply providing students with tablets or a smart phone or even simply learning how to use these tools. The goal will be how to think with these tools. One could argue that colleges have long taught students how to think with cognitive tools, the book being chief among these. Achieving interface with these tools reflects a different order of cognition. Think of the way we use a digital assistant like Alexa or Siri: we query the tool to perform a task—"Play a song"—or to provide information: "What was the score of the game?" But in the scenario described here, students learn how to "converse" with Alexa or some other sort of AI-enabled system. A conversation is a two-way dialogue where interlocutors exchange ideas and information. Perhaps another goal of conversation—or perhaps it is debate?—is to persuade the other to come to a particular viewpoint. Engaging in conversation with machines—as a way to team with them—implies that AI can be "taught," even educated, as well.

It will be important in the future for machines to be educated, part of the process of supporting the bionic worker. This means that the knowledge enterprise will also cater to AI as "students"; the knowledge enterprise becomes a site for training and educating AI. Today, there are some firms that are accelerating machine learning by working on developing "curricula" for AI by providing "experiences." The usual way we think about machine learning is to fill AI with petabytes of data and letting them identify patterns in those data. These are techniques that have produced AI that can play chess and go with an ability orders of magnitude beyond the best human players. But these companies are instead giving AI simulations of experiences from which they can learn, situating symbolic knowledge in a phenomenological context. Imagine a college or university devoted to educating AI by providing virtual experiences from which to learn. Higher education in this setting looks more like a Montessorian classroom. And indeed, this method—of learning via experience— will be of value in educating human learners as well. In order to teach machines to be good teammates—and thus support the bionic worker—knowledge enterprises will be redesigned to educate human and artificial intelligence together. The knowledge enterprise becomes an "interface university."[52]

"The most likely scenario is not that jobs will disappear, but that jobs will change," observes Minouche Shafik, echoing the thoughts of many who have commented on the future relationship between artificial and human intelligence. "Automation can substitute for labour, but it can also complement labour and create new jobs. Routine and repetitive tasks will be automated, machines will augment human capabilities, and those people who have skills that are complementary to robots will fare the best. Those complementary skills include things like creativity, emotional intelligence and an ability to work with people."[53] We might add to that list of complementary skills attributes like imagination, storytelling, awe, wonder, play, and the ability to apprehend beauty, all capacities that are beyond the abilities of current forms of artificial intelligence. Thus, supporting the bionic worker means not only educating for human-machine teamwork but also cultivating these uniquely human capacities.

7. Engage Lifelong Learning

If pursuing lifelong learners is part of a talent magnet strategy, then the need to have a knowledge enterprise in one's town seems obvious. Lifelong learning offerings take three forms: (1) cultural programming, (2) professional development, and (3) "superager" services.

The same impulse that has led millions to watch TED talks online is one that drives knowledge workers to attend lectures and other public programs sponsored by a local college. This impulse for self-improvement runs throughout American history: the Chautauqua and Lyceum movements might be understood as nineteenth-century precursors to today's online TED talks, in that largely middle-class audiences seek knowledge and insights from thought leaders outside of formal schooling. Under the talent magnet strategy, the local knowledge enterprise serves as a guild for thought leaders, accessible to the entire community.

What of such access to thought leaders was planned as part of creative placemaking? A few summers ago, one of us (Staley) was invited to be a speaker at a summer resort. He gave three public lectures over the course of one week and was one of a dozen or so educational lecturers over the course of the summer. The place draws both residents and vacationers not only for the entertainment and the beaches and the comradery but for the intellectual stimulation of the weekly lectures. Lifelong learning is an amenity—part of the infrastructure—of the place. A city or town launching a talent magnet strategy would similarly draw from the guild of thought leaders at the local knowledge enterprise such that such cultural programming is a part of the infrastructure.

The second form that lifelong learning might take is professional development and upskilling. "The term *upskilling* refers to the expansion of people's capabilities and employability to fulfill the talent needs of a rapidly changing economy," according to Laurent Probst and Christian Scharff. "An upskilling initiative can take place at the level of a company, an industry, or a community."[54] The local knowledge enterprise would be the principal institution to engage in professional upskilling.

Large companies have been partnering with educational institutions to provide upskilling services for their employees. The partnership between Starbucks and Arizona State University, for example, was one of the first such partnerships, where Starbucks employees can take online courses at ASU, paid for by their employer. (Notably, Amazon is investing hundreds of thousands of dollars to upskill its workforce, but without partnering with a university.) Knowledge workers—indeed, workers in many different sectors—will be taking advantage of upskilling opportunities, and those places that provide access to knowledge enterprises equipped to provide this service will be attractive places to live. Indeed, one wonders if the location of a robust knowledge enterprise would factor into decisions for companies to locate in a particular area.

The third form of lifelong learning would be serving a market that is just beginning to emerge. As baby boomers age, they are increasingly seeking out experiences that encourage them to vigorously use their brains to stave off the effects of cognitive decline. Cognitive scientists have identified a group labeled "superagers," whose physical brains resemble a 25-year-old's brain. The best explanation offered for this phenomenon is that superagers use their brains to engage in rigorous disciplinary thinking. This goes well beyond doing a daily crossword puzzle; it means engaging in the kinds of cognitive activities traditional-aged undergraduates might engage in. Further, superagers remain physically active, not just walking or strolling but engaging in rigorous—for their age—activities. Many boomers want to stave off mental decline and might turn to such regular cognitive activity as one weapon against such decline.

What if a knowledge enterprise admitted students in their 60s and 70s with the same enthusiasm as they do 18- to 22-year-olds?[55] That is, the "market" for students would be expanded, beyond the traditional-aged student and even beyond the working adult demographic, even further still beyond the curious retiree who delights in an early evening's public lecture event. These would be students seeking a degree—not unlike one their grandchildren might be pursuing—but not because they are seeking job training but instead to keep their brains supple and plastic. They might wish to retire to a place that not only has a pleasant climate or other outdoor amenities but also easy access to an academic culture that welcomes them and seeks to educate for "superager brains."

Lasell Village is a retiree's colony adjacent to Lasell University.[56] As we understand their current strategy, these retirees remain an adjunct to the university, but it does not require much strategic imagination to see how an existing university could create programs and an academic infrastructure for 60- to 70-year-olds. Again, these would not only be course auditors: they would be evaluated on their work and graded accordingly, just as a traditional undergraduate would. Indeed, these superagers would be expected to maintain a minimum GPA to remain at the college.

In considering all three forms, the knowledge enterprise would provide lifelong learning as service to a community.

8. Build an Innovation Cluster

After the Bayh-Dole Act was passed in 1980, universities rushed to develop the infrastructure for capturing faculty research ideas and to commercialize the results. Innovation clusters or business incubators were set up on the edges of many universities, with the promise of cashing in on the federally funded research of faculty talent. These universities looked to the success of Stanford and MIT in cultivating innovation districts. Rural locations could also look to Research Triangle Park in North Carolina for an example of how a strategy of concentrating talent can yield economic benefits anywhere, not just in large cities.[57]

Research Triangle Park has sometimes been faulted for not being as successful in incubating original, local, faculty-driven research but instead drawing existing companies to the region. And yet this would most certainly be of value. Indeed, a college pursuing a talent magnet strategy might create an innovation district with the goal of luring businesses to a region. Proximity to faculty and student talent would be one objective here. The knowledge enterprise might establish a coworking space on the campus with the intention of attracting businesses.[58]

Imagine a college in a rural area offering an incubator space on campus to agricultural technology companies, those innovating in the Internet of Things for the agriculture sector? These companies might be drawn to the region because they are able to provide solutions to the region's unique agricultural problems. In such a scenario, companies would be allowed to "set up shop," as it were, on campus, in the same way a lab or a theater would be so established. Moreover, talent from the company would be invited to offer classes and workshops— to serve as adjunct faculty at the college—thus adding to the talent of the college.

The knowledge enterprise might also establish a maker space as a pillar of its innovation cluster strategy. The maker space would be open to everyone in the community, not just undergraduate students and faculty—an extension of its role as a "third place." But the maker space would also be incorporated into the formal curriculum of the college. Industry-recognized apprenticeship programs and even degrees would be awarded in programs based on making.

Innovation clusters need not be focused solely on incubating the next Microsoft or Uber Eats. The word "innovation" has come to mean a profit-generating enterprise, usually in the technology sector. In our estimation, innovation is left-brain creativity, and creativity is right-brain innovation. Perhaps what we seek is the knowledge enterprise as creativity cluster, a gathering of talent that generates a wide variety of novel ideas.

The success of such a cluster might include new ideas for solving the problem of homelessness, generating a robust form of democracy or a new style of art. Renaissance Florence was one of the most innovative cities in world history: among the many achievements of the city was the development of one-point perspective: a new and innovative way to represent three-dimensional space on a two-dimensional surface, one of the world's great innovations. Changing the way Western culture sees and represents space is an innovation whose success is not easily measured in dollars or whether it generates an initial public offering. Innovation in social entrepreneurship could just as easily be one mark of the "success" of this cluster, drawing in not only faculty and student talent but also knowledge workers; the ferment of ideas—not unlike that generated at the Athenian Agora or the café society of Paris or Andy Warhol's Factory—would be a draw for these knowledge workers.

The innovation cluster might be better understood as a "hothouse." "History's most creative communities enchant us with the almost otherworldly quality of their achievements," writes Barton Kunstler. "Was it an accident of birth, a loaded gene pool that gave ancient Athens its great writers, thinkers, political innovators, builders, and artists? Was fifteenth-century Florence, the heart of the Renaissance, really more creative than Venice or Rome? Or are their different types of creativity, with Florence shining in the arts, Venice in long-distance trade, and Rome in politics?"[59] Kunstler is describing a hothouse as more than an enterprise that engages in tech commercialization: a hothouse produces many forms of innovation. "The hothouse effect," a term coined by Kunstler, "asserts that such singular 'creatives' are more likely to emerge from within a group of skilled practitioners than from isolation." Hothouses might be defined as having these qualities. They

1. sustain a high level of innovative creativity for a significant period of time;
2. draw on the knowledge and innovations of the broader cultural zone to which they belong;
3. spawn geniuses whose achievements climax the work of many other practitioners at all levels of achievement, from the brilliant down to the workaday purveyor of common goods;
4. establish a new idiom, a new way of doing things that informs their creative products and establishes new standards, procedures, and principles in a variety of fields; and
5. achieve recognition from contemporaries and establish a lasting legacy to which future generations continually return and which they emulate.[60]

Any place can become a "creative city" like Athens or Florence, or contemporary cities like San Francisco or New York, if they place creativity at the heart of their placemaking strategy. A college or other knowledge enterprise can serve as the driver of a regional creative city plan if it functions as a creativity center. In functioning as the innovation hub, the knowledge enterprise establishes the "creative milieu" for the town. "A creative milieu is a place—either a cluster of buildings, a part of a city, a city as a whole or a region—that contains the necessary preconditions in terms of 'hard' and 'soft' infrastructure to generate a flow of ideas and inventions," writes Charles Landry. "Such a milieu is a physical setting where a critical mass of entrepreneurs, intellectuals, social activists, artists, administrators, power brokers or students can operate in an open-minded, cosmopolitan context and where face to face interaction creates new ideas, artefacts, products, services and institutions and as a consequence contributes to economic success."[61] The "soft" infrastructure Landry identifies "is the system of associative structures and social networks, connections and human interactions, that underpins and encourages the flow of ideas between individuals and institutions."[62] The knowledge enterprise represents a particular kind of innovation cluster, one that maintains the creative milieu of a town.

David Edwards's "Laboratory" is an example of what a knowledge enterprise's innovation cluster might look like. At the center of The Laboratory is the practice of "artscience," which means combining the aesthetic and scientific methods. The Laboratory hothouse is governed by the idea of "idea translation": "To translate ideas is to move them from some conceptual stage to some later stage in the general process of realization. Realization may be any combination of economic value (new technologies, say), cultural value (new forms of art), educational value (new scientific theories), and social value (new medicines or political policies). In the process of realization our ideas often cross disciplinary boundaries. That is where artscience comes in."[63] Again, the results of an innovation hub can include economic and technological ones but encompass a much broader definition of innovation.

Edwards defines his Laboratory as an "idea accelerator," the goal of which is "to find a way to move ideas more readily over interdisciplinary barriers, which . . . are generally artscience barriers. . . . The idea accelerator is a kind of experimental art center that puts industry, society, and research and education partners in dialog with the public through continual artscience experimentation."[64] In this way, the Laboratory resembles the early twentieth-century German art school the Bauhaus, "where ideas in the arts and design advanced through phases of experiential learning, cultural exhibition, and production."[65] The particular form the innovation cluster might take is defined more by a strategy of idea acceleration than just tech commercialization alone. It would be important to stress that these innovation clusters or the results of innovation be unplanned and emergent, "to embrace ideas so daring that they remain without any clear cultural, commercial, or humanitarian value and to help them attain external value through cultural incubation."[66] The local knowledge enterprise functions as the innovation cluster for the town and region. The work of the cluster is curriculum for the faculty and students of the college, but the knowledge workers lured to the place are also a part of this creative hothouse.

9. Unleash the Commercial Dynamo

Faculty at some universities engage in entrepreneurial activity, as when they work with a campus technology commercialization office to transform the fruits of their research into patents and then to found companies based in that intellectual property. On the other hand, these same institutions often make it difficult for faculty to commercialize their research, burdening them with conflict of interest and conflict of commitment policies. These conflicting policies have the effect of encouraging and promoting entrepreneurial activity on the one hand, while stifling entrepreneurialism on the other. As Costas Spirou observes, "There is a general need [for universities] to rethink the relationship between theory and practice, as well as the management of a continuous, back-and-forth interaction between industry and the academy."[67] At a knowledge enterprise faculty are permitted—even expected—to move seamlessly between the academic institution and the larger commercial world.

We tend to associate such faculty entrepreneurial activity at large research universities in major urban areas. But faculty enterprise can be encouraged anyplace; consider the company Daktronics, founded by two South Dakota State University professors and headquartered in Brookings, South Dakota, population 25,000. At a knowledge enterprise, faculty are encouraged to translate research into productive enterprises. These need not be solely for-profit enterprises. Entrepreneurial faculty—and students—are rewarded for founding B Corporations and nonprofits, their enterprise weighted alongside teaching, research, and service. As part of their growth strategy, faculty-led enterprises seek out talent to move to their regions.

These and other enterprises rely on venture capital, and as a preeminent regional anchor institution the knowledge enterprise serves as a venture capital fund. It might be odd to think of a college acting as a venture capitalist: this surely is not a proper or appropriate function for a college. Further, many colleges are already capital-poor, with small, meager endowments, and so asking these to pivot to acquiring venture funds might be a bridge too far, with capital accumulation seemingly outside of the competency of most institutions. Recall that a generation ago the thought of a college as a real estate developer similarly seemed outlandish, and yet many colleges are indeed playing such a role today, expanding their physical and economic presence by buying and managing hotels and restaurants.

A knowledge enterprise committed to a talent magnet strategy therefore also acts as a capital accumulator for a region. Enterprises in the knowledge economy require capital, and if a regional talent magnet is going to thrive, some organization must serve this role. Some institutions might begin by reallocating funds from their endowments, but, again, this may prove challenging to many incumbent institutions, as endowment funds are often tied to specific initiatives and thus not easily shifted to other purposes. Some colleges might turn a portion of their fundraising efforts toward raising series-level funding, which might require a new administrative position, a vice president for venture capital, for instance. The responsibility for securing venture funds might fall upon the president of the institution; fundraiser-in-chief is a title that defines many presidential positions today. That fundraising is at least in part devoted to venture fundraising. Again, such an enterprise will very likely anger underpaid or contingent faculty, who would exclaim with exacerbation that yet another administrative position has been created to further nonacademic goals. Students and their parents might chafe at the thought of their tuition being used in support of such purposes. But inasmuch as the knowledge enterprise is committed to encouraging enterprise, it must also play the role of capitalizing such enterprise.

10. Rewild Your Population and Land

Any knowledge enterprise committed to a talent magnet strategy of rewilding must understand how its culture—the lived experiences of its faculty, staff, and students—impacts the environment. James J. Farrell observes that the culture of most colleges and universities mirrors the larger, unsustainable consumer culture: "Even as environmental policies and participation change, there's still not much change in everyday life [of many colleges]. The *culture* of college isn't changing much at all, and neither is American culture. . . . [C]ollege students still live like most Americans, and they graduate into a world that's simply not sustainable. . . . Like other Americans. They're nourished by nature and agriculture, but they don't return the favor."[68] How students, especially, live their lives in college—outside of anything they learn in a formal curriculum—merely replicates the thoughtlessly poor decisions the wider society makes with regard to the stewardship of the planet. "Institutions of higher education have always prepared students to succeed in the so-called real world," say Farrell. "Our colleges and universities now need to teach students how to live responsibly on the planet as well."[69]

The college experience could be redesigned such that it becomes a place where students learn new experiences, especially how to live sustainably. "College is a place where students could think twice about American culture and ecosystems, but most students still don't, despite the fact that people are causing climate change—transforming the good Earth into a different planet," observes Farrell.[70] "Students learn a lot in college, but most students aren't learning what they need to create a restorative society, a hospitable earth, and a future with college campuses securely above water. Colleges now need to provide the knowledge and practices humans need for the future, to show in word and deed how a sustainable society might work. A college that wants to remain relevant to its students will teach them how to be leaders in the ecological transition of the twenty-first century."[71] In the redesign proposed here, the college becomes a separate sphere outside of the dominant consumer culture where hitherto unexamined ecological behaviors are made transparent. Students interact with the environment all the time without consciously considering the consequences of their actions. For example, Farrell points to "the hidden curriculum of the cafeteria," "a place where [students] come into contact with their animal nature, the basic need for sustenance."[72] Outside of a formal class, students are made aware of their encounter with systems of food, such as how the hamburger they consume at dinner arrives at their plate and the ecological impact of that supply chain (to say nothing of the effects of consuming the hamburger on their own bodies). These myriad everyday encounters with the environment— eating, buying clothing, consuming social media—are made apparent, not necessarily in any formal curriculum but by cultivating a culture of reflection on one's lived experience. As these hitherto unexamined assumptions are laid bare, students are invited to reflect upon the impact of their choices, perhaps drawing their own conclusions about the necessity to change their behaviors. This learning process can be accomplished through both the visible and the hidden curriculum of the college. "Students may take a few credits in environmental studies," says Farrell, "but they *live* their environmental values every minute of every day and exemplify them to their friends."[73]

Such a culture change involves more than hosting a program or granting a degree in environmental science, although these are acceptable practices. Nor does it assume that every student must major in or otherwise take a class in an environment-themed discipline or coursework in rewilding specifically. Although, again, a knowledge enterprise committed to rewilding certainly could require such coursework as a part of general education. Rewilding as a practice will largely be treated as an extracurricular value, perhaps even transcurricular: how students live and work at the college is scrutinized and guided toward an environmental consciousness. The culture of the institution is rewilded.

Farrell's model for this ideal college is one that produces "designing minds," which David Orr defines as "minds that are prepared to design a good society in harmony with nature." Orr suggests that higher education should be designed "To equip young people with a basic understanding of systems and to develop habits of mind that seek out 'patterns that connect' human and natural systems; 2. To teach young people the analytical skills necessary for thinking accurately about cause and effect; 3. To give students the practical competence necessary to solve local problems; and 4. To teach young people the habit of rolling up their sleeves and getting down to work."[74] This schematic could form the basis of a general education program for the knowledge enterprise. Further, these ideas are put into practice as students learn to design, build, and maintain a rewilding strategy for the region. Working with faculty experts, students work on projects to rewild the campus, to bring the college and nature into balance. This would be another example of the "localization" of faculty research. In so maintaining this ecological balance, the knowledge enterprise thus becomes a model for how to rewild a city and a region. Working with regional planners, the knowledge enterprise leads the region in rewilding initiatives. Rewilding is not only a technical or engineering solution; rewilding also involves changing the culture, habits, and mindset of an area, and this wider culture change is led by the students and faculty of the knowledge enterprise.

11. Turn Housing into an Affordable Service

Becoming a knowledge enterprise as talent magnet changes the definition of a "residential campus." Most colleges and universities are already in the housing business, of course, meaning the provisions for lodging for transient undergraduate students. In a talent magnet strategy, the knowledge enterprise is also in the business of housing non-student adults, those knowledge workers drawn to a region. In this formulation, housing is both affordable and a way for knowledge workers to exchange knowledge. One function of any college or university is to provide an environment for the exchange of ideas and knowledge; the new forms of housing described here allows the knowledge enterprise to extend this mission.

The economic geographer Arnault Morisson observes that there are new social environments forming in global knowledge economy cities. Morrison is specifically looking at Paris, but the forms he identifies can be found in other places. "In the Knowledge Economy, new social environments are deliberately being created combining places in order to facilitate networking and the exchange of knowledge."[75] Spaces for the exchange of knowledge, of course, already describes the activities of a traditional college or university, but these spaces typically cater only to traditional 18- to 22-year-old undergraduates.

Specifically, Morrison sees a blending of first (home), second (work), and third (convivial) places into new configurations, which are especially pronounced in cities of the knowledge economy. These new forms include one that he identifies as a "fourth place." "Since the late 2000s," Morrison observes, "new social environments—such as hacker spaces, maker spaces, Living Labs, FabLabs, shared living spaces, co-living, and co-working spaces—have been emerging in the post-industrial cities. The emergence of new social environments is the result of concurrent trends fostered by the Knowledge Economy, namely, the integration of work and personal life; the importance of informal networks; the importance of tacit knowledge; the millennials' preference to live in urban centers; and overall new organizations of work."[76] Morrison describes the first kind of novel social environment as the coliving space, which combines a first place (home) and a second place (work).[77] He identifies such an arrangement in Paris: the startup HackerHouse, in addition to workspaces, has accommodations for entrepreneurs.[78] Some colleges and universities have built such coliving spaces on or near their campuses. At Otterbein University in suburban Columbus, Ohio, for example, university leaders are planning a development that includes 240,000 square feet of office space, 100,000 square feet of medical office, 25,000 square feet of retail space, and 627 multifamily units. This is not exactly coliving in the knowledge economy sense described by Morrison—in that it is not clear how those residential units plus the working spaces will be connected to the talent of the university. But it does demonstrate how some colleges are already gesturing toward this talent magnet housing strategy. More on point, in 2016, the University of Utah launched Lassonde Studios, a five-story structure where the first floor contains 20,000 square feet of space where students can "connect, test ideas, build prototypes, launch companies and learn by doing." The remaining four floors consist of dormitory living space for the so called "Lassonde 400."[79] This arrangement is intended for undergraduate students of the University of Utah; a talent magnet version would be to open up coliving spaces intended for the entire community, specifically affordable housing that gives knowledge workers access to innovation spaces and the talent of the local knowledge enterprise.[80]

Combining a second place and a third place is what Morrison terms a coworking space, a common feature of cities plugged into the knowledge economy. As described by Morrison, "The function of coworking space is to create an atmosphere conducive to work and network in order to favor the exchange of knowledge and to foster collaboration opportunities."[81] We have described previously the idea of knowledge enterprises establishing such coworking spaces on their campuses, available to local residents as well as traditional undergraduate students.

A comingling space results when a first place and a third place are combined. Morrison describes Le 29 Hôtel (très) Particulier in Paris, which "mixes shared apartments and shared common spaces offering to the residents and guests cultural events and concierge services. . . . The function of the comingling spaces is to favor social interactions and networking opportunities between its residents."[82] Again, these spaces are designed as places not only to live but to facilitate the exchange of knowledge, which is why knowledge enterprises as talent magnets are in the business of providing these comingling spaces.

Combining all three types of places produces a fourth place. "Opened in 2017," reports Morrison, "Station F is a 34,000-square-meter innovation center that combines restaurants, bars, a post office, fablab, and 3,046 working desks for 1,100 startups. In 2018, Station F will open Home, a 100 shared apartments residence for the entrepreneurs and knowledge workers working at Station F."[83] In another part of Paris we find the Stream Building, which

> offers Zoku mini lofts with shared spaces, co-working space, a shared rooftop, bars, and restaurants. The Stream Building is divided into four categories: Stream Work, Stream Play, Stream Eat, and Stream Play [sic]. The fourth place blurs the frontier, within the same space, of the first (home), second (work), and third place making the space, a place in itself. The function of the fourth place is to foster networking, to promote mingling, and to favor collaboration, face-to-face interactions, and the exchange of tacit knowledge.[84]

In the talent magnet strategy advocated here, the knowledge enterprise builds fourth places that draw faculty and students to reside there but also caters to knowledge workers. The college's fourth space holds classes in this space but also lectures and workshops for the community. Inasmuch as one function of a fourth place is the exchange of tacit knowledge, this is certainly within the scope of mission of a knowledge enterprise, and one reason why it is in the housing-as-service business.

The knowledge enterprise must take the lead in working to rezone the campus and other parts of the city to accommodate these new forms of housing. "Policymakers," councils Morrison, "should favor the creation of the fourth place and new social environments such as coliving, coworking, and comingling spaces by promoting mixed-use zoning that incorporates different dimensions of places and by providing incentives in cities where the market is too weak to foster the creation of these new spaces."[85]

Morisson's study was focused on Paris but draws the conclusion that these new forms of spatial arrangements are becoming a feature of the nodes—here, meaning global cities—of the knowledge economy. If one goal of the talent magnet strategy is to plug into the larger knowledge economy, the creation and maintenance of affordable fourth places by the knowledge enterprise must be one of the strategic goals of any town or small city.

12. Rediscover the Lost Art of Placemaking

No one has better articulated a vision for how the deliberate and strategic location of a college can contribute to creative placemaking than the architect Cedric Price. Consider his vision for the "Potteries Thinkbelt," a mid-1960s design for a new kind of university in the north of England. Price wanted to make the university central to and enmeshed with the political economy of the region. Indeed, his plan was to physically expand the university such that it would encompass the entire region. The region in question was northern Staffordshire, an area that was at one time a thriving industrial dynamo centered on the manufacture of pottery (hence the name of the project). By the 1960s, the area had suffered a long decline, some describing it as a "wasteland." Price proposed a revitalization scheme with higher education as the new industry for the region.

Rather than a traditional ivy-covered campus hermetically sealed off in some corner of the region, Price proposed a radically decentralized and mobile campus. Using the existing transportation network, classrooms would be distributed throughout the region, with students and faculty moving between them via road and rail. "All the locations in his scheme were arranged along the railway routes to boost the university's integration into existing regional infrastructure," writes the architectural historian Tanja Herdt. "His [Price's] design envisioned that rail tracks that once carried goods and raw materials between industrial sites would transport mobile teaching modules in dedicated university trains."[86] Like our idea of the 15-minute campus, the Potteries Thinkbelt was not confined to a single location but was to be widely accessible. "The layout of the Thinkbelt," wrote Price, "which will encompass the whole area and spread over about 100 square miles—allows advanced education to take full advantage of present day national and individual mobility. And its form and organization are adjustable for the future."[87]

Price understood two things: (1) that the new university did not need to pay homage to previous examples, either its mission or its appearance, and therefore mimic what already existed and (2) that the university would be embedded in its region and would exist as much to be an economic driver as it would be an intellectual center: that knowledge and economics would be entwined. "Further education and re-education must be viewed as a major industrial undertaking," Price argued, "not as a service run by gentlemen for the few."[88]

"When the next round of university building starts," wrote Price in the 1960s as indeed a new round of university building was under-way in England and elsewhere, "perhaps we should treat education less as a polite cathedral-town amenity."[89] Price could have been ad-dressing our current town-gown moment, especially as exists with small liberal arts colleges and their small (usually rural) towns. His-torically, many of these schools have been largely aloof from the con-cerns of their regions; conversely, the location of a small college might be little more than a badge of honor and an expression of civic pride, a decoration, perhaps, but not as an economic driver.

Economic growth and creative placemaking are central to the tal-ent magnet strategy we are proposing: that knowledge enterprises are not just located in cities or towns but, indeed, can be drivers for creative placemaking for those cities and towns. Price asserted that "the project indicates that education and the need to exchange infor-mation may be able to equal defense, energy and commercial needs as *generators of urban location and form: cities caused by learning*" (em-phasis ours). And elsewhere he wrote: "Defence, energy and com-merce have in the past been sufficient generators of cities. This proj-ect assumes that education and the need to exchange information may have a similar generative force: *cities can be made by learning*"[90] (emphasis ours). The knowledge enterprise is not simply a feature of a talent magnet strategy but a primary engine of such a strategy. Price was suggesting that the knowledge enterprise that was to be the Potteries Thinkbelt could produce the city/town: that the causal train of urban development extended from university outward toward town. This upsets what we normally think of as the town-gown relationship.

In this way of thinking, the knowledge enterprise is embedded in and integral to the local political economy. To be clear: the city or town exists not simply as a service to students. The typical college town might have shops, businesses, and services that cater to the students and that constitute the economy of the region. More than just a cluster of consumers, the knowledge enterprise serves as an innovation cluster, third and fourth space, node to the knowledge economy, knowledge worker recruiter—the catalyst of a regional talent magnet. "The [student] housing will perhaps be of quicker benefit to the surrounding community than even the Thinkbelt's educational industry," Price imagined. "But, over time, the whole of the Potteries will be revolutionized. Not only will derelict land be used again, and the old eyesores go: there will also be a major national industry to replace what they will inevitably lose. Other areas could eventually learn from the example of this vast experiment— which would simultaneously save the country money and *gain it brains*"[91] (emphasis ours). Or gain it talent, as we would say.

"The requirements of a student population approximate closely to the future pattern of a literate skilled and highly mobile society," a description that resonates with our current moment.[92] Price was writing in the UK in the 1960s, where the idea of broad access to higher education was only dawning. But he nevertheless saw the implications for regional economic development of intertwining knowledge with placemaking. To be clear: we are not proposing to simply copy Price's unrealized design. The Thinkbelt was a specific solution to the issues a particular region at a unique moment in time. We are, instead, taking lessons from Price's insights, deriving analogies for the design of a knowledge enterprise that catalyzes a talent magnet: that a college need not mimic existing forms, nor serve existing purposes. The Potteries Thinkbelt provides the idea that a college can be reimagined to serve as the keystone institution of a region's talent magnet strategy. Which is why we refer to these keystone institutions as the knowledge enterprise, to disassociate them from what we usually think of as a typical college or university.

Conclusion

In serving as a talent magnet, the knowledge enterprise asserts itself as a principal regional anchor institution. However, this does not mean that it should mimic the ills brought about by some urban universities. Davarian L. Baldwin argues that some urban universities—or UniverCities, as he describes them—rather than serving as anchor institutions are nothing more than for-profit developers, with a host of dire consequences for their communities. "Urban colleges and universities," especially, "are increasingly setting the wage ceiling for workers, determining the use and value of our land, directing the priorities of our police, and dictating the distribution of our public funds in cities all over the country. . . . [P]ublic discourse remains overwhelmingly silent about the consequences of turning the US city into one big campus."[93]

Although some urban universities have historically been devourers of the surrounding neighborhoods—and especially displacing people of color—the movement toward universities as anchor institutions has frequently meant profiteering, not community service or inclusive placemaking. "An older cadre of activists and educators looked to urban schools as a beacon for enlivening the values of civic engagement," Baldwin writes. "The classroom and the research center, they believed, could be reoriented to address the needs of the city. Meanwhile, a growing class of administrators, coming out of the corporate world, identified universities as central command posts for generating needed profits in new research and real estate markets."[94] Both activists and administrators have evoked the term "anchor institution" to describe their missions, yet Baldwin maintains that the two campus entities rarely work together and, indeed, says that the latter's initiatives usually usurp the former's. "And the failure to reconcile what have become parallel approaches to revitalization continues to shape how university-driven development is done in our cities," he concludes.[95]

When we say that knowledge enterprises in small towns and secondary cities can serve as anchor institutions of a talent magnet placemaking strategy, we wish to make clear that they should not replicate the ravenous behaviors of some urban universities, bringing "Univer-Cities" to smaller towns. Instead, we are arguing that knowledge enterprises should seek to balance and reconcile these two approaches: to be both an incubator of civic engagement and an economic driver, all in service to the community.

This is why we have coined the term "university as utility." A utility is an organization supplying the community with electricity, gas, water or sewage. The university as utility would be an organization supplying the community with public goods, especially regarding the broad accessibility of knowledge as a placemaking asset.[96]

3

Archetypes of a
Talent Magnet / Knowledge
Enterprise Strategy

HOW DOES A COLLEGE OR TOWN LEADER move from conviction of the need for change to begin a process that has a good chance of achieving a meaningful and positive transformation? Who should initiate the move? Could this even be a third party, either an institution with an interest in a particular location, or a community that comes together to create or re-create a place? Our thesis is that a sustainable town-gown strategy must have a triple-win approach, combining social, environmental, and economic growth. It will progress through systematically improving its ability to attract, retain, and nurture talent, thus becoming a "talent magnet." Each place is a unique terrain and thus must find an idiosyncratic solution. The solution will in large part emerge from a process of trial and error, combining top-down goal setting with unleashing a bottoms-up energy for regeneration.

In this chapter we cover the gamut from fledgling places, with no town or college, all the way to the strongest combinations of city and university. The problems may be very different: weaker places and colleges could face a struggle for survival. With stronger colleges and places, the struggle may be to find a broader social purpose and meaning.

Archetype One: Settlement

Imagine a place in which there is a small or even a nonexistent settlement and no college. A committed group of "founders" reach an agreement to create both a college and a village or town of some scale. This idea harkens back to earlier town-and-gown formation stories such as the foundation of the town of Oberlin, Ohio, and Oberlin College, in 1833, in pursuit of a Presbyterian mission to imbue greater religious principles in a European settlement.

According to the Foundation for Intentional Community, there are over 900 "intentional communities" across the United States, organized as ecovillages, communes, cohousing, student coops, spiritual or religious groups, or shared communities.[1] Many of these communities are subscale, undercapitalized, and unlikely to persist across multiple generations. They lack the infrastructure, knowledge enterprises, and innovation to thrive in the knowledge economy.

With the new potential from remote work and remote learning, a new model of town and gown settlement could emerge. An existing intentional community or settlement could seek to form a college and to simultaneously attract a core group of remote workers. Alternatively, a group of remote and other workers could gather online, aggregate their combined assets and income, and negotiate with landowners and existing places a potential mass settlement. To strengthen the long-term viability of place, they would aim to establish a fledgling knowledge enterprise, one that teaches traditional subjects, perhaps, but that features some of the characteristics of a talent magnet as described earlier. This nascent knowledge enterprise might serve as a community "third place" before it develops specific academic programs, or it might be focused on rewilding, environmental issues, or addressing a problem of local consideration, a research problem tackled by its faculty.

In the United States, there are 19,000 incorporated villages, towns, or cities, of which 16,000 have fewer than 10,000 people, and 3,000 have more than 10,000 people.[2] In addition, there are 4,000 census-designated places (CDPs) that are unincorporated but recognized by the Census Bureau to have a critical mass of population density, with a combined population of 39 million in 2010 (implying an average population of about 10,000 people per CDP).[3] The 1990 census estimated that a further 66 million Americans live outside of either an incorporated place or a CDP.[4] If we assume an average population of 5,000 per "location," this yields an additional 13,000 places for an estimated total of 36,000 places in total across the United States.[5] Some sources suggest that there are as many as 108,000 places in the US.[6]

We could posit that 10 million Americans move to the 3,600 most compelling places (10% of all places) based on the quality of their talent magnet strategies as they seek to reduce their cost of living and to improve their quality of life. This implies that each of the "winning" places has the potential to attract on average 2,778 new settlers. If we assume an average prior population per place of 10,000 inhabitants and that inward migrants have the same income per capita as the current population, this migration will generate a 28% average lift in GDP per "winning" location, and an opportunity for place-based reinvention.

Consider the combined potential of a founding group of 1,000 families, with significant remote worker capability, and with an interest in forming an environmentally, socially, and economically sustainable community. We assume that the initial settlers will have an average income in the top 20%, since remote work flexibility is today heavily correlated with income.[7] Minorities are significantly underrepresented in remote work flexibility, so the founding team would proactively recruit for a diverse social mix of families.

The collective potential of this intentional community is $100M in annual pre-tax income, $500 million in combined wealth, and $1 billion or more in potential debt capacity.[8] This could imply a virtual balance sheet of $1.5 billion from the founding "settler" families. This virtual balance sheet can be combined with that of the community they move to and further expanded through population and income growth.

The intentional community would collectively develop a "town purpose" strategy, based on their common interest. As an example, the town purpose could be a "Swiss Lake Town," oriented around natural interaction with the surrounding environment. In the United States there are 111,000 lakes and reservoirs, providing a range of possibilities.[9] "Laketown" would be zoned for clustered urban/rural development along a "gentle density" model. Spiez, on Lake Thun in Switzerland, could be a template. At 6.5 square miles, it has a population of 12,000 people and an average density of 2,000 per square mile. "Laketown" would be broadly designed around a "soft city" model, maximizing for community, walkability, local commerce, flexible work, knowledge development, and innovation.[10] Its development is to be managed via a corporation, with a mandate to combine social, environmental, and economic growth. Its choice of location, its negotiation strategy with landowners and its future zoning could include restricting the use of Internal Combustion Engines and optimizing around human-centered transit. The Corporation would be founded as a knowledge enterprise, with an explicit goal to place the new community into an academic context.

The intentional community would then seek to find a place to move to. It might find a willing partner in a lake town that wants to reenergize its economic growth model, a group of homeowners, a native American tribe, a philanthropic entity, a corporation, or a state. The "Laketown" thesis may not appeal to those accustomed to low-density lake homes. But the combined leverage of the potential settlers, and the diversity of options, suggests that a match between settlers and a destination can be found. For efficiency, the incumbent population on the other side of the negotiation table would need to similarly organize and gain community approval. There must be strong commitment on both sides to create a combined community of intent.

"Laketown" would zone for up to 40,000 people (or 13,000 families, assuming 3 people per family). They might target for an initial new settlement of 3,000 people or 1,000 families, on top of an existing population of 1,000 families. To this end the group invests $100 million in purchasing land including lake frontage,[11] $50 million in infrastructure, and $200 million to build 1,000 new dwellings.[12]

Recognizing the opportunity to extend healthy life expectancy and reduce health care costs, the town enters into a risk-sharing agreement with the state on health care management. The town design and ethos, by promoting walking, clean air, community, and affordable living, reduces the costs of health care and increases the outcomes, aligning with a growing focus in the United States on tackling the social determinants of health.[13]

The 3,000 new settlers now begin to combine with the incumbent population of 3,000. The negotiation process prior to and after settlement should include joint planning and citizen-building exercises, akin to how, in the business world, there is significant planning when companies merge. These should include individual and group processes of "future authoring" and the formation of small teams with specific missions feeding into the overall town purpose. Whereas the initial emphasis has been "top down," the locus of action now must shift to bottoms-up leadership. These teams should have very tangible objectives. They should have access to success-based financing from the knowledge enterprise to turn ideas into core assets.

One key joint objective is to proactively recruit a diverse mix of additional residents, to grow to a near-term target population of 10,000 and to balance for missing skills and social profiles. The town seeks to gain the broadest diversity in terms of race, age, orientation, skills, and interests. It asks of all settlers to focus on what they bring to the place, as much or more than what the place brings to them. The goal is to inject the settlement with a growth mindset and strong community spirit.

The knowledge enterprise plays a critical role in sponsoring migrants, offering low-cost entry into housing, skill acquisition, company formation, and overall triple-win development. It helps to train the population in physical skills in construction, agriculture, fishing, music, and art, thus reducing labor costs for town construction projects, developing latent skills, and balancing the "left-brain" predominance of the settlers with "right-brain" development. The knowledge enterprise is a major landlord and asset owner, benefiting from the economic growth and land revaluation that unfolds as the settlement grows into a talent magnet. Its ownership and governance should be broadly distributed and based on a combination of capital contribution, sweat-equity investment, long-term commitment, and a mandate for diversity. It should operate somewhere between a pure capitalist, a philanthropic, and a government model.

"Laketown" aims to innovate in K–12. In 2021, 22 states in the United States are in the process of implementing tax-credit scholarship laws, giving parents greater control of their children's schooling.[14] Home schooling in the United States grew from 4% adoption in 2019 to over 8% in 2021, with the strongest growth among African American and Hispanic families.[15] Virtual schooling, pod schools, and other innovations have been broadly adopted during the COVID-19 lockdowns. Models for schooling include the International Baccalaureate, aiming for students to become "inquirers, knowledgeable, thinkers, communicators, principled, open-minded, caring, risk-takers, balanced, and reflective," or Knowledge Is Power Program (KIPP) schools, based on the character traits most predictive of academic success: zest, grit, optimism, self-control, gratitude, social intelligence, and curiosity.[16] Other schools may be themed around the Montessori system, based on collaborative and play-based learning.[17]

For higher ed, the "Laketown" knowledge enterprise offerings begin in areas ranging from the liberal arts to process automation, new business formation, lost crafts and skills, or lake rewilding. Areas of focus are tied to town purpose and global demand for skills. The town population, now at a combined 6,000 people, generates 360 traditional college students, half of whom leave to study away, and half of whom study locally.[18] The new knowledge enterprise attracts another 360 traditional college students from away and 300 nontraditional (older) students, combined for more than 1,000 students per year, providing a critical mass of demand. To maximize postgraduate student retention and skills advancement, the town partners with the knowledge enterprise to support the formation of companies related to the core fields of study of the knowledge enterprise.

An American or international university could take a leadership role in supporting the development of the local knowledge enterprise, with an orientation around sustainable growth. For example, a Swiss university could become an anchor in developing one or more US

"Laketowns" along a Swiss model, including application of Swiss environmental practices. The Swiss Federal Institute of Technology in Zurich is the highest-rated university in Switzerland and is ranked fifth in the world in environmental science.[19] The city of Zurich is a world-class example of a "talent magnet city." Zurich's population has tripled in size, from half a million people in 1950 to 1.5 million people in 2020.[20] Despite strong growth, it is regularly ranked among the top 10 most livable and sustainable cities in the world. Switzerland has not always enjoyed clean air and water. In the 1960s only 14% of Swiss households were connected to a sewage system, farmers overused fertilizers and pesticides, and manufacturing plants released polluted water, leading to foam, algae, undrinkable water, and generally polluted lakes. Today 97% of households are connected to public sewage, industrial plants have adopted high quality filters, and farmers have reduced their use of fertilizers through sustainable farming practices.[21] Signaling its interest to continue to lead on sustainable growth, in January 2021 Switzerland announced an ambitious net zero strategy, with the goal of reducing all emissions by 50% by 2030.[22]

As corporations move deeper into education, they could also become involved. For example, UiPath Academy, a free "university" oriented around robotic process automation and sponsored by UiPath, could partner with the "Laketown" knowledge enterprise in developing a localized robotic process automation program to help prepare students to leverage the potential of automation, supporting the bionic worker in the process. As digital customer academies become a core strategy lever for many companies, there could be strong competition among corporations to partner with the "Laketown" knowledge enterprise.

The "Laketown" knowledge enterprise would provide start-up facilities and budgets. It would encourage town residents and new migrants to turn passion projects into academic founding teams of two or three people, then into a succession of ever more committed endeavors. A part-time class could become a summer immersion course, then a one-year certificate, then evolve into an accredited degree. By managing the educational platform, integrating knowledge into the core design of "Laketown," and keeping costs low, the capital costs would be minimal. The knowledge enterprise would thereby be positioned to support success-based expansion. The growth of the knowledge enterprise could attract corporations and universities around the world, looking to use this model to cost-effectively experiment with expansions in their own franchises.

As "Laketown" develops, its approach could attract interest from other places, colleges, and intentional communities. The model could be replicated in rural and urban locations, across a range of settings. One can imagine a broad range of styles, based on natural attractions, history, manufacturing capacity, culture, and many other factors. In addition to the 110,000 lakes in the United States, there are 73,000 mountains in the United States that could accommodate "mountain towns," 93,000 miles of shoreline for "beach towns" and "coast towns," 12,000 ports and marinas for "port towns," 250,000 rivers spanning 3.5 million miles for "river towns."[23] There are mill towns, arts towns, manufacturing towns, remote towns, farm towns across the country. There are myriad opportunities to combine places with knowledge enterprises.

Archetype Two: Reimagination

Deep Springs College, nestled in a cattle and alfalfa ranch in a valley in the Sierra Nevada, is a small institution focusing on teaching its students a "life of leadership and service." It admits only 15 students each year, all on full scholarships. There is no nearby town or even hamlet, with the closest city being 40 miles away. Deep Springs Valley may feel like the last place for expansion. The valley has a saline lake, Deep Springs Lake. Saline lakes as a class are at risk of environmental degradation, as covered by a 2021 article in *Deseret* around risks to the Great Salt Lake of Utah.[24] But with such a challenge, there is also an opportunity.

Fresh water aquifers are on a path of exhaustion in 40 countries, including the United States, India, and China, with agriculture accounting for 70% of global fresh-water withdrawals.[25] Saline aquifers and lakes offer comparable global farming capacity to that of freshwater, and this capacity will increase as depleted freshwater becomes saltwater. According to Saline Agriculture Worldwide, farming with salt-tolerant species and adaptive techniques could bring an incremental 70 million to 120 million hectares into cultivation.[26] Salt-water farming is a fast-emerging sector, with areas of specialization in the Netherlands, the United Kingdom, Spain, India, and Bangladesh. A new primer on the space, *Future of Sustainable Agriculture in Saline Environments* (2022), suggests an immediate opportunity from salt-resistant farming of $1 billion a year.[27] One could imagine a strategy whereby Deep Springs College expands to include a new program in sustainable saline agriculture. It could attract or incubate new businesses in this area, providing space on site for these companies and inviting executives to teach classes. Through this expansion, the size of the settlement could grow, built around a new practice and market in saline agriculture. An intentional community could decide to settle with a mission to develop this kind of farming and reach an agreement with Deep Springs and other local landowners.

Black Mountain College in rural North Carolina operated between 1933 and 1957. As stated in its memorial website, "Black Mountain College was born out of a desire to create a new type of college based on John Dewey's principles of progressive education."[28] It operated on a communal basis and focused on the development of the arts. Although the college did not survive to a second generation, the town of Black Mountain grew from a scarce 300 people at the time of the college foundation to 8,000 today, as it became a destination for those looking for art, nature, and self-reliance.[29] The output of Black Mountain's staff and students is still remembered through a research library and a dedicated journal.[30] Western North Carolina, centered around Asheville, has become a popular remote worker destination, driving the average cost of a home from $315K in 2018 to $399K at the time of writing in mid-2021. Black Mountain itself has seen home price increases, from $260K in 2018 to $320K in mid-2021.[31] The town of Black Mountain could develop a town and gown strategy with a triple-win approach of social, environmental, and economic growth. It could aim to double its population to 16,000 people through "gently dense" expansion of the downtown core, reduced vehicle use, and expansion of dedicated walkable and bikeable paths, harnessing the power of e-bikes to overcome the local hills. It could rekindle the iconic Black Mountain College into a next-generation knowledge enterprise, building on the local art and music scene but also tapping into opportunities for online art and music instruction, 3D printing, design thinking, and urban regeneration. It could establish itself as a "creativity cluster," which is an apt description of the original Black Mountain College. Where the original attracted the world's leading artists, writers, and designers, a Black Mountain College 2.0 could establish itself as a hothouse of creativity, not only in the arts but in a variety of domains that thirst for creative and innovative ideas.

The North Carolina Conservation Network, in its 2019 report on the environment, identified critical concerns in areas such as air quality, species biodiversity, water quality, and in the impact of pollution on child development and racial inequity. The town could promote the Black Mountain knowledge enterprise as having an environmental focus, where an "environmental consciousness is treated as a trans curricular value." This environmental ethos is also aimed at regional concerns, by partnering with one of the 60 environmental groups across the state.[32] The knowledge enterprise could also seek to partner with top universities in environmental sciences, such as Harvard, Stanford, Oxford, or Imperial College, London.[33]

The state of Vermont is a rural, sparsely populated, rapidly aging state. It has 16 currently operating colleges or universities; it has lost 6 colleges since 2010, with a further 3 at risk of closure. Vermont, long a weekend retreat for stressed-out flatlanders from New York and Boston, was a net beneficiary of the "Zoom-town" effect. Remote worker migration to Vermont in 2020 and 2021 has reversed prior population decline.[34] We could envision a strategy in which one or more of the recently defunct colleges, as well as the remaining at-risk colleges, develop town and gown revitalization strategies predicated on quality of life and the potential of remote workers to become the new economic engine.[35]

Green Mountain College in Poultney, VT (population 3,300), is among the latest casualties, closing in 2019 and dealing a blow to a town with below-average income for which the college was a key economic driver. Green Mountain sold for $4.5 million at auction, well below the target price of $22 million.[36] The new buyers, local entrepreneurial couple Raj and Danhee Bhakta, aim to reinvent Green Mountain College as an agricultural-worker college. Danhee is also launching a private K–12 school. One could envision the opportunity to leverage the campus and assets to host a knowledge enterprise: becoming a center for corporate retreats, for instance, and engaging in other changes to attract a community of remote workers. Remote workers could be attracted by cheap accommodations in student digs, with the college building a "fourth place." The Green Mountain knowledge enterprise might also offer professional mentoring services for these remote workers. With 155 acres, Green Mountain could provide the foundation for an intentional community. Poultney combines the charm of the Vermont mountains with nearby Lake St. Catherine. One could thus imagine a "mountain town" model, appealing to skiers, outdoors enthusiasts, new farmers, and those with health concerns such as asthma. Poultney is 90 minutes from Burlington, Vermont, an iconic post-COVID "Zoom town."[37] New York City and Boston are accessible by car or train, for those requiring episodic in-person presence in key cities.

As a state, Vermont could think much more boldly. With potentially 20 million American workers and their families up for grabs, Vermont could aim to attract 20,000 to 100,000 families with a state-level "town and gown" strategy, using a combination of its current colleges, revitalization of the recently defunct and at-risk colleges, and the formation of new colleges. Vermont's GDP in 2020 was $28 billion.[38] The addition of even 20,000 new families would create a potential GDP contribution of $1.4 billion, or a 5% increase, assuming the settlers earn at the average US household income level of $68,000 per year. However, supporting such a large-scale migration would require a comprehensive strategy, building on the 12 key rules of talent magnets and their application via knowledge enterprises. It would require Vermont, its key stakeholders, its universities, and its towns and cities to reverse engineer the needs of potential migrants, to develop planning and zoning strategies, to create financing mechanisms, and to replicate across multiple locations in the state the kinds of strategies proposed in this book for transforming a college into a knowledge enterprise.

Archetype Three: Town and Gown Regeneration

"Make the corn-belt a carbon belt," wrote Dan Imhoff, small-scale farmer and regenerative farming activist in December 2020 in a column published by *The Progressive*.[39] In the piece, he argues that the massive US agricultural subsidies to support the existing farming model should instead be used to finance and support a shift of hundreds of millions of US acres toward sustainable and renewable practices, thus improving the environment, using farms as carbon sinks, and helping improve farm profitability.

The US corn belt, largely coterminous with the Midwest region, covers over 350,000 square miles of the traditionally most productive agricultural land in the country and is the production center for its number one crop. The corn belt spans from the Dakotas on the west to Ohio to the east, from Wisconsin and Minnesota to the north to Kansas, Missouri, and Kentucky to the south. In 1900, following the agricultural revolution of the prior century, the Midwest region of the United States contained 35% of the US population, but this has since declined to 20%, largely in line with reduced farm yield and consequent reduced economic prospects.[40] Declining topsoil, climate volatility, and continuing application of the exhaustive farming model looks set to continue this trend in depopulation. A 2021 study estimated that one-third of the land in the corn belt had lost the critical topsoil that had historically made it so productive.[41] The Nature Conservancy estimated in 2020 that 10 billion tons of soil are lost every year in the United States, much faster than can be replenished by nature, and that annual social and economic losses resulting from this soil forfeiture exceeded $50 billion per year. Farm profitability is projected by the US Department of Agriculture to decline through to 2030.[42]

And yet the Midwest region is perhaps on the cusp of a major new social, environmental, and economic growth wave. Global demand for food is set to grow by 50% by 2050 according to a 2020 study by Deloitte.[43] There are numerous advances in technology, promising increased precision and efficiency, as covered in a 2020 McKinsey study, "Agriculture's Connected Future: How Technology Can Yield New Growth."[44] McKinsey argues that tech can help generate $500 billion in additional global agriculture production by 2030 while reducing some of the most harmful practices and sources of waste, largely maintaining the current business model. In contrast with McKinsey, Forum for the Future also released in 2020 a report titled "Growing Our Future: Scaling Regenerative Agriculture in the United States," arguing for a mass shift to a regenerative model and proposing a series of strategies for this change to happen at scale.[45]

The Midwest region enjoys strong natural bounties. The Mississippi River system drains the corn belt while providing low-cost access to markets and low-cost capital to its population. The river system was estimated in 2015 to generate over $400 billion in annual GDP.[46] Global strategist Peter Zeihan argues in his book *The Accidental Superpower* that the Mississippi River system, by allowing cheap transport of commodities and people via waterways, has been a key contributor to economic growth and the creation of an integrated American culture and thus claims an even more strategic role.[47] The Great Lakes, at a combined surface area of 94,000 square miles, is the largest system of fresh water in the world, representing 21% of total supply. Land, water, and cheap transport represent a compelling combination of assets.

The Midwest, with a population density of 90 people per square mile, is also substantially less crowded than the coastal areas. The Northeast "megalopolis" from Boston to Washington contains 17% of US population in 2% of its landmass and has an average density of 1,000 people per square mile. Lower density and below-average population growth in the Midwest have kept housing costs very afford-able relative to incomes, typically in the ratio of two to three times in-come, compared to five to six times or higher on the coasts. The region has the potential to double or quadruple its population by be-coming a talent magnet without reaching the density of coastal re-gions. With remote workers and others seeking high-quality and low-cost lives, the natural abundance and cheap living in the Midwest are compelling.

Colleges in the Midwest might wish to pursue a talent magnet/knowledge enterprise strategy, especially given the challenges many of these colleges currently face. Clayton Christensen and Michael Horn have predicted that 25% of all colleges could be at risk, including many in the Midwest.[48] Even colleges not at risk may want to consider an ex-pansion strategy to extend their missions and as a path to evolve into a knowledge enterprise.

The natural bounty of the Midwest is, however, at risk. The Mis-sissippi River, while much improved from the toxic levels of the 1970s, still received a C grade in the 2020 report from America's Wa-tershed Initiative, with concerns around frequent and extreme flood-ing, aging infrastructure, chemical pollution, nutrient runoff, urban-ization, and agricultural intensification. Water quality reported in 2020 declined relative to 2015, according to a report by the same organ-ization.[49] The Great Lakes, while also much improved from the 1970s and 1980s, are similarly facing environmental challenges, especially from agricultural runoff coming from the rivers that flow into them.

In this context, how could a college and town work together to take on a regional problem (declining farm productivity, agricultural run-off), a global problem (water pollution, loss of soil, feeding the world), and their own futures? There are almost 700 colleges or uni-versities across the corn-belt states, many sited in towns or cities, and potentially any combination of town and gown could take on these challenges. For illustration purposes we have picked a small college in the town of Defiance, Ohio.

Defiance sits at the confluence of the Maumee and Auglaize Rivers, squarely in the Ohio section of the farm belt. The EPA classifies the

Maumee River system, which drains over 5,000 square miles into Lake Erie, as being "at risk" from pesticides and nitrates from agricultural runoff.[50] A 2020 article on pollution in Lake Erie, specifically blamed the inflow of water with high nitrate and pesticides from the Maumee River that runs through Defiance as a key barrier to cleaner lake water.[51]

In line with slow regional growth, town population in Defiance peaked at 16,000 in 2010 and has stayed flat since then. With average house prices at $138K and average household income at $49K, a 3:1 ratio, Defiance has a better housing affordability ratio than the US average. Defiance College is ranked No. 49 in the Midwest.[52] The city of Defiance also hosts Northwest State Community College.

There is no immediate call to action for either the town or the college of Defiance to change, but the long-term warnings are there. The college may get squeezed out between megabrands and disruptive offerings, and the town faces long-term risks from pollution and from its reliance on a fragile and environmentally unsustainable farming model. How could the town and college of Defiance pursue a triple-win growth strategy, and what would this look like? Could Defiance College transform itself into a "village commons" devoted to regional economic development and talent incubation?[53] What is the potential role of the college and town in exploring new models for agriculture and contributing to eliminate the harmful loss of topsoil and runoff? Could this evolve into world-class leadership in new scientific, economic, environmental, and social disciplines?

We could envision a strategy along the following lines:

The central challenge of the region is to evolve to a future agricultural and environmental model. This likely combines some of the technological advances covered in the McKinsey report with changes in practices as advocated by Forum for the Future and other regenerative farming advocates and a focus on future global demand for food, as covered by the Deloitte report. Defiance College and the town of Defiance could partner with agricultural tech start-ups, institutes, consulting firms, and other groups across each of the relevant domains of a future agricultural model to sponsor the formation of a new agricultural college. Similarly, they might form an environmentally oriented program, with particular focus on the riverine systems feeding into lakes and the intersection of water and agriculture. These schools could begin as lightly funded programs, with plans for them to expand based on their success in attracting students and sponsors.

In many ways, although perhaps a radical departure for a traditional liberal arts school, the initial prescription is a typical expansion path for adding new faculties or schools in traditional universities. However, the overarching goal is to evolve the town into a talent magnet and the college into a knowledge enterprise, so they will need to think bigger and go much further. For example, by structuring these new programs as autonomous business units rather than academic departments, they are freed up and under pressure to create their own business models. By analogy, many start-ups backed by venture capital begin as projects inside larger companies or universities and are then spun out into separate entities to pursue their destiny. This allows the best projects to achieve greater long-term impact by accessing expansion capital.[54]

Once the school has built a strategy to spin out or spin in new programs, it may be in position to replicate the process with additional concepts (e.g., a school focused on aquaculture, an outdoors-oriented school, a rewilding school), or to attract educational entrepreneurs and their founding student classes with an interest in a completely different field. Defiance College could evolve toward a platform model, still providing its own fully integrated brand (the traditional college offering) but also enabling the development of other institutions.

The town would need to ensure it becomes an attractive destination for short-term visitors and future residents. Its plentiful access to riverside and outdoor destinations is highly appealing from a real estate perspective, and it could convert some of its current grid system into a network of protected bike paths, while simultaneously slowing down the speed of traffic within the urban center. It should ensure that it has the quality of communications network and multigenerational fourth-place housing that knowledge economy migrants will expect.

As the town improves on its "product," it needs to proactively recruit migrants to settle. It may initially need to run a strategy along the lines of Tulsa Remote, sponsoring a group of migrants to come and stay for a year in the town. This kind of initiative could be funded by philanthropic entities, as was the case in Tulsa. A remote strategy is as much about redefining the sense of place and putting the town on the map as it is about raw numbers. For Tulsa, with a population of 774,000, the 100 immigrants it attracted in the first year of its program had a negligible numeric effect but a massive public relations impact.[55] For Defiance, 100 new migrants would have a more measurable impact. It is important to target this program in a way that attracts "high multiplier" knowledge workers (such as entrepreneurs), but also a broad mix of skills and social backgrounds. All those recruited should be attracted by the potential to 'settle' and help contribute to the future of the town.

As the college evolves into a knowledge enterprise and the town-level improvement strategy gains traction, it may be possible for Defiance to attract an intentional community looking to settle in a new area. For example, one could envision a new generation of organic farmers, river enthusiasts, and others who want to be part of turning around the runoff problem and build their lives in a cleaner river system. They will not require these processes to be completed, but they will need to feel that there is long-term commitment to evolving the town to fit the mission of the Intentional Community.

As in many college towns, most of Defiance's students today move out of the town when they graduate, even as remote and flexible work become more mainstream. Defiance would benefit from creating compelling reasons for its students to remain in town after graduation. Some initiatives include coursework in fields that are most conducive to remote work (such as computer science), providing bridge programs, internships, and apprenticeships to enable students and recent graduates to work with settlers attracted to live in the town, recruitment of knowledge industries to the town, and accelerator and incubator programs to launch businesses spun out of the fields of expertise in the new knowledge enterprise.

The town and college should plan on success and thus ensure that they can expand housing as demand increases. They should focus on intensifying density in the urban core rather than supporting sprawl. This reduces the costs of living and commuting, increases the profitability of small local stores, maximizes the benefits of community, and increases the level of productivity and innovation. Housing strategy should include flexible models to accommodate short- and medium-term settlers and those who are splitting their residence with another location.

Financing will be required to scale some of the emerging opportunities. For example, shifting a farm to a regenerative model likely requires at least $250K–$500K in working capital to manage the transition. Building additional housing will similarly require capital and skills. Creating a community bank and a venture capital fund managed by the knowledge enterprise will be important to sustain and accelerate the overall place-based strategy.

A key event for the town and gown collaboration is to achieve a significant milestone, such as migrating 10% or more farms to a regenerative model or reaching a significant reduction in river pollution. As these stages are accomplished, they become powerful signals for a new iteration of the opportunity. Perhaps the challenge is now to go from 10% to 50% in farm regeneration or to make the water fully potable and swimmable. There may be an opportunity to expand some of the micro-colleges and to extend them to different locations. The capital requirements for the next iteration will be higher than for the first phase, but the growing credibility and traction will also expand the sources of funding.

Through this kind of approach, there is a pathway for the town to grow, for the college to gain additional revenue sources and diversification, and for an ecosystem to emerge around solving the biggest challenges of the surrounding environment.

Archetype Four: Town, City, or Region Reinvention through a Strong College

In this scenario, the college is strong (in the sense that it has a combination of endowment size, high-quality applicant pool, operating profit, and brand to endure) but the town is suffering. The college takes on a supportive role in leveraging its assets (endowment, students, faculty, research, global connections, real estate, alumni) to work with the town in developing a regeneration strategy. This strategy is what James Martin and James E. Samels refer to as *The New American College Town*, where the college is directly involved in regional economic development.[56]

As covered by Martin and Samels, several colleges have pursued town reinvention strategies, including Colby College (Waterville, Maine), Albion College (Albion, Michigan), St. Francis College (Brooklyn, New York), Connecticut College (New London, Connecticut), Lehigh College (Bethlehem Valley, Pennsylvania), SUNY Broome Community College (Binghamton, New York), University of Nevada (Las Vegas, Nevada), and Portland State University (Portland, Oregon). Colby College is a top-tier small New England college in the state of Maine. Its hometown of Waterville, which at many points proved pivotal in the survival of the college, fell on hard times as traditional industries declined. Population declined from a peak of 19,000 in 1960 to a low of 16,000 in 2010.[57] Recognizing both the obligation from the past and the mutual benefit, David A. Greene, after taking on the role of Colby president in 2014, spurred an ambitious fundraising campaign to strengthen the school's endowment and to collaborate with other key stakeholders to regenerate its host city. This includes investment of up to $100 million from the college and college support in revitalizing the downtown.[58]

Similarly, when Kevin Drumm became president of SUNY Broome Community College in Binghamton in 2010, the city's population had declined from 75,000 people at peak to 45,000 people. SUNY Broome was dependent on the local tax base, so this decline put the school in jeopardy. Drumm developed and implemented a visionary strategy to revitalize Binghamton, in part by enlisting collaboration from the larger Binghamton University.

President Drumm at SUNY Broome had fewer resources than President Green at Colby College, and in both cases, it is still early to talk about a large-scale turnaround. But there are positive signals. In the case of Waterville, Maine, population has begun to grow again, and house prices have risen from about $100K in 2015 to $187K in 2021, a signal that there is growing interest in the town and that it could benefit from the remote work trend.[59] In Binghamton, New York, the population is still in decline, but house prices have also increased since 2015, from $111K to $147K in 2021.[60] Both towns are roughly three hours from their respective key metropolis (Boston and New York), close enough for episodic travel. Waterville has an emerging start-up scene, and Binghamton has an active start-up incubation program coming out of Binghamton University's research.[61]

How could the new remote work paradigm accelerate the opportunity for town revival, and what should colleges wishing to further evolve as knowledge enterprises do next?

It is critical to evolve emerging start-ups into scale-ups. For this, the optimal strategy is to develop a locally oriented venture capital fund with about $75M to invest. The purpose of this fund should be to accelerate the pace of spinouts and other start-ups from the knowledge enterprise and surrounding town, scale the most successful of these, and encourage spin-ins (i.e., get companies to move part of their operations to the region and integrate these businesses into the local college or university). The local venture capital strategy should be pursued in partnership with all the key stakeholders in the surrounding region (companies, hospitals, institutes, major landowners, government departments). A small number of colleges have endowments that are large enough to anchor the venture fund. Colby's endowment is $1 billion.[62] A contribution of $10 million over a 10-year period is manageable within its portfolio strategy and likely sufficient to cornerstone a fund and attract external investment, including from local sources, companies invested in the region, alumni, and others. It could also join up with the nearby colleges of Bowdoin ($2 billion endowment) and Bates ($350 million endowment) to gain further financial depth and a broader diversity of domains.[63] The fund should be pointed at the intersection of areas of strength of the college and town, growth markets, and social problems that the region can participate in solving.

Binghamton University and SUNY Broome are in a different situation, with weaker endowments but potential support from large local employers. Binghamton University's endowment is only $118 million and SUNY Broome's is $36 million, probably insufficient to cornerstone a venture fund. One option for undercapitalized institutions is to launch a campaign to increase their endowment, with the innovation strategy and venture capital fund as a key element. They will also need to work closely with major local employers such as Lockheed Martin (market cap at time of writing $95 billion), United Health (market cap $393 billion), and BAE Systems (market cap $26 billion).[64] Large enterprises could benefit from developing a talent magnet strategy. A successful strategy will provide them with a deeper pool of local talent and an innovation ecosystem that they can leverage to develop new markets or products. Binghamton University has specializations in fields such as small-scale microelectronics, data centers, energy management, and materials. These could potentially represent areas of collaboration with one or more of its largest employers and a foundation for a cornerstone investment in a new venture fund.

Stakeholders in the region should be encouraged to become supportive of the local start-up scene, sharing with local start-ups their areas of commercial interest and becoming first customers and lead users of new technologies. The goal is to create the elements of a "living lab" in the region, a continuous flow of ideas, money, and people, between the university, the start-up companies, accelerators and venture capital firms, large companies, and others. This is hardly a new idea, and there are perhaps thousands of similar efforts around the globe. However, an effective process to create this kind of ecosystem could add 1,000–2,000 technical jobs, create opportunities for graduates to stay in the college town to join local start-ups, and drive a secondary wave of service jobs. Over time, as some of the companies reach scale and get acquired, they will likely recycle talent and capital and generate a new wave of start-ups.

The college, town, and other stakeholders should form other entities to support innovation and development in the region. For example, the knowledge enterprise could have a mission to support talent magnet goals through the provision of housing and related real estate services. The knowledge enterprise could be partially capitalized via land contributions by major landowners in lieu of cash, as well as through cash investments. It would be tasked around long-term value growth. Early in its formation, it would be able to acquire land at low cost, given the weakness of the town. As the town becomes more desirable, the value of the land will increase. The knowledge enterprise may also be granted zoning overlay rights to develop with higher than historical density, in exchange for hard commitments to maintaining its rental and home prices low. Real estate–oriented options are covered in a July 2021 paper by the Brookings Institute titled "The Emerging Solidarity Economy: A Primer on Community Ownership of Real Estate," which describes various strategies and approaches such as community land trusts, limited equity co-ops, community stores, cooperatives, and neighborhood real estate investment trusts.[65]

As start-ups, community real estate entities, local venture firms, and other initiatives gain critical mass, they should raise their ambitions. As an example, Waterville, Maine, is not yet on the passenger railway, the Downeaster Line, which today stops 56 miles south in Brunswick, Maine. Central Maine has long petitioned for extension of this vital line, but this is subject to the vagaries of Amtrak and legislative priorities.[66] A central Maine knowledge enterprise that had started to build its own economic power base would be in position to accelerate the extension of the train line. For example, it could subsidize part of the service, funding this subsidy through real estate construction and rentals. The Downeaster was extended into Brunswick, home of Colby rival Bowdoin College, in 2012. Since then, house prices in Brunswick have grown from $215K to $421K in 2021, more than twice the level in Waterville.[67] Access by train to Portland and Boston, combined with other development, would drive additional land value and support a train subsidy. The knowledge enterprise can also plough back some of its profits into funding protected bike lanes and other initiatives. As a major landowner it will be a primary beneficiary of the additional demand and therefore can take a broader view of many investments. It is critical that the knowledge enterprise stay focused on maintaining housing affordability by ensuring that there is sufficient supply to avoid spikes in house prices and rentals.

On the venture capital side, future extensions could be growth funds, designed to support the most successful companies funded at seed and Series A financings in the next leg of their scaling journeys. There could also be specialized funds built around unique areas of expertise in the knowledge enterprise and formation of microfunds to enable emerging managers to build their investment experience and capability. With COVID-19, there has been a radical shift in the "desired location" of entrepreneurship, from being concentrated in a small number of privileged regions to being anywhere. As covered in a May 2021 *Forbes* article, "The Rise of Global Tech Entrepreneurship," there is now a global race to launch and grow the best companies, often with remote-first principles and companies managed virtually.[68] Many colleges and towns in the United States are within a close enough radius of major finance centers that founders can regularly meet with venture capitalists even if they are not based in a traditional hub. US-based companies have full insider access to the US economy, typically the largest market in every new category, whereas global competitors lack these advantages. Hence, rather than thinking that three hours from Boston or New York is a long way, these regions must act and think like they can operate within these cities' areas of influence and determine spaces and activities where they can best complement activity in the hub city. This could include outsourcing some of the high-cost activities from existing hubs or developing specialties in markets that have not yet gone mainstream. As technology expands into almost every area, most innovation is in the future, not in the past.

As an example of specialization, Colby College announced the formation of the Davis Institute for Artificial Intelligence, focused on integrating AI with liberal arts education.[69] The institute, funded by an alumni family with a strong prior relationship with the college, will focus on applications of AI into economics and finance, computational social sciences, computational biology, bioinformatics and genomics, the environment and oceans, and ethics.[70] Tapping into partnerships with finance powerhouses such as Goldman Sachs and leading knowledge centers such as the Art Institute of Chicago, Colby is able to "act local and harness the cloud." The new institute will create its own spin-off effect in local company formation and in further sponsoring an entrepreneurial milieu.

The COVID pandemic, by reshuffling work to be anywhere, is creating a unique opportunity for a reversal in the pattern of big-city concentration. Towns and cities that have struggled with growth but have strong colleges are now in a very good position to participate in the emerging innovation economy. However, they need to develop and gain financing for ambitious projects and must not accept a "business-as-usual" mindset. This strategy supports their underlying community and bolsters the broader college mission but equally will be critical to maintaining the core academic mission and business model as it faces increasing challenges from alternatives.

Archetype Five: Strong Town, College Formation

In this scenario, the town is strong enough and committed enough to go through a reinvention exercise but does not have a strong knowledge enterprise asset. The town itself or a major stakeholder in the town recognizes the benefit of creating a college and supports development of a dedicated strategy.

An example of this strategy is the University of Minnesota's campus in Rochester, Minnesota.[71] Rochester is home to the world-famous Mayo Clinic, but lacked a local university until 2006. UM Rochester was set up as a dedicated, science-oriented campus, to train and prepare students for careers at the Mayo Clinic and other health care organizations.[72] This was done without massive capital investment by leveraging existing city or commercial assets. Rochester's attraction of a university has worked well. UM Rochester is ranked by College Factual in the top quartile of American universities.[73]

The world-class status of the Mayo Clinic and the capital-efficient way in which the Rochester campus was developed are somewhat unique. Other attempts to create a "college town" by attracting an academic institution have been less effective. About one hour away from

Rochester is Red Wing, Minnesota, a charming town of 16,000 people, popular with outdoors enthusiasts, on the banks of the upper Mississippi.[74] As reported in *Inside Higher Ed*, in 2014 a local group set out to attract a four-year college to the town.[75] The group was formalized into the Red Wing Area Higher Education Partnership, with the goal of forming a university with up to 2,000 students. It sent written requests to 75 colleges and universities making the case that it could serve the needs of large local employers, including nearby Mayo Clinic, as well as key employers in the Minneapolis–St. Paul–Bloomington conurbation of 3.7 million people, also about one hour away. The group believed that a college would further increase the town's economic prospects by adding the "college town" flavor. There are few rigorous models on the impact of a college on town economics, but a 2020 review of New England colleges by the Boston Federal Reserve suggested a median multiplier value of 1.7 for every dollar spent at the college.[76]

The Red Wing local group estimated that setting up a new university, premised on a traditional model for developing a college campus, would cost between $20 million and $50 million in capital. Taking a midrange number of $35 million in investment and assuming that a new college would reach an initial target of 1,000 students implies an investment of $35K per student per year. Although the group attracted some interest, a new university has thus far been unattainable. A list of new colleges since 1990 by CollegeExpress.com indicated 43 new institutions formed in the past 30 years, or only 1.4 per year. The current blueprint for starting a college is unlikely to support much growth. Even an innovative new model such as Minerva, started by Silicon Valley execs, has raised $128 million to date while educating 618 students in its latest academic year, implying over $200K in investment per annual student.[77]

Today there are about 4,000 higher education institutions in the United States and 36,000 "places" (hamlets, villages, towns, or cities), for a ratio of 9:1.[78] With predictions of 25% or more colleges or universities under pressure, there is a likelihood that the number of institutions declines to 3,000, or a 12:1 ratio of colleges to US places. Given the pressures on the finances of existing colleges and the high capital costs to start new colleges, it may feel challenging for even the strongest cities to attract a new college or university.

We can explore an analogy between the beer industry and the college sector. The traditional beer sector went through an intense consolidation phase, with the number of traditional breweries declining from 468 to 101 between 1945 and 1980, even as demand more than doubled and larger breweries were able to benefit from economies of scale.[79] In 1980 one would likely have predicted that the trend would continue. And yet from 1980 to 2020, the number of breweries has grown 80-fold, reaching a total of 8,800, largely through an explosion in microbreweries.[80] The microbrewery is a radically different economic model from the traditional mass brewery. For example, Molson Coors's capital expenditure in 2020 was $575 million across eight breweries, or $72 million per year per brewery. In contrast, a microbrewery requires between $500K and $1 million in start-up costs, perhaps 20% of this amount in annual capital expenditure.[81] As a result of this growth explosion, the ratio of microbreweries to places in the United States has gone from 400:1 in 1980 to 5:1 today. If it feels like every town in America has a microbrewery, it is because this is increasingly the case.

The conventional approach to starting a new college implies significant capital investment, along the lines of the $20 million to $50 million commitment that the Red Wing group estimated. Until recently, a college would also need to build a fully integrated value chain, everything from curriculum development to dormitories, sporting facilities, a minimum number of academics, and an administrative staff. It would need to go through an accreditation process, which can easily take five years and cost over $1 million.[82] In fact, by requiring a critical mass of infrastructure, staff, and capitalization, the credentialing process has necessarily raised the minimum entry cost for starting a college to the range of $20 million or more.

In contrast, a minimally viable microcollege would approach the start-up process in a way closer to that of a microbrewery. It could begin with a founding core of 3 academics and 2 support staff, teaching 20 students on site and another 40 primarily online. Average US salaries for postdoctoral teachers are $47K in the United States, so the annual fixed staffing bill for five "founders" could be in the range of $300K per year.[83] A town that aims to attract a microcollege could make town facilities available rent free. Businesses in the town could provide funding and part-time employment for the students, and people with unused rooms could provide low-cost accommodation for out-of-town students (in the United States, there are 44 million homes that have empty bedrooms, suggesting ample room for this kind of arrangement).[84] If the business aimed for $500K in initial annual revenue, to cover other expenses, bonuses, and to create retained earnings, it could charge on-site students $12.5K and on-line students $6.25K, for a blended cost of $8.3K per student. Given these assumptions, an initial investment of $1 million would be sufficient to get this microcollege model going, which implies an annual investment per student of $17K. These per-student numbers may seem low, but it is useful to note that Harvard charged $500 in tuition in 1950, 15% of the average family income of $3,300 at that time.[85] With today's household income at $68K, a comparable fee would be around $10K per year.

As indicated, it is unlikely that such a microcollege would initially receive regional accreditation. However, it could use a range of strategies to manage around this restriction. For example, a college aiming to compete at the top level could establish strict entry criteria, using standardized tests and requiring high incoming grades. It could seek to partner with an accredited "platform," such as a local university, a foreign university whose credentials might be accepted by employers in the United States, or an online platform. If there are strong local employers, the microcollege could partner with a group of companies in curriculum development, selection criteria, acceptance, class development, internships, and other ways to ensure that the incoming students have a high probability of securing a job after graduation. It may also begin by specializing in courses for which traditional credentials are not required. With the need for lifetime education, it could also focus on providing new skills for highly credentialed older students aiming to reinvent their careers.

A 2020 survey by nonprofit social impact organization Strada Education Network indicated that Americans looking for college solutions are focused on very practical needs. In this survey of 16,000 Americans across a spectrum of income and other demographic variables, the most important criteria impacting the choice of provider were impact on work opportunities, a strong ability to give support, and providing a strong sense of belonging to the student, the latter especially critical for those with traditionally less of a family background in higher education.[86] Traditional credentialed degrees are still important for some contexts, but there are sufficient exceptions to foster a wave of innovation that is not handicapped by the restrictive nature of credentialing processes.

Some of the larger platforms are exploring options for localization. According to a 2020 survey by *University Business*, 50% of the parents of traditional-age students now have a strong preference for their children to stay nearby, more than in prior times.[87] Some colleges are adapting their strategy to be able to serve the market closer to home. Penn State has been among the most ambitious, with 24 campuses, largely distributed over its home state of Pennsylvania.[88] These campuses began as feeders into its main campus, allowing students to study for their first two years in a satellite location, closer to their home, and to complete their degree at the main location. Around 2010 the university expanded the satellite offerings to include four-year degree options, without requiring students to transfer to the main campus in the final two years.[89] As we cover in archetype six, the localization strategy could evolve into a national growth path for an ambitious university.

In the world of alternative K–12, pod school companies are starting to explore expansion from their original locations. Prenda is an Arizona-based provider of pod schooling for K–12 that was started in 2013. As of 2021 it claimed 400 microschools and growing. Prenda has raised over $19 million, implying an average cost per location of $47K.[90]

While one cannot compare a K–12 school with higher ed, the broad point is that as a society we have sufficient infrastructure in most towns to accommodate a new microcollege. With many postdocs earning low wages at their current universities, there is a ready supply of teaching capability, which can be complemented by people living in the town with valuable skills or people with skills (such as retired or semiretired professors, consultants, executives, musicians, artists, farmers, manufacturers, and others) wanting to move into a town for a new act. Many students and their parents are frustrated with the range of available options and are more open than ever to explore alternatives. Employers and other participants in the local economy would be beneficiaries of a microcollege. The initial direct expenditure impact of a microcollege would be limited, perhaps $1 million a year in direct and indirect revenue. However, a successful microcollege could expand organically and perhaps grow over the course of a decade from 20 local students to 200 local students, reaching a spending impact of $5 million to $10 million a year.

The impact of having a college in town, as we have argued across this book, would go far beyond the spending increase. It would attract talent in many ways, beginning with teachers and students moving specifically for the college offerings, but also others that might want to live in a place that has a college, especially if it combines this offering with other aspects of a talent magnet, such as the availability of a vibrant third-place culture, a creativity incubator, and support for the "bionic worker." A place such as Red Wing, with one or more microcolleges, could become a particularly attractive location for empty nesters, people with remote work options, or entrepreneurs starting a business. Microcolleges could also be set up with the explicit purpose of solving a problem that the town is dealing with, whether environmental, such as flooding or pollution; social, such as racial inequity; or economic, such as loss of a major employer. Thus the microcollege policy could become a central element of the placemaking strategy.[91]

Building on how microschools and millions of start-ups have often developed out of people's homes or garages, a first iteration of a microcollege could even be as simple as someone with something to teach finding an initial group with a hunger to learn and getting together for a regular series of discussions, perhaps starting with 1 teacher for

10 students. It could be an evolution from an existing institution such as a museum, an art gallery, a coworking space, a maker space, a book group, a garden or park, or a factory. It could begin as a summer course. It could start as an attempt by town representatives, public and private, pursuing the same mission as Red Wing but going for an iterative approach. Perhaps it would have been better for Red Wing in 2014 to have started with a modest first effort, aiming to get better each year, with the idea that by 2022 they might be in position to make a bid for the more traditional "macrocollege."

Every hamlet, village, town, city neighborhood, or city district can consider whether they have something to teach the world, whether there is a founding group with the energy to get something started, and how their place can best support the formation of a knowledge enterprise. Ultimately, we believe there is no minimum or maximum scale for a knowledge enterprise. Just like purposeful lives can be pursued by all regardless of their circumstances, so can a knowledge enterprise begin as a "one-room school."

Archetype Six: Multilocal Knowledge Enterprises

Southern New Hampshire University has evolved from a third-tier regional school into a major educational power. SNHU has grown from 3,000 students in 2003 to over 135,000 students in 2019, with a 2023 target of 300,000 students.[92] Its revenue and profit evolution have been very strong. By comparison, SNHU's revenue (all student income) had grown from 21% of Harvard's revenue in 2012 to 89% of Harvard's revenue by 2020.[93] If we project SNHU's stated goal to reach 300,000 students by 2025 and assume that Harvard stays on its historical growth trend, SNHU's student-based revenue will reach parity with Harvard's by 2022 and be 25% larger by 2025.[94]

For Harvard, student fees are only a small component of its income. In 2020, only 17% of its total revenue came from student fees and of this, 9% from degree seeking students and 8% from continuing education. Harvard teaches 24,000 students each year.[95] In 2020, Harvard generated another 17% from research, 46% from philanthropy (including contributions from the Harvard endowment), and 20% from nonacademic sources, based on its 2020 annual report.[96] We will pick up on knowledge enterprise options for top-tier universities like Harvard in a later chapter, but for now the key point is that SNHU has shown an ability to reach more students and generate faster revenue growth than the oldest and arguably best-known university in the country. We are not arguing that SNHU and Harvard are today in the same league. However, SNHU's growth and profitability give it the firepower and momentum to make additional moves.

As SNHU looks to evolve further, where could it be going? Some signs of its future evolution include moving into nondegree education, focusing instead on microcredentials.[97] In March 2021, SNHU announced its acquisition of Kenzie Academy, an online technology and microcredential leader. Paul Leblanc, president of SNHU, said about this transaction: "We have long known that alternative credentials are critical to helping people upskill, prepare for the future of work, and be lifelong learners. As the COVID-19 pandemic continues to displace workers, these shorter bursts of learning at affordable price points will be critical for learners to advance their careers and improve their lives in the new economy."[98]

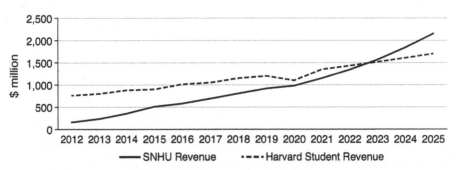

Figure 1. Student fee revenue, 2012–2020 and projections to 2025, Harvard and Southern New Hampshire University (SNHU) (in $ millions).
Source: SNHU information drawn from ProPublica, https://projects.propublica.org /nonprofits/organizations/20274509; Harvard information is drawn from Annual Financial Reports, https://finance.harvard.edu/annual-report.

SNHU is expanding its provision of affordable on-site and hybrid degrees. In 2020, SNHU announced its plans to offer a fully on-site degree for $15K a year and a hybrid on-site/online degree for $10K per year, representing a discount from its prior degree prices. It will also expand its on-site student base in Manchester, New Hampshire, from 3,000 students to 4,500 by 2025. SNHU also partners with other institutions in developing online degrees, combining its expertise in online processes with its partner's specific skills. For example, it offers an online MBA in music management jointly with Berklee College of Music.[99]

Building on this direction, we could see an interesting potential partnership for SNHU (or equivalent groups with similar capabilities, such as Western Governors University, Arizona State University, or Harvard University) to act as a "platform" partner in seeding localized microcolleges. This strategy would likely include three elements: the platform partner, such as SNHU, could step into campuses or colleges at risk of closing or recently shut down and develop a localization strategy, likely in combination with property-oriented partners that could manage the real estate component. This might include evolving the campus into a hub for a local education strategy, combining online, on-site, and hybrid learning. Even with online programs, there is a strong preference by students to study at a "local" school and to have the opportunity to occasionally go on site. In a 2020 survey of online students by education company Wiley, local factors were important in the ranking of why students chose a particular program. For example, for 27% of students, being able to attend both online and on-site classes was important, for 22%, proximity to where they live or work was important, 13% valued familiarity with the school, and 11% valued their employer having a relationship with the school.[100]

A second variation of this localization strategy would be to support higher-ed entrepreneurs, towns, and other groups that are looking to transform existing colleges into knowledge enterprises. The platform company could provide technological and back-office capabilities to support the educational mission of these academic entrepreneurs. They could also provide access to loans and financing, recruiting, and career services for these new establishments. An analogy to this strategy is how Amazon launched Amazon Web Services as a business to enable other companies to access comparable efficiencies in cloud operations to what it could achieve. Highly efficient knowledge enterprises could add a "university as a service" offering to further extend their mission and grow their revenue. Today many universities partner with online program managers (OPMs), a market dominated by players such as 2U, Pearson, and Wiley.[101] However, OPMs in many ways replicate the "macrocollege" structure and are primarily focused on monetizing existing college and university assets online. A more disruptive enabler might focus on creating a wave of new collegiate entrepreneurs.

Third, platforms could eventually become incubators and accelerators of microcolleges. In this model, each microcollege maintains its own mission and character, but the platform takes care of common elements. In this sense, platforms could be analogous to other companies that are enabling the creative economy, everything from Etsy ($24 billion market cap, supporting craft artists) to Gumroad (supporting digital creators) or, in the education sector, companies such as Thinktific and Teachable. According to *Business Insider*, in 2021 "creator economy" start-ups raised $1.3 billion in venture capital.[102]

The US higher ed market generates around $600 billion per year in revenue.[103] The United States is extremely well positioned to lead globally, as long as it continues to evolve. If every one of the roughly 36K unique US "places" were to develop a microacademy with 200 students per year, at a revenue per student of $15K per year, this would aggregate nationwide to 7 million students (roughly 36% of today's higher-ed population) and $108 billion in revenue (18% of today's higher ed revenue). Consider that 40% of working Americans need to reskill by 2025 out of 160 million working Americans (64 million, or roughly 13 million per year, assuming 1 year to reskill).[104] There are a further 29 million retired boomers, many of whom are capable and willing to move to a town where they can reinvent themselves through education, others having to do so for financial reasons.[105] Global education is projected to grow from $5.4 trillion in 2020 to $7.3 trillion in 2025, by which time 3.5 billion people around the world would be learning online, providing a vast additional online market for these microcolleges.[106]

What else would it take to convert a multilocal expansion by a university platform into the creation of a plethora of talent magnets? As we have argued throughout the book, every town, city, or rural area will have its own unique context and character. An effective multilocal expansion (for example, helping to save a dying college or launching a new microcollege where none exists) needs to be complemented with a "town and gown" collaboration program in which key local stakeholders work to support both the new academic mission and other missing elements (such as building sufficient density, providing walkable and bikeable neighborhoods, and ensuring sufficient innovation and economic growth). Combining the power of one or more national platform with the energy potential among 36,000 places in the United States could unlock a revolution in college and town reinvention the likes of which has not been experienced in the country since the nineteenth century.

Archetype Seven: Evolving Strong Town and Gown Pairs into Their Next Phase of Development

Greater Boston is the quintessential college city. In the Aggregate Ranking of Top Universities (which ranks the top 400 global universities drawing from *Times Higher Education*, the QS World University Ranking, and the Shanghai Ranking), Boston-area universities ranked number 2 (Harvard), number 3 (MIT), number 72 (Boston University), number 175 (Tufts), number 239 (Northeastern), number 283 (Brandeis), and number 342 (Boston College).[107] A 2020 article by *Times Higher Education* indicated that Boston has over 100 colleges and universities and over 250,000 students.[108] Greater Boston is ranked eighth in the United States in economic output, producing $468 billion annually, and it scores at the top in domestic product per capita. It is ranked the second most expensive city to live in in the United States, an indicator both of its popularity and its inability to create sufficient housing to meet demand in an affordable way.[109]

Can we thus say that greater Boston is a talent magnet and that its key academic institutions are knowledge enterprises, or is there further to go? As we define each of these terms, the answer is that they are not yet done and that there is much further that they can and must go.

Greater Boston and its universities can vastly deepen their collective impact on the surrounding community, with a primary focus on the New England and US Northeast region. The US Northeast has a combination of city layouts, transport networks, access to capital, knowledge economy, and start-up activity that positions it to evolve first and fastest into a talent magnet region. As an example, a 2020 review of cities above 250K population with the potential to become "15-minute cities" ranked Boston as number 4 among 25 cities, behind Miami, San Francisco, and Pittsburgh.[110]

However, thus far Boston is failing at the most basic level. A November 2020 article on city costs indicated that Boston is the second most expensive city in the country per square foot.[111] As an example of a currently missed opportunity, in a 2020 paper the Brookings Institute proposed a strategy of medium dense development around railway stops, showing its potential to drive a material improvement in affordability by shifting from the prevailing single-family home toward a more diverse mix.[112] As covered by a 2020 report by the Boston Foundation, expensive housing is a key source of inequity and financial insecurity, impacting low-income Bostonians and minorities.[113] Boston is positioned 42nd out of 330 global cities on air quality by Numbeo, outranked by world-class cities such as Zurich and Copenhagen. Trends for Boston have been improving, but air quality is also a source of inequity in Boston, and particles such as nitrous oxide and carbon dioxide are in particularly high concentrations in poor neighborhoods.[114] Although with relatively good walkability relative to most American cities, Boston is rapidly falling behind global competitors such as Paris or London. Therefore, if Boston wants to become among the top global cities, it will need to substantially improve in housing affordability, walkability, and air quality.

Moreover, beyond improvements in the city itself, Boston should partner with other cities, towns, and regions in New England. New

England states, many with historically weak population growth and rapidly aging societies, need to develop their own talent magnet strategies. Greater Boston, with its powerful network of universities and critical assets such as rail networks, should support this growth.

Greater Boston and its key university platforms should also support the reinvention of the collegiate ecosystem across New England. As discussed earlier, many New England colleges are at financial risk. Top Boston-area colleges, with large endowments and powerful education platforms, have the capability to drive a revolution in town and gown collaboration across New England.

What if Harvard took $1 billion out of its $53 billion endowment and invested $50 million each in 20 of the colleges across New England currently at risk of closure, seeking to secure a transformation of each college into a knowledge enterprise?[115] We note that becoming a knowledge enterprise is not about scale or strength of the institution but about how the institution harnesses its available assets to improve its surrounding community. What if the investment were also aimed at supporting the evolution of each college town into a talent magnet? This would be structured as a for-profit investment, aiming to increase the value of the underlying assets by improving the performance of the college and the talent attraction of the surrounding town. Thus, the $1 billion could further compound into $2 billion or more. It would also allow Harvard to extend its platform and expertise far deeper into New England and evolve into a hub-and-spoke model. If, at some point in the future, an emerging player such as SNHU were to acquire a top college brand and launch its own multilocal strategy to compete in the upper end of the market, Harvard University will be that much better positioned to answer the new challenge. If this strategy works in New England, it could be extended beyond. This strategy allows Boston to evolve from a single power center into the hub of a constellation of powerful cities, and to simultaneously relieve the concentration of housing and population demand.

We now move to explore a state-level strategy building on the case of New Hampshire.

Archetype Eight: State-Level Strategy

How could a state evolve toward being a talent magnet? How might it work in collaboration with other regions that have evolved further? What is the potential magnitude of economic, environmental, and social growth that it could achieve through a dedicated strategy? What is the role of knowledge enterprises in this evolution?

Consider, for example, a partnership between the state of New Hampshire (surface area 9,350 square miles, population 1.34 million), covered in chapter 1, and the similarly sized country of Switzerland (surface area 15,940 square miles, population 8.6 million). New Hampshire is blessed with over 1,000 lakes, comparable to the 1,500 lakes in Switzerland, and is similarly mountainous. Switzerland, long settled and a key path for crossing central Europe, can be defined today as a world-class talent magnet country.[116] Switzerland has over triple the density of New Hampshire (540 people per square mile versus 150 people per square mile), gaining economic efficiency without sacrificing environmental and social quality. Switzerland is ranked globally at number 2 in life expectancy, number 3 in environmental quality, number 4 in happiness, and number 9 in social purpose. The high Swiss score in life expectancy compares with the United States' poor number 28 ranking, despite Switzerland's spending only 12% of its GDP on health care, compared to 16% of GDP in the United States. Switzerland's GDP per capita has grown from $20K in 1980 to $83K in 2020, while its population has grown by 2.5 million people, from 6.2 million to 8.7 million, growing total GDP from $124 billion in 1980 to $722 billion in 2020 and reaching a total net worth of $4.7 trillion. In the same 40-year period, New Hampshire added about 0.5 million in population, from 0.9 million to 1.4 million, saw average income grow from $22K to $54K, and GDP growth from $20 billion to $74 billion. New Hampshire's net worth is about one-tenth that of Switzerland, at an estimated $490 billion.[117] The Swiss growth model shows that GDP and population growth can be combined with improvements in social and environmental metrics.

What if the state of New Hampshire opted for a "moon-shot" strategy, aiming for a triple-win growth model combining social, environmental, and economic growth, in part by understanding global best practices and copying features of what has worked elsewhere? The goal would be to simultaneously raise health outcomes, improve productivity, and reduce environmental degradation, anchored around a symbiotic partnership between towns and knowledge enterprises.

In looking for models, in addition to Switzerland, we could point to the success of Singapore, Israel, Taiwan, and South Korea. Each has achieved substantial growth in population, GDP per capita, life expectancy, and environmental quality between 1980 and 2020. Several factors stand out: each of the comparison countries has achieved significant economic growth, combining population expansion with growth in GDP per capita. All have achieved superior total GDP growth in the past 40 years, in many cases spectacularly so. Each has achieved substantial improvement in life expectancy, to the point where New Hampshire has gone from a leader to a laggard, with the comparison countries now enjoying two to five extra years of life. Each is much denser than New Hampshire and has seen a significant increase in density, suggesting that there is substantial potential for density growth in New Hampshire without impairing economic, social, or environmental growth. New Hampshire has better affordability and pollution levels. It also has easy access to 330 million internal migrants and is inside the largest economy in the world. Therefore, in many ways it is better positioned than these other countries to achieve growth.

At the core of environmental and economic sustainability is higher population density. A 2020 analysis of New Hampshire's population by Urban3 shows very sparse levels of density, outside of the coastal strip and a few former mill towns.[118] Urban 3 shows that the urban sprawl growth model is a fundamental drag on the value of New Hampshire real estate. The most valuable real estate is in the few downtown cores, whereas much of the sprawl surrounding towns generates very low value per acre. Variables such as vehicle miles, lane density, impervious surfaces, and municipal services costs decline by

30%–60% with each doubling in population density on a per-capita basis.[119] As discussed in a 2010 study by the Federal Reserve Bank of New York, looking at 363 US metropolitan areas, doubling density increases total factor productivity growth by 2%–4%.[120]

Our hypothesis is that housing can remain affordable if there is an adequate and timely plan for housing supply. For example, a 175-year study of UK house prices by Schroders shows that pricing in London stayed below a ratio of four times income until the 1990s, as supply met demand. It was the increasing restrictions on new supply in the past 30 years that drove that ratio to 11 times income in 2021.[121]

New Hampshire is within a close driving radius of the East Coast states of Massachusetts, New York, Connecticut, and Rhode Island, with a combined population of 32 million people and GDP of $2.7 trillion. At a net worth/GDP ratio of 6:1, this implies combined $16 trillion of addressable wealth in its "back yard."

A bold growth strategy for New Hampshire, building on the principles developed in this book, could include several elements. If New Hampshire aimed for 2.5% annual growth in population (vs. a 0.4% historic rate), this would take its population to 2.2 million by 2040 (implying a density of 235 per square mile, still at 50% of the current Swiss level).[122] Growing per-capita income by a Swiss level of 4.5%/year would take income to $130K in 2040. GDP would grow at 7% per year, to $286 billion by 2040. Assuming a 6:1 wealth/GDP ratio, this implies net worth grows from $490 billion in 2020 to $1.6 trillion by 2040, or $1.1 trillion of value growth by 2040.[123] For example, consider construction. Adding a net of 800,000 people implies 270,000 new homes. Assuming replacement of 25% of the existing housing stock of about 600,000 homes, or a further 150,000 homes, implies total construction of 420,000 new homes. At an average cost of $200K/home and an average value per completed home of $300K, this is an opportunity for $84 billion in direct investment and $126 billion in new asset formation. The potential for substantial economic growth and wealth creation suggests that private capital could be raised to fund growth acceleration in New Hampshire. Private investment can combine with local, state, or federal funding as well as with philanthropy and other asset classes. New Hampshire could also anchor growth around the concept of talent magnet towns and cities, with knowledge enterprise partnerships. In essence, this requires encouraging towns and cities to evolve to a compact and growing downtown core, optimized around walkable and bikeable cities, leveraging existing colleges and creating new ones. It implies developing a talent attraction strategy while simultaneously reimagining the potential to unlock the talent, skills, and caring of each community. It means investing in world-class digital capability and ensuring that each town is best positioned to participate in the global cloud and knowledge economy. It requires addressing zoning and regulatory constraints that have outlived their use, while ensuring that there are limits on environmental degradation. The combined undertaking requires a Marshall Plan or Manhattan Project level of focus, commitment, and organization hitherto associated with prior generations but that can be rekindled with the right local leadership. It does not require the state or the towns to go cap in hand for state or regulatory investment. If the plans are triple win, economically, socially, and environmentally viable, they are fundable. If not, should they be funded by taxpayers?

Another goal could be to double the size of the ten largest cities, with a focus on creating transit-oriented development (TOD), combined with walkable/bikeable infrastructure and improved transit. The top 10 cities in New Hampshire have a combined population of 436,000 people. Doubling average population to 872,000 would create a critical mass of know-how and innovation. A good example of TOD is a $588 million project proposed in September 2020 for Manchester, New Hampshire, that would involve creating "new condos, apartments, offices, shops, parks, and plazas all within a 5- to 10-minute walk of a new shuttle service, new bus hub, and a future commuter rail station."[124] This project is complemented by a July 2021 proposal to extend the Massachusetts Bay Transportation Authority train network to include stops in Nashua and Manchester in New Hampshire. The combined effect of rail, medium-density housing, and mixed-use neighborhoods creates many elements of a talent magnet.

In our world, local champion SNHU would likely play a critical role in providing the knowledge enterprise element, but we would hope that other platforms would aim to build their own microcolleges. The rail opportunity could be much larger. Passenger railways are thought inherently unprofitable, but this may be tied to their lack of participation in the underlying real estate value. MTR Corporation in Hong Kong is a highly profitable corporation and generates over $7 billion a year in revenue and $1–2 billion in annual profit by combining transit with real estate development, based on agreements with the state to gain low-cost access to land that gains value through rail development. The train system covers 131 miles, serves 5 million people, and has very low fares, as it can be subsidized via property development.[125] Transit financing in New Hampshire could be supercharged with an ambitious population expansion plan. If the population of the four largest New Hampshire towns on a path from Concord to Nashua (Concord, Manchester, Salem, Nashua) doubled through TOD and other projects from today's 240,000 to 480,000, at an average income per capita of $40K, this implies $9 billion in incremental growth for the state. If we assume a cost of $250K/mile to run a service from Concord to Boston over 80 miles, this implies a cost of $20 million/year (note that the Downeaster line from Brunswick to Boston covers 135 miles and costs $23 million/year to run, or $170K/mile). The ratio of increased GDP to annual cost to operate would be 450:1, suggesting that the train service could potentially be fully subsidized. Beyond this corridor, the New Hampshire train authority owns over 200 miles of active railroads and rights, as well as further inactive rights of way.[126] A transit network could become a new critical "spine" for the state, integrating with the highway and road network. It would also critically need to integrate with expansion in biking network and support of multimodal systems to make it seamless to switch from one mode of transport to another. Finally, the state could seek to reduce driving. New Hampshire's population drives about 10K miles per person per year, up from 7K in 1980. While this is below the US average of 14K miles per person per year, it is 30%–40% higher than the European average, which is at around 6K–7K miles per person per year.[127]

Knowledge enterprises are critical conduits for state-level transformation. A wealthier, healthier, less-polluted New Hampshire would require academic institutions to help with new skill formation, attracting expertise, deepening global academic partnerships, and extending the "college town" experience from a few towns to a much broader subset of locations. Academic institutions can provide knowhow for environmental improvement and new technology-based start-ups to drive high productivity jobs.

Conclusion

In this chapter we have covered a broad range of *archetypes* of town/knowledge enterprise partnerships, beginning with as close to a blank canvas as possible and evolving through to a state-level strategy. We have covered a small number of states, preferring to go deeper into a few situations and explore the art of the possible. But the types of growth models can be used across any state in the United States and in countries around the globe. In the next chapter we talk about the potential actions that can be taken by ordinary citizens, students, and teachers, by representatives of academic, civic, philanthropic, and business groups, and by entrepreneurs seeking to make the world a better place.

4

———

What Is to Be Done?

IN THIS CHAPTER WE PROVIDE GUIDANCE to people interested in the ideas in this book and who want to begin the journey for their place to become a talent magnet anchored by a knowledge enterprise. We begin with actions by the least powerful and then evolve up the power and control hierarchy. We also begin with recommendations at the level of the individual and then evolve toward institutional recommendations, including some ideas on new institutional structures that could be critical enablers. In each case we explore how fledgling or developed academic institutions can play a critical role in place-based strategies.

Town Citizens

We covered in chapter 1 the idea of a series of citizen-based groups that could be formed around the resolution of one specific challenge. Although we proposed in that chapter that the formation of citizen groups could be a *result* of a top-down strategy, that is not necessary. Individuals with agency and ideas could begin by forming a group in an area of interest with no other mandate or request. Through concerted action, citizens could eventually help to *cause* the formation of a top-down strategy.

Consider the example of Laramie, Wyoming. According to a community profile on Main Street America's website,

> Twenty years ago, the historic core of Laramie was struggling. There were few thriving businesses. Only one or two restaurants remained open, and several dilapidated buildings were so far gone that they required demolition. Despite being home to the state's four-year university, with more than 14,000 students, there was limited interaction between town and gown: Students hardly participated in life downtown at all. They ate on campus, socialized on campus, and stayed on campus.

> Worst of all, there was no unified vision for what downtown could become, says Trey Sherwood, executive director of the Laramie Main Street Alliance, an Accredited Main Street America program. "No one could figure out what to do. City officials had one idea, local merchants had another, the downtown development authority yet another."

> That all changed when Wyoming Main Street provided the funds for a new, comprehensive downtown plan. Suddenly local stakeholders were sharing priorities, reviewing lessons learned and identifying short- and long-term goals.

> Sherwood then led the effort to bring government and private entities together under a single Main Street America umbrella, "moving from multiple boards and multiple non-profits pushing for revitalization, to a single one-stop shop. Now we can focus effectively on precisely what to do."

> Part of the answer came from six blocks away at the campus of the University of Wyoming. The university's art museum was about to close for renovations, and public access to the collection would be restricted for months. So local leaders came up with a novel solution: What if, instead of canceling gallery exhibitions, the community of Laramie became the gallery? Curators could mount a sculpture exhibition in public spaces where the works of art would be accessible to everyone— students, merchants, residents, and tourists.

> The bold proposal became a booming success, and inspired Laramie's award-winning Mural Project, an ongoing public art display that

transformed the look and spirit of downtown and became a magnet for investment.

When property owners saw murals beautifying a building nearby, they said, "My building needs attention, too," and private money began flowing to the historic district.

The domino effect has been nothing short of astounding. Laramie now boasts 272 locally owned businesses in a historic district that covers nearly 30 blocks. There are 35 restaurants and bars and about 70 retailers, including specialty gift shops, clothing stores and art galleries. But there are also professional offices, nonprofits, start-ups and—significantly—nearly 100 residential units.[1]

The Laramie example illustrates the power of an individual to kick off a local movement, as well as the often-latent opportunity to leverage the assets of an existing university to integrate it more deeply into its surrounding community.

There are 1.6 million charitable organizations in the United States and 63 million volunteers, and thus one potential starting point could be to spin out a group from a charitable organization or from a volunteering effort.[2] Leaders must establish a core of mission-based colleagues, with a diverse range of skills, contacts, and other assets to help them maximize the chances of success, and for the effort to endure. The leader could begin by inviting for dinner or to a coffee conversation some candidates to test their interest and capability to drive significant change. Over the course of several conversations, they can gauge who can be central to the group, who might be a helpful peripheral partner, and who is unlikely to add value. A useful winnowing test would be to ask candidates to complete a task. The velocity and effectiveness of task completion gives a sense on their skills, commitment, and speed. It is also important to select for diversity at all levels: age, income, race, orientation, background, thinking approach, and so on. This ensures that the mission will be as inclusive as possible and that it will gain the maximum access to skills.

The new group should collectively establish a goal and area of focus. This group might have begun with a very specific idea, but as it recruits a base of colleagues, the goal will likely evolve. If it is clear through the process of goal formation that there is no consensus around the group, it may be a sign that the group needs to split or that some need to leave. The group must have a very strongly agreed-upon strategy. If successful, this could become a core component of their and other participants' future lives, and therefore this is not a casual endeavor but the beginning of an important commitment.

Once this stage has been completed, the onus must shift from strategy to action. Scoring initial wins, even if small, is important to the group evolving from talking shop to becoming change agents. Key wins could include recruiting key external stakeholders, completing a successful event that creates public interest for their cause, raising seed capital, and organizing a local initiative. Momentum from a first win should lead to a sequence of progress. We discussed previously how citizens of Red Wing sought to attract a college. They got as far as to form a dedicated group, develop a proposal for a college, send request letters to several candidate partners, and get some to respond, even though ultimately the effort failed. What would a redo look like today?

The group might still define their long-term goal as the establishment of a traditional macrocollege. However, the formation of a microcollege cluster could be a good interim step. A microcollege is a small-scale institution, with scores of students and perhaps a dozen faculty. The group could, for example, aim to attract several microcolleges to the town. To this end, it would search for a platform partner that could support the formation of the microcolleges, define the broad mission of each, recruit a founding group of teachers and prospective students, and secure seed funding to support their initial wave. As an additional step, these microcolleges might begin as community third and fourth places, before the first students and teachers arrive. Perhaps the microcolleges are created to initially serve as an innovation cluster for the town.

Assuming that the initial microcolleges are successful, a second wave of development would aim to grow them to the next level of scale. At this stage, the colleges may have largely developed their own agency and mission. The citizens group could then disband, shift to an advisory role, or set its sights on a higher objective, such as expansion into a macrocollege, launch of additional microcolleges, or a broader strategy to evolve into a knowledge enterprise. This could include developing mechanisms to spin out businesses from the microcolleges, deepening the economic footprint of the colleges on the surrounding region or tackling a regional challenge such as social inequity. As the economic magnitude of the project grows, what might have begun as an unpaid effort for the town group could evolve into a source of employment for them and some of the other volunteers.

This volunteering effort can also expand horizontally and vertically. The group might influence other citizens, who seize upon the example to create civic-minded groups to resolve other challenges. If the group reaches a certain size, it could likely spin out groups that want to pursue a variation of the main theme. Others across different locations might be impressed by the group's progress and want to copy what they are doing. A successful group in one domain, especially as it attracts imitation, could lead to a broader civic discussion around the idea of developing a talent magnet and thus lead to a higher-level strategy.

Every movement begins when somebody picks a goal and commits to it. In *Dedicated: A Case for Commitment in the Age of Infinite Browsing*, Pete Davis argues that our society encourages optionality and "browsing," but that those counterculturalists who reject this premise, pick an area, and commit to it, create the most meaning and purpose in their own lives, and contribute more substantially to the social whole.[3]

Environmental Intentional Community Organizers

According to a 2020 Pew Charitable Trust survey, over 60% of Americans are concerned over the impact of pollution on life in their local community, suggesting a foundation for the formation of a community with an orientation toward environmental objectives.[4]

A founding group could set out to organize an online intentional community, with the goal to settle in, or help re-create, a low-carbon, walkable and bikeable, medium-density town and beyond this, to actively reduce pollution of all types in the region surrounding this town. Its initial goal is to recruit 100 members, then to create a working group among the most committed and to work together to expand the group to 5,000 supporters, with the collective skills required to execute on the planning, building, and settlement of the town. Ultimately the aim is a critical mass of 1,000 committed and financially capable "founding settlers" that have the capital and income viability to become an initial economic engine.

As the online community expands, a series of subgroups could be formed, tasked with planning and executing on different aspects of the mission. One group is focused on searching for the ideal location for settlement, building a database of candidate communities and landowners with an interest in partnering and researching which states and counties have the greatest flexibility in the zoning changes required to achieve their goals. Another group develops a conceptual master plan, to be adapted to a short list of eventual candidate locations. A third team works on developing the financing models and securing the right financial partners. Other teams study the zoning and regulatory process required for settlement, the construction process, the creation of new services, integration with the existing community, plans for talent attraction, and so on. All this activity is done on a volunteer basis. A diversity of backgrounds and skills make the project viable. The aim is to combine the energy of people with deep domain experience and practical skills with others who are willing to think and act on the impossible.

The process of developing short-list settlement partners will include many variables: Is there a strong majority interest from the townspeople in taking part in such a merger, and in the mission of the project? Does the legal environment support the zoning changes required to make the mission work? Are there sufficient facilities to support the health care, schooling, and other needs of the settlement? Are there sufficient local skills for the construction process required to accommodate the initial families, and if not, how can they be procured?

The concept of settlement feels alien to our contemporary culture. We feel that this is something that was done in the past, by others. Our life has been built around convenience, and starting anew is everything but. Nonetheless, the instinct to roam and move around is still within us. Humans are a nomadic species and optimally walk in the range of six miles or more per day.[5] Hiking has exploded since 2019, with AllTrails recording a 171% increase in the number of hikes between 2019 and 2020, as people could redeploy some of the lost time previously spent commuting and seek an activity that allowed social distancing.[6] Other latent instincts, skills, and desires can also be reanimated as we wake from the slumber of commuting and consumption.

Convincing a host location to allow a wave of new settlers to move in and dramatically change the nature of the town will also be far from easy. It is also in our nature to resist strangers, especially those who want things to change. Hence, the first settlements of ecological intentional communities (EICs) have tended to be subscale efforts on private land. At a practical level, it makes a lot more sense to take advantage of the deep pool of existing infrastructure and adapt it to meet a new town ethos, than to start anew.

The locations for new EICs might be somewhat paradoxical. Around 250 malls are projected to close by 2025.[7] Perhaps the ultimate product of the suburban experiment could become the foundation for an ecological community. Malls have substantial infrastructure, fewer negotiating partners, and those that close will become an economic and social blight for the community. They could be reenvisioned as a high-density neighborhood, and an EIC could negotiate an overlay agreement specific to that mall. Thus far, most of the mall conversions have stayed within the current car-centric paradigm, as captured by a 2020 study by the National Association of Realtors, indicating that only 7% of conversions shifted into residential areas, and in all cases, these were car-centric models, but this could change with shifts in regulation and consumer preferences.[8]

But there are many other locations with existing infrastructure. A 2019 study of northern New England by the Federal Reserve Bank of

Boston estimated that 27% of the 56 towns evaluated were experiencing population decline.[9] In many cases, this decline is associated with increases in the average age of the townspeople, a decline in the number of school children, and an overall loss of vibrancy. Even though some of these towns may have benefited from a temporary COVID boost to their population, they still face structural challenges. Similar population declines have been experienced across the rural Midwest.[10] Many cities in the Rust Belt and elsewhere are experiencing their own hollowing out.[11] This means that there are sufficient candidate locations with the infrastructural capacity to accommodate a significant group of immigrants.

But it is one thing to conclude that a place should, rationally, embrace the economic revitalization that could come with new settlement and another to negotiate the complex task of creating an ecological intentional community.

Strong Towns, an organization whose mission is to replace the 100-year experiment with sprawl and top-down development in the United States with an incremental bottom-up movement, is a good first port of call. The ethos of Strong Towns will align with any group looking to build a better place, and they have considerable resources through their podcasts, blogs, and other digital assets.[12] The Congress for the New Urbanism provides a database of developments that conform to the general principles of "new urbanism," searchable by region, type of development and other metrics.[13] The American Planning Association is a good resource for planning information, contacts, case studies, and so forth. For example, it has an extensive section on green communities, as well as an advisory arm.[14]

Settlers should track zoning progress across the country. Over the past year, major zoning changes have been approved in Portland, Oregon; Berkeley, California; Charlotte, North Carolina; and Minneapolis, Minnesota. Among the most ambitious and comprehensive is the Charlotte 2040 Plan, which is anchored around the concept of 10-minute neighborhoods "where residents can access key amenities such as supermarkets and childcare within a 10-minute walk, bike ride or transit trip." The local college could similarly be redesigned into a

10-minute campus, spread throughout the community. A community with an approved plan could potentially accommodate an EIC or be a good anchor location around which to build a satellite EIC.

Settlers can also consult with some of the top universities in the field of urban planning, as they will likely become influential mechanisms of transmission and development for new approaches to city development. MIT, Berkeley, Rutgers, UCLA, and UNC–Chapel Hill are among top-ranked universities in this area.[15] Government departments can also be of help. FEMA has useful information on aspects of green building, especially as they pertain to resilience. The EPA has also been proactive in supporting sustainable communities.[16]

The role of colleges or universities in an ecological intentional community is central. There is a wealth of know-how being created around renewable energy, low-impact manufacturing, regenerative agriculture, and many other areas that will fit closely with the ethos of an EIC. One option is to place an EIC within or close to a university with a commitment and practice consistent with the mission. This might require partnering with an institution that is willing and able to alter its mission to be more like a knowledge enterprise, especially one that places environmental consciousness at the center of its pedagogical mission. There are rankings of colleges based on environmental progress from sources such as B.E.S.T. College and Collegexpress.[17] For example, building on our hypothetical evolution of Defiance, Ohio, in an earlier chapter, this could be a potential destination. Alternatively, the EIC could build links with one or more academic centers of excellence with alignment to its mission and from there explore the formation of a partnership or eventually a jointly sponsored microcollege.

While the prospects of creating a new ecologically friendly settlement may seem daunting, the combination of social, work, economic, and environmental changes experienced since 2019 have shifted core assumptions around the American way of life. Now is as good a time as any to take the plunge.

Town Officials

Someone running for mayor of a small town could propose a platform for town and gown regeneration. Imagine a town facing population decline, pollution, and social challenges around aging and race. The local college is on the ropes, unlikely to survive the next decade of change. At one level, as a government official one has a lot more standing, connections, and power than an ordinary citizen. But it is also a more complicated environment, having to balance the competing needs of taxpayers, voters, parents, retirees, key institutions, regulators, the state, and unions.

A good way to start the town journey is to look at what other places have achieved. In 2009, the University of North Carolina School of Government published a detailed study of 50 small towns, all with fewer than 10,000 people, that had demonstrated effective community economic development.[18] These success cases fell into four archetypes based on the key anchor to the development strategy: recreational destinations, historic downtowns, proximity to a college campus, or proximity to a metropolitan area or transport link. From UNC's review of what worked across these case studies, they derived rules for small-town success that are broadly consistent with the themes in this book: be highly proactive and willing to take risks, harness existing assets in creative ways, pursue a comprehensive strategy rather than piecemeal efforts, start small and celebrate initial wins, innovate with new governance and partnership models, and recognize that community and economic development are the same thing. And, perhaps most centrally, build a robust knowledge enterprise.

Another source of inspiration is the Walton Foundation's work on what are termed "Micropolitan" locations, 531 places, each with between 10,000 and 50,000 citizens, scattered across the United States. The foundation evaluates every year the most successful "Micropolitan" regions based on an array of metrics and assesses which are progressing or regressing and what factors may be driving change, thus providing a "pulse" for small-town America.[19]

For those starting on the journey, it is critical to realize that they are not alone. There are thousands of other small towns with peers on comparable paths that can provide support and trade ideas, as well as national organizations with the very purpose of supporting place-based regeneration. For example, Main Street America is a group formed as a division of the National Trust for Historic Preservation, focused on rehabilitating historic main streets. Main Street America estimates that since 1980 it has helped rehabilitate over 300,000 build-ings, generated $89 billion in reinvestment, and created 687,000 jobs across over 1,000 communities.[20] Another group, EnterpriseCommu-nity.org, also a 40-year-old nonprofit, has helped build or rehabilitate 791,000 homes and facilitated over $63 billion in investment.[21] These groups can not only help with strategy and planning and peer net-works but may provide financing for some elements of the town transformation.

It is important to enlist the philanthropic and community spirit of your town. Americans give over $400 billion a year in charity, and there is over $1.7 trillion in philanthropic endowments that can sup-port elements of your town strategy.[22] Local businesspeople and high-net-worth families have often been key players in stories of place-based regeneration. In many cases, local families and businesses will com-bine charitable donations of cash, land, buildings, and other resources with investment in new business growth in the community. In the book and HBO documentary *Our Towns*, James and Deborah Fallows document many cases of town regeneration led by prominent local families.[23] The Fallows's project provides an inspiring account of the diversity and creativity of town regeneration across the country in many different contexts.

Town managers also need to enlist the energy and creativity of or-dinary citizens of all stripes. They should recruit citizen leaders and ask them to create working groups to tackle specific elements of the plan. These individuals are not necessarily defined by their qualifica-tions, titles, or wealth but rather by their ability to lead and inspire others.

However, what worked in the past may not be enough. We make the case in this book that the town regeneration strategies that worked well in prior eras are insufficient for the future and that they should be adapted to an era where the knowledge economy and remote work are central. Critically, towns need to carefully consider the knowledge enterprise aspect of their talent magnet strategy. If there is an institution of higher learning already in town, the goal might be to partner with the college president to transform the college into a knowledge enterprise, one committed to helping to execute a talent magnet strategy. If there is no such institution, the town may have to seek out a partner organization to help create a knowledge enterprise. The approach for academic partnership will depend on a variety of factors: What are the key initiatives being pursued by the town, and what is their intersection with academia? What are the unique features of the town that could attract the interest of academic partners? What institutions have the skills, networks, and interests to become logical partners? Are there institutions or corporations or individuals in town that could provide a foundation for a new microcollege or department? Are we able to attract and recruit talent from out of town to help seed a microcollege? What are key current and future skills required by the largest local employers, and could they be convinced to partner with the town to form a microcollege? Can you convince a group in town to take a lead in attracting an academic institution?

A useful analogy for new microcolleges is the charter school movement in K–12. According to the National Alliance for Public Charter Schools, in the United States there are 7,500 charter schools nationwide, educating 3.3 million students and employing 215,000 teachers. Charter school funding has totaled $440 million, or $59K per school on average. The Walton Family Foundation estimates typical start-up grant requirements of $100K to $350K for a charter school, whereas a recent New Hampshire award to support 27 new or improved charter schools would suggest a cost per school of about $1 million.[24]

There is not a clear consensus in the US political and social environment about the costs and benefits of charter schools. A detailed study of the costs of charter schools and traditional public schools across the United States in 2020 concluded that charter schools, on average, cost 33% less than traditional public schools. A 2021 paper published by the National Bureau for Economic Research concluded that charter schools on average deliver slightly better academic results than traditional public schools, though the gap was not statistically significant. It also concluded that charter management organizations such as KIPP schools generated significantly better results than the average charter school. Although the performance, cost, and social impact of charter schools is a contentious topic, studying what works and what does not can be very helpful for places looking to start a micro-college. As we have researched material for this book, we have not come across a private, public, or charitable organization whose exclusive focus is on starting new colleges or on supporting existing colleges to transform, the equivalent of a group such as Main Street America in supporting the revitalization of historical downtowns. Paradoxically, perhaps, some university systems are involved in charter schools but not in creating the collegiate equivalent. For example, in New York State, the State University of New York system has its own charter school support organization, SUNY Charter Schools Institute.[25]

There was a brief attempt at starting a charter college movement, led by then governor Paul Cellucci in Massachusetts in 2000. He was supported by a paper developed for the Pioneer Institute of Boston by Robert Berdahl, professor emeritus of higher education at the University of Maryland, and Terrence MacTaggart, chancellor of the University of Maine system, titled "Charter Colleges: Balancing Freedom and Accountability."[26] However, there was fierce resistance from the Massachusetts higher ed establishment, and the concept failed to progress. Even so, the charter college concept was developed before the explosion of the educational technology (ed-tech) sector, the remote work wave, and the growth of widely available broadband. Perhaps a new wave may be about to start.

The first higher-ed move as town mayor could be to form a team with a focus on developing and executing a knowledge enterprise strategy. The town should seek to recruit a team leader with the capability to make change happen, attract others, persuade townspeople and business leaders, and liaise with academics. It should encourage early successes to build momentum. For example, the group could start with a program for local employers with talent needs or convince a local institution to spin out a test microcollege. The town might also lead the transformation of an existing college into a knowledge enterprise, recognizing it as an asset as vital to the smooth functioning of the town as any other utility or service. Indeed, whatever institution the town partners with, it should develop a formal agreement that the college/knowledge enterprise receives funding from the town in exchange for providing "knowledge services" to the community. For example, the knowledge enterprise serves as the node to the larger cloud-based knowledge economy, including the provision of broadband connectivity for the region. The knowledge enterprise maintains an innovation incubator for the town. As other elements of the town revival strategy come together, it may become clear what new academic opportunities could emerge as it considers the development of a university-as-a-service model.

COVID-19, by accelerating the move of higher education online, and through changes in our economic model, has created new academic openings across every category. For example, manufacturing has bounced back rapidly in the United States and is now experiencing labor and skill shortages.[27] Rust-belt towns with a manufacturing base could seize on this shift to build knowledge enterprises oriented around filling these gaps. Travel is also set to change, with tourists favoring small towns, sustainability, experiences, all trends that could potentially benefit small towns. With lines blurring between short-term travel and medium-term nomadism, emerging needs for medical and wellness tourism, new interest in craft and farming tourism and ecotourism, new skills could be developed by travel-oriented knowledge enterprises adapted to these new needs. Health care and wellness, among the largest and fastest growing sectors in the United States, are also set to continue to change dramatically, suggesting the need for new academic models to train health and wellness professionals.

McKinsey estimates a $250 billion telehealth sector by 2025, requiring fundamentally different care delivery, suggesting the opportunity for new training approaches.[28]

As the town gains a stronger academic infrastructure, it should set its sights on further evolution along the knowledge enterprise spectrum. New schools could get involved with business formation and social causes in the town from an early stage, and in some cases a microcollege could be designed and launched as part of a broader mission, such as the creation of an ecotourism sector. If the economic opportunity is large enough, and if the town can tap into local stakeholders, it could create financing vehicles, including venture capital and development organizations. For example, if a town has good transit connections to regional employers, it could develop a "green bedroom community," designed to provide low-impact and high-quality lives and commuting options, using a housing-as-a-service approach to reduce friction and increase worker options. It could leverage the same platform to attract other demographics, such as empty nesters and remote workers. The development itself could support the use of innovative technologies and potentially result in additional spin-off companies. A vigorous knowledge enterprise can be the driver of these efforts.

Over time, the role of town mayor could evolve toward managing a knowledge ecosystem, encouraging the development of new institutions and businesses, proactively working to attract and develop talent of all types, and the evolution of the town toward becoming a talent magnet.

Academic Leaders

We can imagine a newly appointed president of a college under pressure in the Midwest region. A study by academic analytics company Othot titled "Futureproofing Students against the Demographic Cliff" indicates that the student population in the Midwest will decline to 85% of current levels by the end of the decade.[29] Applications are down, discounts to list fees are up, and the college is at risk of shutdown within the next few years, a "poisoned chalice" indeed. The surrounding town is dependent on the college for 20% of its income, but it too is facing challenges to its future growth. The town, local enterprises, and other institutions are supportive, but they are looking for the college to lead. The college has already set in place strategies to rationalize the course portfolio and improve its base profitability. Now it is looking for a transformational shift.

In many cases, colleges have a potentially very valuable real estate portfolio. If the campus is close enough to town, it could be developed into multigenerational "fourth-place" housing as part of a remote town talent attraction strategy. In addition, the campus and the downtown could be redesigned as a 15-minute walkable and bikeable neighborhood. The college could work with city government to develop a joint master plan with the town, including a rezoning of the combined space to accommodate the new place-based strategy. The college and town could apply for grants and loans through Main Street America and other supportive organizations. One option could be to pool the real estate assets from the college and town into a jointly owned development company and secure financing from local banks and other institutions to support a "town and campus" transition.

To stave off the demographic cliff decline, a college president could propose a seemingly radical new strategy for the college: that it will no longer focus exclusively on educating 18- to 22-year-olds, although that enterprise will continue to remain an important part of its mission. It will take strong leadership to bring the board of trustees around to the necessity of this kind of thinking, but the institution must transform into a knowledge enterprise. The president might have been brought in to be a "custodial leader," ensuring stable undergraduate enrollments, satisfying the alumni, raising funds for yet another capital campaign, and generally trying to maintain the legacy of a century-old institution. But what is demanded today is for the new leader to be a "change leader," charged with transforming the institution into a knowledge enterprise, one who will assure the growth and vitality of both the college and the town in which it resides.[30]

As the new infrastructure and town ethos come into focus, the college would partner with the town on a talent attraction strategy.

The college would secure $1 million in funding from a local philanthropy to provide a $10,000 subsidy for 100 people to live in the town and campus for a year, creating momentum. It would build a database of potential recruits, including alumnae, town residents, second homers, tourists, and others who might be attracted to place a stake in the town. Using similar methods as those used to attract undergraduates to the campus, the college would reach out to candidates directly via surveys, teams of students, and townspeople. The initial conversations would be to understand more about them: What are their priorities? What skills do they have? Can they work anywhere? Is there a business they want to start or expand? What is their connection to the town and college?

From this research, it is important to pursue a multistaged process of talent attraction. The focus initially may be on "high-multiplier" talent: people who are interested in starting a restaurant, small store, remote business, coworking space, café, or micro-mobility store (electric bikes and scooters), as well as people who could be convinced to move their business or open a branch. Another move is to develop a business incubator on campus, inviting executives from these companies to teach classes and even develop full programs at the college. As the "15-minute neighborhood" comes into focus, the next move could be to build a public relations and media campaign to generate inbound interest. It is useful to design programs that make it very easy for people to come and test living in the town. These include vacation stays, semester transfers for college students, sabbatical programs, time sharing, plentiful hotel accommodation, room rentals, and so on. By making the experience of living in this neighborhood unique, the bet is that once someone spends a few days in the town, there is a possibility of convincing them to spend a lifetime.

Another priority is to research the work and learning needs of the surrounding community, including employers, workers, parents of future workers, and those who might consider moving to the area. From this research, a college could develop an educational strategy aimed at those living within a 100-mile radius of the college. The goal is to provide a blend of online, hybrid, and on-campus options, meeting pockets of need with academic offerings. The effort should seek to meet the learning needs of all ages and stages, including midlife career changers, empty nesters, those who never completed college, and working parents. Noting a preference by online students to study from a "local" college, the college could provide high-quality and low-cost online certificates, microdegrees, and full degrees that can all be largely done from home but with many pathways to encourage some on-campus presence and sense of belonging.

Through this effort to democratize college, the town and college campus becomes the "knowledge market town" of the surrounding region, the natural center for learning and intellectual exchange. The market town, as defined in medieval England, was the place in which the surrounding rural hinterland came to trade, gossip, get services, and secure provisions. The goal of a knowledge market town is that anyone in the region feels that the local college is his or her alma mater and that it and the town are at their disposal as their lives unfold. This strategy is a critical way to evolve the college's social mission. But equally, this allows the college to expand its revenue sources and to reach a much broader demographic than the traditional college student model of the past.

Business Leaders in the Manufacturing Sector

In this scenario we can consider the potential options for the CEO of a manufacturing business in the Rust Belt, in a town that is struggling to grow, which has a local liberal arts college that will soon face demographic decline in its target student population. The past decades have been tough for manufacturing, but as the United States now restructures its supply chain to increase resilience, speed of response, and value added, demand for manufacturing is stronger than ever. The challenge today is a lack of qualified workers.

Manufacturing is a critical foundation for the US economy. An April 2021 study by the consultancy McKinsey highlights how important this sector is: "In the United States, manufacturing accounts for $2.3 trillion of GDP, employs 12 million people, and supports hundreds of local economies. Although it represents just 11 percent of US GDP and 8 percent of direct employment, it drives 20 percent of the nation's capital investment, 30 percent of productivity growth, 60 percent of exports, and 70 percent of business R&D."[31] McKinsey then outlines a vision for a substantial renewal of the US manufacturing sector, adding between $275 billion and $460 billion in GDP per capita by 2030 and creating upward of 1.5 million new American jobs. It proposes a combination of investments in new technologies, process improvements, training in new skills, and an overall integrated strategy, in contrast to today's fragmented approach. Today, there are an estimated 593,000 manufacturing companies in the United States, each on average employing 20 people and generating $4 million in revenue. Using our estimate of 36,000 "places" in the United States, that would imply an average of 16 manufacturing companies and 333 factory workers per average location.

Another consultancy, Deloitte, estimates that 1.9 million jobs will be added and that 2.1 million US manufacturing jobs will go unfilled by 2030, for a total of 4 million potential jobs.[32] Manufacturing jobs are estimated by Deloitte to have a job multiplier of 2.74, suggesting close to 11 million direct and indirect jobs as a result of new manufacturing job potential (in other words, if all 4 million potential manufacturing jobs are filled, over 11 million jobs opportunities would be created through the multiplier effect). Assuming that these 11 million jobs are evenly distributed over 36,000 "places," this implies 305 potential added manufacturing-induced jobs per place. Shifts in manufacturing approach, including automation, 3D printing, artificial intelligence, and microfactories, suggest a critical need for current and future manufacturing workers to acquire new skills, through a combination of schooling and on-the-job learning. How could one or more enterprises get together to support new skill formation in their town, and what role could nearby colleges and towns take?

The CEO gets together with other local manufacturers, and they jointly develop a regional manufacturing plan for the year 2030. The goal is ambitious, aiming to triple manufacturing employment in the region. They determine that they need to train or reskill 3,000 workers and to evolve the region into a pattern of continuous innovation and adaptation. The manufacturing group reaches an agreement with the local liberal arts college and town to create a new program focused on supporting the learning needs associated with the 2030 plan. The town provides buildings in the downtown area, and the liberal arts college helps support the curriculum development, recruits the faculty, and manages the new manufacturing training program.

The downtown is weak, with space utilization below 50%. As part of the strategy, students from the college get involved in rebuilding and reimagining the downtown. The college and other local stakeholders invest in several downtown construction projects, as well as in turning the combined college and downtown area into a 15-minute neighborhood. The river that spawned the town mills is turned into a key attraction for tourism and outdoors activities. Artists are encouraged to reimagine some of the larger industrial plants, and the town also becomes an artistic destination, aided by the establishment of a creativity incubator by the college.

To position for future evolution in manufacturing, the group reaches partnerships with top global centers of excellence, including Manufacturing USA and the Fraunhofer Institute in Germany. Partnering with the town and the college, they develop a talent attraction strategy, aimed at recruiting into the town and region a broad range of people with skills relevant to current and future manufacturing needs. In partnership with the town, regional investment groups, and global manufacturing partners, the manufacturing group sponsors the creation of a regional institute within the college, to help develop local areas of specialization.

As the community develops skills in new areas of innovation (logistics, autonomous systems, robotics, artificial intelligence, connectivity, additive manufacturing, and digital twins), the collective of manufacturers, the knowledge enterprise, and the town raise their ambition, with the goal of developing a thriving Industry 4.0 ecosystem.[33] This begins by spinning out new businesses, then adding a small ($5 million) accelerator fund, and then developing a $75 million early-stage fund. The venture fund helps to position local starts-ups on the

American and global stage and to increase their impact on innovation in the region. As some of the investments scale, capital starts to move into the town from American and global investors. Global manufacturing companies become interested in the capabilities being developed, acquiring companies, and building R&D centers in the region.

What was a place on the ropes evolves to become a knowledge town. Manufacturing is a core engine of growth, software is a close second, but the town also develops as an artistic and tourist destination. This attracts empty nesters, remote workers, and college alumni, drawn in by the new vibe. Building on this interest, the college sponsors the formation of new academic offerings to serve the needs of new settlers, expanding the liberal arts college into a knowledge enterprise. As it hits the demographic cliff in traditional students in the mid-20s, the college has now diversified into a more economically sustainable "lifelong learning" model. It has expanded its online and hybrid offerings, and its impact reaches across a broad swathe of the surrounding region, including serving rural and urban customers of all ages and sociodemographic statuses.

Over the course of the next decade, the town becomes successful and vibrant, with utilization of available space reaching 95%. As this happens and the price of housing and land increases, it leads to a new role for the knowledge enterprise—creating an affordable fourth place—to ensure that the town can continue to evolve in an ecologically sustainable way, with a medium dense core. The knowledge enterprise invests to ensure that there is sufficient housing to meet evolving town needs. By the year 2030, the town is well positioned into the future, and the industrial companies of the region are prepared to adapt well to the new challenges of the 2030s.

Philanthropic Leaders

Beyond core needs such as hunger, shelter, and basic medical care, key giving priorities for Americans include providing education, securing the environment, and supporting local causes.[34] As a philanthropic leader, how can one best respond to the disruption coming into the community? Should philanthropies get involved if they see the nearby towns and colleges at risk? What is the role of philanthropies in town and gown revitalization?

As covered in a 2020 analysis by the Milken Foundation, there are a broad range of philanthropy strategies, from traditional grants to venture philanthropy, social enterprise, and traditional investment.[35] Typically, many philanthropies seek to maintain or grow their endowment from investment activity and then use the annual returns for giving purposes. Endowments search for the best returns through a portfolio of public and private assets. Often, they are not particularly oriented around local investment, in part because there is almost always a better return option or more worthy grant initiative elsewhere. There has historically been a disconnect between the giving and the investing side: whereas giving was explicitly about impact, investing was hard-nosed capitalist.

Environmental, social, and governance (ESG) principles are beginning to factor in investment strategies. ESG principles now guide over 33% of global assets under management (AUM), a trend that is likely to accelerate.[36] Thus, we can expect to see a broader convergence between the investing side and the donating or giving side of philanthropy.

We may also see a renewed interest in locally oriented investment on both the giving and the investing side. Today there are an estimated 700 community-oriented foundations.[37] Cambridge Associates estimated total AUM at community-oriented foundations to have reached $87 billion in 2017, and it will likely have passed $100 billion by 2021.[38] Although this is a fraction of the total philanthropic AUM of $1.7 trillion, it could be an area of growth and innovation.

On the investment side, the historical pattern was to invest in companies whose headquarters were heavily concentrated in leading cities such as New York, Los Angeles, Chicago, or Boston. This is where the bulk of hedge funds, private equity, top corporations, and top talent have been based and where the best returns have been available. This includes investing in public markets, private equity, and assets such as real estate. As discussed earlier, these places represent a third of the country's wealth but occupy only 0.1% of the US landmass.

However, with a move toward wealth, talent, and knowledge decentralization, we will see a rebalancing away from the 0.1%. In 2020 and 2021, the strongest growth in real estate values was in secondary cities.[39] As towns and colleges evolve to become talent magnets/knowledge ecosystems and thus attract a growing share of wealth creators, the financial returns from local investment are likely to grow. For a philanthropic leader, especially with a community mandate, there is an opportunity to explore new shifts in strategy, in giving, in investing, and broadly in the mission.

A good point of departure might be getting involved in a talent attraction strategy, as the George Kaiser Foundation did with the Tulsa Remote program, contributing over $1 million in the first year alone.[40] This program has now attracted over 50,000 applicants, caused over 800 people to move to Tulsa, and firmly placed the city on the map of "tech hubs."[41] A second area of activity could be to use the same $1-million investment to support the launch of a microcollege.

Using both funding capacity and organizational assets, philanthropies could also support the town and knowledge enterprise in tapping into national charitable organizations, such as Main Street America (active in 1,200 communities in the United States), Habitat for Humanity (active in 1,400 localities in the United States), Corporation for Supportive Housing (330,000 houses, $1 billion invested), HomeAid America, Keep America Beautiful (active in 600 communities in the United States), and many others. Blogging site Stacker in 2019 put together a list of the 50 most impactful locally oriented charities.[42] As a professional fundraising organization, philanthropies could be well positioned to support the town in applying for grants and other forms of financing.

Using the philanthropy's standing in the community, it could work with the town and college to launch a dedicated endowment to support place-based regeneration. Typically, college, town, and philanthropic funding are managed in separate silos, but the time might be right for a new cross-silo structure, managed by the knowledge enterprise, focused on triple-win growth in the community.

From the investment side, there could be a range of ways in which to participate in local regeneration. A talent magnet strategy will drive an increase in the value of local land and housing. Therefore, philanthropic endowments could profitably shift some of their real estate investment activity toward their local town. Just as Colby College's endowment combined supporting the town with meeting its own investment requirements by investing in the surrounding community and driving up land value, so could local philanthropic endowments pursue a similar policy. If philanthropic institutions own land within the town, they could contribute land and cash in exchange for an equity share in a local development corporation, participating in its value growth and impact. As described in some of the scenarios in this book, a knowledge enterprise oriented around supporting local triple-win development can grow in size and scope and thus further increase the value of local assets. This is not to suggest that philanthropies should abandon prudence in their financial investments but rather that they should adapt to the new reality. As evidence grows of the power of decentralized growth in the United States and the financial potential for well-run community-oriented projects, it would be prudent to make this part of an investment portfolio.

College or University Endowment Leaders

College and university endowments are in a special category. With combined assets of $637 billion in 2020, endowments represent around 37% of the total $1.7 trillion in philanthropic assets in the United States.[43] Most endowments have a local mission revolving around their college and are primarily focused on providing student aid, which represented 48% of average endowment spending in 2020, with the remaining 52% supporting academic programs, faculty positions, and campus operations (respectively 17%, 11%, and 7% of total spending).[44] Top school endowments have massive size and impact. For example, Harvard's endowment of approximately $42 billion as of 2020 contributed 5% or $2 billion to school revenue that year, roughly twice as much as Harvard's student revenue of $1.1 billion.[45] With 23,000 full-time students at Harvard, this represents $87K in average endowment contribution per student, compared to $48K in average fees.

The distribution of endowments is heavily skewed. Out of 4,000 higher education institutions, 705 report their endowment size, suggesting that for many of the remainder the endowment is of limited size. Out of the 705 reporting, 80% of the assets are concentrated in the top 111 institutions, which average $4.5 billion in assets each. The remaining 594 reporting institutions average $214M million in average assets. Therefore, the potential impact on the local community will vary substantially depending on the size of the endowment, both in absolute terms and relative to the size of the underlying population.

Many endowments have historically applied an investment strategy that had a limited focus on sustainability and local issues. Reviewing NACUBO-TIAA's 2020 analysis of endowment investment strategies, one can see that endowments' portfolio allocation is a mix of public market, private equity, fixed income, alternative investments, and real estate, with varying strategies for maximum yield based on size and other factors, but generally with very limited focus on local development.[46]

There are some examples of community-oriented university investments from endowments. As covered by *Impactivate* in July 2021, the University of Maine is an investor in the $100 million Maine Economic Improvement Fund, and several other colleges and universities are mentioned as making local contributions to environmental and social projects.[47] Town and gown partnerships such as Colby College's with Waterville should also be included, and perhaps collectively these add up to a few billion dollars in commitments. However, relative to the $637 billion in total university AUM, the total amount of endowment capital going toward local investment is small.

Sustainability has also historically been a low priority for endowments. In a 2020 article Adam Schor at Metropolitan State University of Denver argues that US endowment investors have historically not included ESG factors in their investment strategy. Quoting a 2016 survey by Commonfund,[48] only 25% of endowments at the time considered ESG or socially responsible investing in their investment strategy, and only 3% used impact investment guidelines.[49] Impact investment, according to Emerson, goes beyond ESG and socially responsible investing to include "intentional deployment of resources across the entire capital continuum wrapped around itself, transcending the dualism of doing good and doing well."[50] The 2016 survey states: "The survey found 71% of respondents seeing returns from impact investing as a substantial or moderate impediment to implementation. Additionally, 37% saw concerns about fiduciary duty as a substantial or moderate impediment."[51]

There has been a shift in sentiment. In March 2021, Commonfund completed a new survey of its members, all nonprofits representing colleges and other institutions, with combined AUM of $1.1 trillion. In this survey, 50% of respondents indicated that they believe they could combine sustainable investing with reaching their target investment returns and would factor ESG principles in their investment decisions.[52] However, many college funds are concentrated in highly illiquid investments with long-term commitments, and the global pace of change could leave endowments behind. European investors have moved earlier and much more aggressively into ESG investments, and they are now being followed by top US-based fund managers such as BlackRock, Fidelity, and others. Many of these top US firms have reached the conclusion that ESG-type investments deliver, on balance, improved results relative to non-ESG investments, by focusing companies on taking steps that improve their resilience, reduce their costs, and lower their risks. A metastudy of 1,000 papers by NYU's Stern School of Business on the impact of ESG investments concluded that such investments were positively aligned with investor and corporate returns, with 33% of papers showing positive correlation, 14% negative correlation, and the remaining 53% showing either a neutral or mixed impact.

Regardless of how rapidly the perspective and actions of university endowment managers change, the global shift is likely happening faster. As an indication of the growing impact of ESG investment, global ESG AUM investments have grown from $13 trillion (22% of all assets) in 2016 to $35 trillion (36% of assets) in 2020, and many expect that ESG investment will pass 50% of all assets by 2025.[53] As an indication of future trends in US asset investment, Larry Fink, CEO of BlackRock, the world's largest asset manager with $9.5 trillion in assets, focused on what he described as a "tectonic shift" toward sustainability in his 2021 letter to CEOs: "As more and more investors choose to tilt their investments towards sustainability-focused companies, the tectonic shift we are seeing will accelerate further. And because this will have such a dramatic impact on how capital is allocated, every management team and board will need to consider how this will impact their company's stock."[54]

Adam Schor makes several compelling arguments for a substantial increase in the allocation of university endowment money toward impact investing. First, he argues that impact investing does not necessarily impose a returns sacrifice (the NYU Stern study and the perspective of BlackRock and many global investors would go further and claim a net positive relation). Second, he argues that many impact investments are inherently less risky than other endowment investments, which include significant allocations to high-risk venture capital, private equity, or hedge funds. Based on his modeling, he concludes that even if investor returns on impact-oriented projects were not as good as nonimpact projects (he uses 10% as a modeling assumption for average rate of return for impact investments, by adjusting for reduced risk, it would still make sense to allocate up to 30% of assets toward impact investing, or a tenfold increase relative to current levels. He uses as a measure the Sharpe ratio, which compares reward, measured as average excess IRR over a risk-free rate, divided by the standard deviation of outcomes (the higher the Sharpe ratio, the better the investment strategy). Third, he argues that if we consider the broader benefits to an endowment from impact investing, for example increased donations by students and alumni, the case for impact investing becomes even stronger.

How then could a visionary chief investment officer of an academic endowment decisively shift the investment approach toward impact, especially to help the surrounding community that has been a critical part in the history and mission of the college? On the public equity and fixed-income side, the move to ESG investment is relatively advanced; therefore, endowments can work within the mainstream while staying vigilant against the perils of "greenwashing," where claims of impact are exaggerated.[55] Private equity is also rapidly moving in the direction of ESG investment, as leaders recognize the potential for improved returns through ESG practices. Venture capital and real estate investing have been slower to embrace the ESG trend and therefore could be areas for an endowment to prioritize. But even with areas such as cash management, there is potential for improvement.

Schor proposes several ways in which endowments can begin to shift their approach in cash management, fixed income investments, and equity investing. He suggests that "cash could be kept in local banks, where it could support activities such as housing loans, rather than in national accounts." In particular, he advocates putting money in community development finance institutions and similar local financing groups, which often can leverage deposits for additional federal grants. He also advocates "fixed income lending for low-income and affordable housing and for community entrepreneurs unable to access traditional bank networks, perhaps because those in need do not fit a traditional profile." Finally, he proposes "equity-like exposure via venture capital investments for entrepreneurs in the university community, as defined by the mission statement or investment policy statement." He suggests that an endowment could use an "outside-managed fund for this exposure or could harness local resources, including its faculty and students, to source ideas."[56]

Our view is that an endowment could get potentially very high leverage from supporting the formation of a locally oriented venture capital fund, aimed at maximizing the potential of start-ups launched out of the college or town. As we discussed above, a $75 million seed venture fund could likely require only $10 million from an endowment as a cornerstone investment, and fund managers would be encouraged to raise the remainder from other funding sources, including enterprises, high-net-worth individuals, university alumni, local institutions, and city funds. There are 274 endowments with over $250 million of assets under management, and potentially any of these could take a role in forming a fund.

A fundamental challenge for a venture capital firm is the power law in venture returns. Venture capital returns are heavily skewed toward the best performing firms, and it is very difficult for new firms to break into top rankings and to compete on the same basis as established firms. Historically, these top firms have been based in places such as Silicon Valley, New York, or Boston. A new fund in a small town in America would thus also be handicapped by location. Therefore, there would likely be strong pushback from the endowment investment committee in getting it involved in a new, local fund.

However, for a fund in the $75 million size range, a capital-efficient strategy provides a good balance between reward and risk. In this strategy, the fund focuses on disciplined and success-based financing of entrepreneurs who aim for exits in the $50 million to $100 million range, in contrast with the mainstream venture capital strategy of betting on outliers. Roughly 90% of venture-backed exits happen at below $100 million in value. Many limited partners do not want their fund managers to focus on this part of the market. In many cases the limited partners are betting in venture for the possibility of very high multiples, and they have sufficient diversification across a range of funds to balance out the high risks of such a strategy. This leaves an opening for a contrarian strategy, that also is appropriate in emerging categories with still underdeveloped exit markets. By focusing with discipline on the "long-tail" segment of the exit market, a fund can aim for an IRR in the 15%–20% range, with a high level of consistency. An endowment can still seek the outsize returns of top venture capital investments while finding some room in their portfolio of investments for a strategy that fits within the future evolution of its knowledge enterprise.

With decentralization of work, learning, and innovation, a seed stage fund in small-town USA has a better shot of success than at any time in the past. The historical difficulty for start-ups operating in a remote location, to raise capital, get key hires, or get acquired have dramatically eased since 2019. Technology companies and late-stage private equity investors are serial acquirers of start-ups, and both groups are becoming increasingly comfortable with buying and operating remote teams and companies.

In parallel, large American companies are increasingly retrenching from globalization and shifting toward domestic supply and domestic markets. In March 2021, Niccolò Pisani published an article in the *Sloan Management Review* around the future of globalization postpandemic for the largest global companies. He made three claims: (1) the home region of global companies will become ever more important as they pull back from global supply chains and markets; (2) very few companies will have the ability to globalize; and (3) global competition will increasingly shift toward digital competition.[57] Any start-up based in the United States, no matter how remote, has the benefit in operating in the largest market for almost every product category. As large firms pull back and refocus on national supply and domestic markets, there are opportunities for start-ups to partner with them across a range of activities.

Towns with low costs, high quality of living, and a minimum infrastructure and knowledge enterprise are well placed to compete. In this sense, an enlightened college endowment that recognizes the shift in the terrain and works in partnership with the college and the town to evolve their location to a talent magnet and emerging knowledge enterprise can also gain confidence that a dedicated venture capital fund can succeed, especially one that can leverage the unique skills of the college and community. If the fund managers for this locally oriented venture capital fund can achieve solid IRRs for their first fund (above 10% net IRR, ideally in the 15%–20% range), they position themselves to raise future funds without requiring the same level of support as the initial fund. If the fund underperforms, this has a limited impact on the overall portfolio return of the endowment.

Even in this downside scenario, the college could use the activity and interest associated with the fund to drive an increase in alumni donations that would more than make up for any performance loss. In the case of Colby College, early on in his tenure, President David A.

Green launched "Dare Northward," a campaign to more than double the size of the endowment, in recognition that the college would need sufficient capital to achieve its ambitious objectives.[58] Colleges and endowments could use a talent magnet/knowledge enterprise strategy and the formation of a local fund as key elements of a major donor campaign. Increasing the endowment from $250 million to $500 million through such a campaign, appealing to the connections of thousands of alumni to their alma mater, and their participation in a compelling strategy for the future, the $10-million allocation into the venture capital fund will be a minor commitment.

What about a college with a smaller endowment or with no endowment? The $250 million cutoff point eliminates 95% of colleges from contention in forming a fund. Building on our arguments thus far, we would propose that the endowment, college, and town could work together to develop a strategy for capital formation. The goal would be to create an endowment with the specific mission to support triple-win growth in the region, evolve the town toward a talent magnet, the college toward a knowledge enterprise, and the combination into a regional "knowledge market town." The endowment would represent these combined interests rather than exclusively those of the college. The campaign would be aimed at alumni, current parents, local stakeholders, and global enterprises and investors interested in participating in, and learning from, the related opportunities. Funds could be raised as donations or investments, for general purposes, or for specific purposes and vehicles. If the goal would be to capitalize up to $500 million, with a starting endowment of $25 million, one pathway could include a general-purpose endowment of $250 million, a land and property management corporation with $100 million, a venture capital fund with $75 million, and various other vehicles and initiatives with the remaining $75 million (including institutes, accelerators, special-purpose development projects).

In this strategy, the endowment's mission statement and guidance would be oriented around a triple-win mandate, looking to achieve strong IRR while focusing on projects with high environmental and social components. This may appear a naïve sentiment, but we estimate that roughly half of today's economy has been underinvested by venture capital and mostly in areas with the most opportunity for societal improvement. Thus we believe that there are strong opportunities for economic returns. Venture capitalists, like other professionals, tend to specialize and stay very focused on what they do well, and many of the areas requiring social improvement have generally been underinvested.

The notion that social impact and economic growth are connected is not a new idea. Even the much-maligned internal combustion engine was a godsend in the early twentieth century as cities struggled to escape from the pollution of horse-drawn carriages.[59] The mistake was to allow the internal combustion engine–based model to so dominate the economy that it crowded out much of the rest of society, but at its foundation it was both a massive new market and a social good.

Consider today the digital twin market, projected by one analyst to grow from $5 billion in 2020 to $85 billion in 2028.[60] One application of digital twins is to create virtual models of future towns, including information on zoning, investment processes, rental, and service models. These models could then be auctioned off to financial investors interested in putting money into the various future return streams. Some investors may want to focus on early-stage development, riskier but with higher potential returns, whereas others may aim for more predictable investment in financing rental markets or in some of the new service models that could emerge. If a locally oriented venture capital fund were to back investments in early-stage digital twin companies, whose software could be used to support town regeneration strategies, the endowment would gain early visibility on a range of future investment options. The more central to a growing ecosystem, the greater the adjacent investment opportunities for the endowment.

Where could the strategy go from here? If the shift toward decentralized innovation continues to accelerate and the college and the town gain further traction in the talent magnet/knowledge enterprise strategy, the surrounding region could start to generate a self-fueling cycle of entrepreneurship, economic growth, inward migration, and capital value growth. In an upward cycle, the value of the regional ecosystem could grow substantially across all asset categories, including private company valuations, local real estate, sponsored development corporations, and other vehicles in which the endowment can invest. As the endowment increases its participation based on evidence of improving outcomes, it can participate in triple-win growth, creating economic, social, and environmental equity and fusing the financial power of the endowment into the new mission of the overall institution.

US endowments have thus far managed to skirt some of the contradictions between being nonprofits (and getting many societal benefits from this status) and yet largely ignoring social and environmental considerations in their investment process. Given also that most of the endowment proceeds are, in essence, ploughed back into the university cost structure, including salaries and accommodations for senior staff, there is a case for reconsideration.

Conclusion

We might summarize the common themes of this chapter by providing these visions of possible futures that could emerge by the year 2030:

- *Microcolleges.* Echoing recent growth in microbreweries, microfactories, charter schools, and pod schools, we hope to see, and help drive, an explosion in microcolleges, started at low cost, bringing a new sense of energy and experimentation to the world of higher education.
- *Transformed colleges.* We believe that many colleges recognize that their current model will not endure. We hope to inspire their leaders to pursue reinvention along the lines of the examples discussed in the book, expanding their reach in the community, evolving to adapt to the new economic, social, and environmental priorities to become knowledge enterprises, and reach a renewed role as cornerstones of their community.

- *Transformed towns.* As captured in the book, there is a wave of experimentation among American towns that has been ongoing, led by local change makers, often supported by national organizations such as Main Street America. We aim to inspire and help towns to seize on the opportunity to become talent magnets, including creating a significant knowledge enterprise at their core.
- *Transformed businesses.* Small and large businesses are powerful engines for change. We aim to see an explosion of innovation, with new companies being formed and existing companies adapting to the new realities of the knowledge economy and the new societal and environmental priorities of American citizens.
- *Transformed philanthropy.* There is a massive opportunity for philanthropic entities to harness both the financial assets and time of Americans, in taking an active role in town and gown regeneration. Charity begins at home, and philanthropies can become critical in local renewal.
- *Transformed endowments.* We hope to see a dramatic shift in the role of university endowments in sustainability in general and specifically in local renewal. We also hope to inspire the growth of new endowments, including ones that blend the interests of the college and the surrounding community.
- *Civic initiatives and societies.* We hope to inspire ordinary citizens to form together, as they have done in prior times, to help define and build a better future in their towns, in their colleges, and in other institutions.
- *Intentional settlers.* We aim to inspire a wave of settlement by those that have been thinking about taking a more active role in forming or re-forming their ideal community but have not yet made that move.

CONCLUSION

———

History Does Not Repeat but It Does Rhyme

ALMA COLLEGE, LATER RENAMED FRANKLIN COLLEGE, was a Presbyterian abolitionist college founded in New Athens, Ohio, in 1818. Nestled in the Appalachian foothills, Franklin educated some of the nation's foremost abolitionist leaders.[1] Although an exceptional institution, Franklin College was hardly unique in the nineteenth-century American higher education landscape. Owing to a quirk of history, many of the United States' liberal arts colleges are located in small towns and rural areas. Many of these schools were founded in the nineteenth century as denominational colleges, where a college education was as much about teaching religious devotion, morality, and good character as it was about imparting knowledge and certifying skills. The belief among their founders was that this moral and character education could not happen if the college were in proximity to the vices and temptations of the city. Moreover, many of the small towns in which these schools were located established a college as much as a matter of civic obligation as of educational necessity. Indeed, this seemed to be one of the impulses of American settlers as they moved across the continent: that as they founded a town or settlement, they would first construct a church and some sort of civic building, followed closely by a school or academy. The proliferation of one-room schoolhouses across the country is also emblematic of this impulse to place educational institutions at the heart of civic life.[2] It seems that at one point in American history, practically every town—no matter the size—had its own small college at its center.

But after a century of operation, Franklin College closed its doors in 1919. This is the other half of the story of nineteenth-century American higher education: that while many institutions were established, many others were simultaneously shuttering. There were a variety of reasons for these failures: most of these colleges were already small, with a student population numbering in the dozens. Most were typically underfunded. Further, denominational colleges were under pressure to secularize, and American society was industrializing and urbanizing such that the appeal of attending school in such an isolated, rural location was less of an attraction. By the early twentieth century, many of these denominational schools were losing enrollment, as well as their reason for being. Those small rural colleges that did survive did so because they were forced to reinvent themselves, to pivot away from their nineteenth-century foundations.

Many small liberal arts colleges, and even some regional public universities, are in a similar situation today. Especially owing to what is being called the "demographic cliff"—a dwindling pool of traditional-age college students over whom schools will have to aggressively compete—and given their relatively high tuitions, an increasing number of colleges and universities face daunting prospects, even the unpalatable option of having to close their doors.[3] On top of that, many of these schools remain tethered to rural areas and other locations of their original founding that are themselves, today, economically declining. Absent a visionary strategy of institutional reinvention—similar to what we have proposed in this book—we anticipate that many more Franklin Colleges will close their doors in the coming decade. Like the situation a century ago, in order to survive and thrive, these institutions of higher education are going to have to do something many of them do not want to do: reinvent themselves again.

This book is about ideas, but it is also a book about action. What we aim to do is to inspire as many people as possible to act, moving their town, college, company, philanthropy, endowment into a more sustainable growth model. We have made the following claims:

- There are tremendous pressures for change in both academic institutions and the places where Americans live. On a broad scale, we have reached the limits of what the societal platform laid out between the Great Depression and World War II can deliver.
- The knowledge economy, integrated into the cloud, represents the dominant economic and social model of the twenty-first century and thus sets the context for any strategy, including collegiate and place-based policies.
- The COVID-19 pandemic has accelerated change across all domains. Specifically, by normalizing remote work and learning, it has reopened what appeared a closed debate around the future of humanity being concentrated into ever larger megacities. We may be entering an age of decentralization.
- In the new context, we believe places of all sizes must develop strategies to become talent magnets, by which we mean that they should pursue policies that optimize their ability to attract, retain, and grow talent of all types by pursuing social, environmental, and economic growth. In chapter 1 we define in detail the principles behind talent magnets and illustrate some ways in which they could manifest.
- For every place there should be a knowledge enterprise, an academic institution whose mission, central purpose, and reason for being is to contribute to—and, indeed, to lead—a region's talent magnet strategy. The knowledge enterprise for a region might be defined as a "university as a service," a public utility necessary for creating a desirable and attractive place. In chapter 2 we look at the application of talent magnet rules to the creation of knowledge enterprises.
- We claim that talent magnets and knowledge enterprises are two sides of the same coin, in a society, economy, and environ-

ment where knowledge sits at the center. A combined talent magnet and knowledge enterprise strategy, when successfully executed, can evolve to create "knowledge towns," places that act as cornerstones of their region's evolution.

- We explore in chapter 3 a range of archetypes for how combinations of town and gown can pursue triple-win growth, beginning with situations where there is either nothing or very little and evolving to very strong combinations of place and university. We argue that regardless of starting position, there is both an opportunity and a critical need for growth strategies.
- In chapter 4 we work through how different personas could take a lead in initiating a sustained shift in the fortunes of their town or institution, from ordinary citizens to those in position to control access to capital and other resources.

Underlying the thesis of the book is the notion that the way to improve our lives is via continued growth. In this sense, we are aligned with the thinking of books such as *More from Less* by Andrew McAfee of MIT, in which the central theme is to improve on economic growth while simultaneously reducing absolute and per-capita resource use.[4] In contrast, a "de-growth" platform, we fear, would be at risk of inducing a triple-loss path, ensuring social, environmental, and economic decline. We have seen this path in many of the utopias and dystopias pursued over the course of the past 100 years.

With strong consensus around environmental risk, there now is conviction among many around the need to pursue net zero strategies. However, there is a risk that a top-down and monocultural approach to net zero, with insufficient bottom-up experimentation, could lead to harmful and unforeseen results, much as the top-down "motor society" culture of the past 100 years created a vast array of negative effects. Also, in pursuing a pure environmental goal without explicitly factoring the social aspect, there is a risk of continuing to fail many within our society.

Therefore, it is critical to both humanize and decentralize the process of growth, and to make its evolution emergent and based on results. This leads us to advocate that the new societal model that we must build should happen whenever possible at the most local level, even while staying fully enmeshed in the global knowledge economy. This is our foundational rule: "Act local but harness the cloud." A thriving knowledge enterprise sits at the heart of this new societal model.

NOTES

Introduction

1. Adedayo Akala, "Now That More Americans Can Work from Anywhere, Many Are Planning to Move Away," NPR (October 30, 2020), https://www.npr.org/sections/coronavirus-live-updates/2020/10/30/929667563/now-that-more-americans-can-work-anywhere-many-are-planning-to-move-away.

2. Based on average US GDP per capita of $63K per Data Commons times 23 million internal migrants equals $1.45 trillion, https://datacommons.org/place/country/USA.

3. There are no perfect estimates, but there are approximately 130 million Americans living in coastal counties, which are typically less affordable, according to https://oceanservice.noaa.gov/facts/population. Per Habitat for Humanity, there are 37 million "housing burdened" Americans, https://www.habitat.org/costofhome/2020-state-nations-housing-report-lack-affordable-housing. A much large percentage would benefit from reduced costs of housing and commuting.

4. World Population Review, "How Many Cities Are in the US," https://worldpopulationreview.com/us-city-rankings/how-many-cities-are-in-the-us.

5. See David J. Staley, *Alternative Universities: Speculative Design for Innovation in Higher Education* (Baltimore: Johns Hopkins University Press, 2019).

6. Michael M. Crow and William B. Dabars, *The Fifth Wave: The Evolution of American Higher Education* (Baltimore: Johns Hopkins University Press, 2020).

7. Bruce Berman, "$21 Trillion in U.S. Intangible Assets Is 84% of S&P 500 Value—IP Rights and Reputation Included," IP CloseUp, June 4, 2019, https://ipcloseup.com/2019/06/04/21-trillion-in-u-s-intangible-asset-value-is-84-of-sp-500-value-ip-rights-and-reputation-included. See also Jonathan Haskel and Stian Westlake, *Capitalism without Capital: The Rise of the Intangible Economy* (Princeton, NJ: Princeton University Press, 2018).

8. "What Is the Knowledge Economy?" Corporate Finance Institute (n.d.), https://corporatefinanceinstitute.com/resources/knowledge/other/knowledge-economy/.

9. See, for example, the October 2020 McKinsey report "How COVID-19 Has Pushed Companies over the Technology Tipping Point—and Transformed Business Forever," https://www.mckinsey.com/business-functions/strategy-and-corporate-finance/our-insights/how-covid-19-has-pushed-companies-over-the-technology-tipping-point-and-transformed-business-forever.

10. Estimate of 100 million knowledge workers, https://www.altvil.com, 45% of knowledge workers working from home. See "Moving beyond Remote: Workplace Transformation in the Wake of Covid-19," *Slack* (October 7, 2020), https://slack .com/blog/collaboration/workplace-transformation-in-the-wake-of-covid-19.

11. Roy Maurer, "Study Finds Productivity Not Deterred by Shift to Remote Work," Society for Human Resource Management (September 16, 2020), https:// www.shrm.org/hr-today/news/hr-news/pages/study-productivity-shift-remote -work-covid-coronavirus.aspx.

12. "It's Time to Reimagine Where and How Work Will Get Done: PwC's US Remote Work Survey," PwC (January 12, 2021), https://www.pwc.com/us/en /library/covid-19/us-remote-work-survey.html.

13. Paul Sawers, "After Embracing Remote Work in 2020, Companies Face Conflicts Making It Permanent," VentureBeat (January 1, 2021), https://venture beat.com/2021/01/01/after-embracing-remote-work-in-2020-companies-face -conflicts-making-it-permanent/.

14. Albany is 3 hours and 40 minutes by train from Manhattan. Average house prices in Albany: "Albany Home Values," https://www.zillow.com/albany-ny/home -values/. Average prices in New York City: "New York Home Values," https://www .zillow.com/new-york-ny/home-values/.

15. Zillow, "Tulsa Home Values," https://www.zillow.com/tulsa-ok/home-values/.

16. Enrico Moretti estimates a number as high as a 5x multiplier, but we propose 2–3x as a more conservative option. See *Sloan Management Review*, "The Multiplier Effect of Innovation Jobs," (June 6, 2012), https://sloanreview.mit.edu /article/the-multiplier-effect-of-innovation-jobs/.

17. Mark Johanson, "The 'Zoom Towns' Luring Remote Workers to Rural Enclaves," BBC (June 8, 2021), https://www.bbc.com/worklife/article/20210604 -the-zoom-towns-luring-remote-workers-to-rural-enclaves.

18. Finding NWA, "Talent Incentive," https://findingnwa.com/incentive/.

19. Ascend West Virginia, https://ascendwv.com/.

20. "Gov. Justice, Brad & Alys Smith, and West Virginia University Launch Ascend WV Remote Worker Program," *WVU Today* (April 12, 2021), https:// wvutoday.wvu.edu/stories/2021/04/12/gov-justice-brad-alys-smith-and-west -virginia-university-launch-ascend-wv-remote-worker-program.

21. Work From Purdue, https://www.workfrompurdue.com/.

22. Ibid.

23. Lindsay Ellis, "The Rise of Remote Work May Reshape College Towns. Here's How These Campuses Are Wooing Transplants," *Chronicle of Higher Education* (June 1, 2021), https://www.chronicle.com/article/the-rise-of-remote-work-may -reshape-college-towns-heres-how-these-campuses-are-wooing-transplants.

24. Richard Vedder, "Why Colleges Need Major Creative Destruction," *Forbes* (April 5, 2018), https://www.forbes.com/sites/richardvedder/2018/04/05/collegiate -incentives-and-creative-destruction-death-of-universities.

25. Jeremy Hobson and Allison Hagan, "Coronavirus May Mark the End for Many Small Liberal Arts Colleges," *Here and Now* (May 13, 2020), https://www .wbur.org/hereandnow/2020/05/13/coronavirus-small-college-closures.

26. See Staley, *Alternative Universities*.

27. Erik Kain, "The Rise of Craft Beer in America," *Forbes* (September 16, 2011), https://www.forbes.com/sites/erikkain/2011/09/16/the-rise-of-craft-beer-in-america.

28. Brewers Association for Small & Independent Craft Brewers, "National Beer Sales & Production Data," https://www.brewersassociation.org/statistics-and-data /national-beer-stats/.

29. "It's Time to Reimagine Where and How Work Will Get Done: PwC's US Remote Work Survey," PwC (January 12, 2021), https://www.pwc.com/us/en /library/covid-19/us-remote-work-survey.html.

30. Salvatore Cipriano, "Harvard 1642: America's First Commencement," *We're History* (May 8, 2019), http://werehistory.org/harvard-1642-americas-first -commencement/.

31. Statista, "Population Density of the United States from 1790 to 2019 in Residents per Square Mile of Land Area," https://www.statista.com/statistics /183475/united-states-population-density; encyclopedia.com, "The Population of Europe: Early Modern Demographic Patterns," https://www.encyclopedia.com /international/encyclopedias-almanacs-transcripts-and-maps/population-europe -early-modern-demographic-patterns.

32. "Urban World: Mapping the Economic Power of Cities," McKinsey and Company (March 1, 2011), https://www.mckinsey.com/featured-insights /urbanization/urban-world-mapping-the-economic-power-of-cities.

33. Geoffrey West, *Scale: The Universal Laws of Growth, Innovation, Sustainability, and the Pace of Life in Organisms, Cities, Economies, and Companies* (New York: Penguin, 2017).

34. Bessemer Venture Partners, "State of the Cloud 2020 Report," https://www .bvp.com/atlas/state-of-the-cloud-2020#2020-Predictions.

35. Statista, "Population Density of the United States from 1790 to 2019 in Residents per Square Mile of Land Area," https://www.statista.com/statistics /183475/united-states-population-density/; Statista, "European Union: Population density from 2010 to 2020," https://www.statista.com/statistics/253445/population -density-in-the-european-union-eu/; worldometer, "Asia Population (Live)," https://www.worldometers.info/world-population/asia-population; worldometer, "Current World Population," https://www.worldometers.info/world-population.

36. International Institute for Environment and Development, "The World's 100 Largest Cities from 1800 to 2020, and Beyond," https://www.iied.org/worlds-100 -largest-cities-1800-2020-beyond; https://www.biggestuscities.com/1950; https:// www.biggestuscities.com/1850; US Census 1850 and 1950.

37. "The 200 Largest Cities in the United States by Population 2022," https:// worldpopulationreview.com/us-cities; United Nations Department of Economic and Social Affairs, Population Division, "Population Facts" (December 2018), https:// population.un.org/wup/Publications/Files/WUP2018-PopFacts_2018-1.pdf; City Mayors Statistics, "Largest Cities in the World," http://www.citymayors.com /statistics/largest-cities-population-125.html; Kim Parker, Juliana Menasce Horo- witz, Anna Brown, Richard Fry, d'Vera Cohn, and Ruth Igielnik, "Demographic and Economic Trends in Urban, Suburban and Rural Communities," Pew Research

Center (May 22, 2018), https://www.pewsocialtrends.org/2018/05/22/demographic-and-economic-trends-in-urban-suburban-and-rural-communities/.

38. Statista, "Distribution of Countries with Largest Stock Markets Worldwide as of January 2021, by Share of Total World Equity Market Value," https://www.statista.com/statistics/710680/global-stock-markets-by-country/; Curious Cat Blog, "Stock Market Capitalization by Country from 1990 to 2010," https://investing.curiouscatblog.net/2012/06/28/stock-market-capitalization-by-country-from-1990-to-2010.

39. We build an estimate of the number of "places" in the US in chapter 3.

40. Treh Manhertz, "Recovery Riches: The U.S. Housing Market Gained $11 Trillion in Value in the 2010s," Zillow, https://www.zillow.com/research/us-total-housing-value-2019-26369.

41. Carmen Ang, "Mapped: The Top 30 Most Valuable Real Estate Cities in the U.S.," Visual Capitalist (December 1, 2020), https://www.visualcapitalist.com/most-valuable-real-estate-cities-us/.

42. "The Economics of Biophilia: Why Designing with Nature in Mind Makes Financial Sense," Terrapin Bright Green (2012), https://www.terrapinbrightgreen.com/reports/the-economics-of-biophilia/.

43. Jack M. Broughton and Elic M. Weitzel, "Population Reconstructions for Humans and Megafauna Suggest Mixed Causes for North American Pleistocene Extinctions," *Nature Communications* (December 21, 2018), https://www.nature.com/articles/s41467-018-07897-1; Environmental Justice Foundation, "Ocean: Protecting Marine Ecosystems and Livelihoods," https://ejfoundation.org/what-we-do/oceans; US Geological Survey, "Groundwater Decline and Depletion" (June 6, 2018), https://www.usgs.gov/special-topic/water-science-school/science/groundwater-decline-and-depletion; Daphne Ewing-Chow, "Earth's Rapidly Degrading Soil Is Bad News for Human Health," *Forbes* (June 24, 2020), https://www.forbes.com/sites/daphneewingchow/2020/06/24/earths-rapidly-degrading-soil-is-bad-news-for-human-health.

44. "Upward and Outward Growth: Managing Urban Expansion for More Equitable Cities in the Global South," World Resources Institute (January 31, 2019), https://www.wri.org/wri-citiesforall/publication/upward-and-outward-growth-managing-urban-expansion-more-equitable.

45. Carlos Bueno-Suárez and Daniel Coq-Huelva, "Sustaining What Is Unsustainable: A Review of Urban Sprawl and Urban Socio-Environmental Policies in North America and Western Europe," *Sustainability* (2020), 12: 4445; doi:10.3390/su12114445.

Chapter 1. Modern Society and the New Definition of Talent Magnets

1. Peter Wagner, "The Modern Enterprise," Wing VC (March 23, 2020), https://www.wing.vc/the-modern-enterprise.

2. "Twilio Study Finds COVID-19 Accelerated Companies' Digital Communications Strategy by Six Years," *Businesswire* (July 15, 2020), https://www.businesswire.com/news/home/20200715005140/en/Twilio-Study-Finds-COVID-19-Accelerated-Companies%E2%80%99-Digital-Communications-Strategy-by-Six-Years.

3. Matthew Haag, "Remote Work Is Here to Stay. Manhattan May Never Be the Same," *New York Times* (August 24, 2021), https://www.nytimes.com/2021/03/29 /nyregion/remote-work-coronavirus-pandemic.html.

4. Each farm has a unique soil footprint, and thus a regenerative farmer must "learn" the optimal mix via trial and error. It typically takes three to four years of intense testing to find the optimal combination. Once this stage is reached, the soil generates higher profitability than mechanized agriculture. See Gabe Brown, *Dirt to Soil: One Family's Journey into Regenerative Agriculture* (White River Junction, VT: Chelsea Green, 2018).

5. A June 2021 survey of 521 firms in London suggests that for companies with knowledge workers, over 50% expect their employees to be working remotely 5 days a week after COVID-19. See Nikodem Szumilo and Thomas Wiegelmann, "Do You Really Need All That Office Space?," *Harvard Business Review* (July 2, 2021), https://hbr.org/2021/07/do-you-really-need-all-that-office-space.

6. OECD (Organization for Economic Development and Cooperation), "What Is Green Growth and How Can It Help Deliver Sustainable Development?," https:// www.oecd.org/greengrowth/whatisgreengrowthandhowcanithelpdeliversustaina bledevelopment.htm.

7. David Sim, "David Sim of 'Soft City': Making the Places We Live More Human," interview by C. Christopher Smith, *Strong Towns* (October 28, 2019), https://www.strongtowns.org/journal/2019/10/28/david-sim-of-soft-city.

8. Alex Baca, Patrick McAnaney, and Jenny Schuetz, "'Gentle' Density Can Save Our Neighborhoods," Brookings (December 4, 2019), https://www.brookings.edu /research/gentle-density-can-save-our-neighborhoods/.

9. Simon N. Young, "How to Increase Serotonin in the Human Brain without Drugs," *Journal of Psychiatry and Neuroscience* 32(6) (November 2007): 394–99, https://www.ncbi.nlm.nih.gov/pmc/articles/PMC2077351/.

10. Hannah Ritchie and Max Roser, "Outdoor Air Pollution," Our World in Data (January 2022), https://ourworldindata.org/outdoor-air-pollution.

11. Wei Wei and Zanxin Wang, "Impact of Industrial Air Pollution on Agricultural Production," *Atmosphere* 12 (2021): 639, https://mdpi-res.com/d_attachment /atmosphere/atmosphere-12-00639/article_deploy/atmosphere-12-00639.pdf ?version=1621319619.

12. "How to Achieve a Walking and Cycling Transformation in Your City," C40 Knowledge, https://www.c40knowledgehub.org/s/article/How-to-achieve-a -walking-and-cycling-transformation-in-your-city?language=en_US.

13. See Jeff Speck, *Walkable City Rules: 101 Steps to Making Better Places* (Washington, DC: Island Press, 2018).

14. Google Spreadsheets, "COVID19 Livable Streets Response Strategies," https://docs.google.com/spreadsheets/d/1tjam1voNLUWkYedIa4dVOL49pyWIPIyG wRBoDOnm3Ls/edit#gid=2048567740.

15. Carlton Reid, "Paris to Create 650 Kilometers of Post-Lockdown Cycleways," *Forbes* (April 22, 2020), https://www.forbes.com/sites/carltonreid/2020/04/22 /paris-to-create-650-kilometers-of-pop-up-corona-cycleways-for-post-lockdown -travel/?sh=3bbe482654d4.

16. "France to Splash Out €43 Million to Build New Cycle Lanes around the Country," *Local* (September 16, 2019), https://www.thelocal.fr/20190916/france -will-lay-out-43-million-to-build-and-improve-cycle-lanes.

17. Elliot Fishman, Paul Schepers, and Carlijn Barbara Maria Kamphuis, "Dutch Cycling: Quantifying the Health and Related Economic Benefits," *American Journal of Public Health* 8 (August 2015): e13–e15. doi:10.2105/AJPH.2015.302724.

18. From C40 Cities Climate Leadership Group, Climate Hub, updated August 2021, which adds: "When the Mayor of Sevilla polled residents in 2006 on whether cycling infrastructure would benefit the city, 90% of respondents agreed. Sevilla then built an 80km network of segregated bicycle lanes in just 18 months, mostly by repurposing 5,000 on-street parking spaces. Crucially, this was done within a single mayoral political term. The cycle network was immediately popular. The number of trips taken by bike per day increased by over eleven times in just a few years. The city is now one of the best in Europe for cycling." https:// www.c40knowledgehub.org/s/article/How-to-achieve-a-walking-and-cycling -transformation-in-your-city?language=en_US.

19. Sebastian Kraus and Nicolas Koch, "Provisional COVID-19 Infrastructure Induces Large, Rapid Increases in Cycling," *Proceedings of the National Academy of Sciences* (March 29, 2021): 118(15)e2024399118, https://doi.org/10.1073/pnas.2024399118.

20. Hannah Thompson, "France in Top 5 for Cycling in the World, Google Maps Data Shows," *Connexion* (June 4, 2021), https://www.connexionfrance.com/French -news/France-in-top-5-for-cycling-in-the-world-Google-Maps-data-shows-for -World-Bike-Day.

21. "Mobility and Transport," European Commission, https://transport.ec .europa.eu/index_en.

22. Sigrid Ehrmann, "Here Come the Superblocks," La Pinya Barcelona (September 29, 2018), https://lapinyabarcelona.com/blog-archive/superblocks.

23. Feargus O'Sullivan, "Barcelona Will Supersize Its Car-Free 'Superblocks,'" *Bloomberg* (November 11, 2020), https://www.bloomberg.com/news/articles/2020 -11-11/barcelona-s-new-car-free-superblock-will-be-big.

24. Jennifer S. Mindell and Saffron Karlsen, "Community Severance and Health: What Do We Actually Know?," *Journal of Urban Health* 89(2) (April 2012): 232–46, doi:10.1007/s11524-011-9637-7.

25. "The Benefits of Having Extended Family Nearby," ReGain (March 3, 2022), https://www.regain.us/advice/family/the-benefits-of-having-extended-family -nearby/.

26. "Pandemic Spreads Volunteering, Study Shows," *Nonprofit Times* (August 31, 2020), https://www.thenonprofittimes.com/hr/Pandemic-spreads-volunteering -study-shows/.

27. James Arentson and Stephen Klimek, "The 21st Century Barn Raising: Case Studies on Community Building from Urban & Rural Minnesota," *Enterprise* (January 31, 2018), https://www.enterprisecommunity.org/blog/21st-century-barn -raising-case-studies-community-building-urban-rural-minnesota.

28. Robert D. Putnam, *Bowling Alone: The Collapse and Revival of American Community* (New York: Simon and Schuster, 2000).

29. David Davenport Hanna Skandera, "Civic Associations," in Peter Berkowitz, ed., *Never a Matter of Indifference: Sustaining Virtue in a Free Republic* (Stanford, CA: Hoover Institution Press, 2003).

30. Niranjan J. Nampoothiri and Filippo Artuso, "Civil Society's Response to Coronavirus Disease 2019: Patterns from Two Hundred Case Studies of Emergent Agency," *Journal of Creative Communications* (May 17, 2021), https://doi.org/10.1177/09732586211015057.

31. Birgit Tremml-Werner, Lisa Hellman, and Guido van Meersbergen, "Introduction. Gift and Tribute in Early Modern Diplomacy: Afro-Eurasian Perspectives," in *Diplomatica* (December 21, 2020), https://brill.com/view/journals/dipl/2/2/article-p185_185.xml.

32. Menno van Dijk et al "Building a Community," *Thnk.org*, https://www.thnk.org/insights/building-a-community/

33. Sarah Ford, "The Business Case for Employee Volunteer & Skills Giving Programs," America's Charities (February 16, 2021), https://www.charities.org/news/business-case-employee-volunteer-skills-giving-programs.

34. Tulsa Remote, https://tulsaremote.com/.

35. Rachel Pelta, "Incentivizing Remote Workers: 4 States Luring Telecommuters," *FlexJobs* (n.d.), https://www.flexjobs.com/blog/post/economic-development-programs-remote-workers/.

36. Taylor Soper and Monica Nickelsburg, "Amazon Tops 75,000 Employees in Seattle Area as Company Looks Elsewhere in Region for Growth," *Geek Wire* (January 6, 2021), https://www.geekwire.com/2021/amazon-tops-75000-employees-seattle-area-company-looks-elsewhere-region-growth; "The Multiplier Effect of Innovation Jobs," *Sloan Management Review* (June 6, 2012), https://sloanreview.mit.edu/article/the-multiplier-effect-of-innovation-jobs/.

37. Federal Reserve Bank of St. Louis, "All-Transactions House Price Index for Seattle-Bellevue-Kent, WA (MSAD)," https://fred.stlouisfed.org/series/ATNHPIUS42644Q; https://fred.stlouisfed.org/series/ASPUS.

38. Phone interview with Aaron Bolzle, founding executive director of Tulsa Remote, by Dominic Endicott (October 2022).

39. See this recent article on fears of gentrification in Kingston, NY: John Camera, "Citing 'Gentrification,' Kingston Duo Call for a Business Boycott," *Spectrum News* 1 (June 16, 2021), https://spectrumlocalnews.com/nys/hudson-valley/news/2021/06/17/gentrification-concerns-lead-to-boycott-of-business-in-kingston.

40. Jacob Passy, "An Inflation Storm Is Coming for the U.S. Housing Market," *Market Watch* (July 13, 2021), https://www.marketwatch.com/story/an-inflation-storm-is-coming-for-the-u-s-housing-market-11623419869.

41. World Economic Forum, "The Future of Jobs Report 2020" (October 2020), http://www3.weforum.org/docs/WEF_Future_of_Jobs_2020.pdf; Richard Dobbs, Anu Madgavkar, Dominic Barton, Eric Labaye, James Manyika, Charles Roxburgh, Susan Lund, and Siddarth Madhav, "The World at Work: Jobs, Pay, and Skills for 3.5 Billion People," McKinsey Global Institute (June 1, 2012), https://www.mckinsey.com/featured-insights/employment-and-growth/the-world-at-work; Malvina Vega, "19 Statistics about Jobs Lost to Automation and the Future of Employment in

2022," Tech Jury (February 6, 2022), https://techjury.net/blog/jobs-lost-to
-automation-statistics.

42. Anna Mleczko, "How Many Developers Are There in the World in 2022?,"
Future Processing (January 4, 2022), https://www.future-processing.com/blog
/how-many-developers-are-there-in-the-world-in-2019.

43. Sébastien Ricard, "The Year of the Knowledge Worker" *Forbes* (December 10,
2020), https://www.forbes.com/sites/forbestechcouncil/2020/12/10/the-year-of
-the-knowledge-worker.

44. Françoise Carré, Chris Tilly, Chris Benner, and Sarah Mason, "Change and
Uncertainty, Not Apocalypse: Technological Change and Store-Based Retail," UC
Berkeley Center for Labor Research and Education and Working Partnerships USA
(September 2020), https://laborcenter.berkeley.edu/wp-content/uploads/2020/09
/Change-and-Uncertainty-Not-Apocalypse_final.pdf.

45. Harman Singh, "The Future of the Retail Workforce" (July 20, 2020),
Capgemini, https://www.capgemini.com/insights/expert-perspectives/the-future
-of-the-retail-workforce/.

46. "Etsy Statistics, User Counts, Facts and News (2022)," DMR (Digital
Marketing Ramblings) (March 27, 2020), https://expandedramblings.com/index
.php/etsy-statistics/.

47. Holon IQ, "10 charts to Explain the Global Education Technology Market"
(January 25, 2021), https://www.holoniq.com/edtech/10-charts-that-explain-the
-global-education-technology-market.

48. Markus Overdiek, "Worldwide School Closures Could Cause Large Economic Losses," Bertelsmann Stiftung (September 29, 2020), https://ged-project.de
/digitization-and-innovation/worldwide-school-closures-could-cause-large
-economic-losses/.

49. Lynda Gratton and Andrew J. Scott, *The 100-Year Life: Living and Working in
an Age of Longevity* (London: Bloomsbury Information, 2016).

50. Lasell Village, "Live Where Lifelong Learning Means Something Different,"
https://lasellvillage.com/.

51. Staley, *Alternative Universities*, 43–57.

52. Glassdoor Team, "15 More Companies That No Longer Require a Degree—
Apply Now," Glassdoor (November 8, 2021), https://www.glassdoor.com/blog/no
-degree-required/.

53. Casey Eggleston and Jason Fields, "Census Bureau's Household Pulse Survey
Shows Significant Increase in Homeschooling Rates in Fall 2020," US Census
Bureau (March 22, 2021), https://www.census.gov/library/stories/2021/03
/homeschooling-on-the-rise-during-covid-19-pandemic.html.

54. "Biochar Is a Valuable Soil Amendment," International Biochar Initiative
(n.d.), https://biochar-international.org/biochar/.

55. Biochar is a black carbon produced from biomass sources, per the USDA
(https://www.ars.usda.gov/midwest-area/stpaul/swmr/people/kurt-spokas/biochar).

56. Federal Reserve Bank of St. Louis, Economic Data, https://fred.stlouisfed
.org; Michael Hendrix, "Boulder's Challenge: The Colorado City's Future Depends

on Whether Newcomers Can Afford to Live There," *City Journal* (Winter 2021), https://www.city-journal.org/boulder-colorado-affordable-living.

57. Brad Feld, *Startup Communities: Building an Entrepreneurial Ecosystem in Your City* (Hoboken, NJ: John Wiley and Sons, 2012).

58. Feld, page 25

59. Alisa Cohn, "Brad Feld on Startup Communities, the View from 2040, and His One Piece of Advice for You," *Forbes* (October 9, 2020), https://www.forbes.com/sites/alisacohn/2020/10/09/brad-feld-on-startup-communities-the-view-from-2040-and-his-one-piece-of-advice-for-you.

60. Iain McGilchrist, *The Master and His Emissary: The Divided Brain and the Making of the Western World* (New Haven, CT: Yale University Press, 2009).

61. John Hepp, "London as an Urban Model since 1666," in Phillip Drummond, ed., *The London Reader 1: Papers from the First Annual London Studies Conference* (London Symposium: London, UK, 2011); Adam Forrest, "How London Might Have Looked: Five Masterplans after the Great Fire of 1666," *The Guardian* (January 25, 2016), https://www.theguardian.com/cities/2016/jan/25/how-london-might-have-looked-five-masterplans-after-great-fire-1666.

62. Louise Miner and Jeremy Wilks, "Rising Sea Levels—How the Netherlands Found Ways of Working with the Environment," *Euronews* (February 25, 2020), https://www.euronews.com/green/2019/10/14/rising-sea-levels-how-the-netherlands-found-ways-of-working-with-the-environment.

63. "Occupational Licensing: A Framework for Policymakers," Department of the Treasury Office of Economic Policy, Council of Economic Advisers, and Department of Labor (July 2015), https://obamawhitehouse.archives.gov/sites/default/files/docs/licensing_report_final_nonembargo.pdf; Ben Adler, "Starving the Cities to Feed the Suburbs," *Grist* (January 9, 2013), https://grist.org/cities/starving-the-cities-to-feed-the-suburbs/.

64. Peter Weber, "The Rise and Fall of Detroit: A Timeline," *Week* (January 8, 2015), https://theweek.com/articles/461968/rise-fall-detroit-timeline.

65. Christine MacDonald, "Detroit Population Rank Is Lowest since 1850," *Detroit News* (May 19, 2016), https://www.detroitnews.com/story/news/local/detroit-city/2016/05/19/detroit-population-rank-lowest-since/84574198/.

66. J. C. Reindl, "5 Years Out of Bankruptcy, Can Detroit Avoid Another One?," *Detroit Free Press* (December 9, 2019), https://www.freep.com/story/money/business/2019/12/09/detroit-bankruptcy-anniversary/2586744001/.

67. Thomas Sugrue, *The Origins of the Urban Crisis: Race and Inequality in Postwar Detroit* (Princeton, NJ: Princeton University Press, 1996).

68. Angie Schmitt, "How Sprawl Got Detroit into This Mess," *Streetsblog USA* (July 22, 2013), https://usa.streetsblog.org/2013/07/22/how-sprawl-got-detroit-into-this-mess/.

69. Richard Feloni, "Billionaire Dan Gilbert Has Already Bet $5.6 billion on Detroit's Future, but Money Can't Solve His Biggest Challenge," *Business Insider* (August 18, 2018), https://www.businessinsider.com/quicken-loans-dan-gilbert-detroit-2018-8.

70. Scott A. Brave, Ross Cole, and Paul Traub, "Measuring Detroit's Economic Progress with the DEAI," *Chicago Fed Letter* 434 (March 2020), https://www.chicagofed.org/publications/chicago-fed-letter/2020/434.

71. Deborah L. Wince-Smith, "How Pittsburgh Shed Its Rust Belt Image," *World Economic Forum* (August 15, 2014), https://www.weforum.org/agenda/2014/08/pittsburgh-rust-steel-city/.

72. James Fallows and Deborah Fallows, *Our Towns: A 100,000-Mile Journey into the Heart of America* (New York: Pantheon, 2018).

73. John Kania and Mark Kramer, "Collective Impact," *Stanford Social Innovation Review* (Winter 2011), https://ssir.org/articles/entry/collective_impact.

74. Paul Gompers and Silpa Kovvali, "The Other Diversity Dividend," *Harvard Business Review* (July–August 2018), https://hbr.org/2018/07/the-other-diversity-dividend.

75. "Amazon's Two Pizza Rule: One Simple Rule for Maximizing Meeting Effectiveness," *Directorpoint* (n.d.), https://landing.directorpoint.com/blog/amazon-two-pizza-rule.

76. Marilyn Lewis, "Love That Home's View? See How Much More You'll Pay," *Nerd Wallet* (April 4, 2018), https://www.nerdwallet.com/article/mortgages/how-much-does-a-view-affect-a-homes-value.

77. "Natural Capital Accounts for Public Green Space in London," *Vivid Economics* (October 2017), https://www.london.gov.uk/sites/default/files/11015viv_natural_capital_account_for_london_v7_full_vis.pdf.

78. "Iowa Soils," *Iowa Pathways* (n.d.), https://www.iowapbs.org/iowapathways/mypath/2576/iowa-soils

79. Evan A. Thaler, Isaac J. Larsen, and Qian Yu, "The Extent of Soil Loss across the US Corn Belt," *Proceedings of the National Academy of Sciences* 118(8) (February 15, 2021), https://doi.org/10.1073/pnas.1922375118.

80. "What Is Regenerative Agriculture?," Regeneration International (February 16, 2017), https://regenerationinternational.org/wp-content/uploads/2017/02/Regen-Ag-Definition-2.23.17-1.pdf.

81. Claire E. LaCanne and Jonathan G. Lundgren, "Regenerative Agriculture: Merging Farming and Natural Resource Conservation Profitably," *PeerJ—The Journal of Life and Environment* (February 26, 2018), https://peerj.com/articles/4428/.

82. Victor Feldman, "Enrich the Soil, Cool the Planet," *Berkshire Edge* (September 2, 2019), https://theberkshireedge.com/enrich-the-soil-cool-the-planet/.

83. Gabe Brown, *Dirt to Soil: One Family's Journey into Regenerative Agriculture* (White River Junction, VT: Chelsea Green, 2018).

84. "How to Get Here," American Prairie, https://www.americanprairie.org/how-to-get-here.

85. Nate Berg, "Charlotte May Have Cracked the Code on Affordable Housing. Here's How," *Fast Company* (January 25, 2021), https://www.fastcompany.com/90597128/charlotte-may-have-cracked-the-code-on-affordable-housing-heres-how; https://www.iconbuild.com/.

86. Joseph Gyourko and Jacob Krimmel, "The Impact of Local Residential Land Use Restrictions on Land Values across and within Single Family Housing Mar-

kets," National Bureau of Economic Research, Working Paper 28993 (July 2021), https://www.nber.org/papers/w28993.

87. Daniel Herriges, "Will 2021 Be the Year Zoning Reform Reaches Critical Mass?," *Strong Towns* (March 4, 2021), https://www.strongtowns.org/journal/2021 /3/4/will-2021-be-the-year-zoning-reform-reaches-critical-mass.

88. David Brooks, "Amtrak Wish List Includes Passenger Rail to Concord," *Concord Monitor* (April 1, 2021), https://www.concordmonitor.com/amtrak-concord -nh-39776679.

89. New Hampshire House Bill 341 *(Prior Session Legislation)*, Legiscan, https:// legiscan.com/NH/bill/HB341/2021.

90. Congress for the New Urbanism, https://www.cnu.org/.

91. Fred Kent, Kathy Madden, and Steve Davies, "Build Back Better, Together: 11 Transformative Agendas to Restore Social Life in Your Community," Social Life Project (June 21, 2021), https://www.sociallifeproject.org/11-ways-to-reinvigorate -towns-cities-everywhere/.

92. David Sims, "Soft City: Building Density for Everyday Life" (Washington: Island, 2019).

93. Mike Maciag, "Population Density for U.S. Cities Statistics," *Governing* (October 1, 2013), https://www.governing.com/archive/population-density-land -area-cities-map.html.

94. "How to Build Back Better with a 15-Minute City," *c40 Knowledge* (July 2020), https://www.c40knowledgehub.org/s/article/How-to-build-back-better-with-a-15 -minute-city.

95. Matthew J. Moury, "People Move to N.H. in Pandemic," *Concord Monitor* (March 29, 2021), https://www.concordmonitor.com/Pandemic-has-people -moving-to-New-Hampshire-39697738.

96. Michael Mortensen, "Cash Is King as New Hampshire's Real Estate Market Keeps Soaring," *NH Business Review* (May 5, 2021), https://www.nhbr.com/cash-is -king-as-new-hampshires-real-estate-market-keeps-soaring/; Kyle York, "Manchester, New Hampshire: So Hot Right Now," York IE (April 22, 2021), https://york.ie/blog/manchester-new-hampshire-so-hot-right-now/.

Chapter 2. The Knowledge Enterprise as an Alternative University

1. Costas Spirou, *Anchoring Innovation Districts: The Entrepreneurial University and Urban Change* (Baltimore: Johns Hopkins University Press, 2021), 17.

2. Judith Rodin, *The University and Urban Revival: Out of the Ivory Tower and into the Streets* (Philadelphia: University of Pennsylvania Press, 2007), 44.

3. Spirou, *Anchoring Innovation Districts*, 17–18.

4. James Martin, James E. Samels, and Associates, *The New American College Town: Designing Effective Campus and Community Partnerships* (Baltimore: Johns Hopkins University Press, 2019), 10–21.

5. Lisa Prevost, "Colleges Invest So 'What's the Town Like?' Gets an Upbeat Answer," *New York Times* (February 25, 2020), https://www.nytimes.com/2020/02 /25/business/colleges-downtowns-investment.html.

6. Spirou, *Anchoring Innovation Districts*, 18.

7. Richard Florida, *Cities and the Creative Class* (New York: Routledge, 2005), 152–53.

8. Michael M. Crow and William B. Dabars, *The Fifth Wave: The Evolution of American Higher Education* (Baltimore: Johns Hopkins University Press, 2020), 29.

9. Roberto Mangabeira Unger, *The Knowledge Economy* (London: Verso, 2019), 10.

10. Ro Khanna similarly argues that the knowledge economy should be decentralized: "This book imagines how the digital economy can create opportunities for people where they live instead of uprooting them. It offers a vision for decentralizing digital innovation and wealth generation to build economically vibrant and inclusive communities that are connected to each other." See Ro Khanna, *Dignity in a Digital Age: Making Tech Work for All of Us* (New York: Simon and Schuster, 2022), 3.

11. Unger, *The Knowledge Economy*, 4.

12. Ibid., 7.

13. Ibid., 7.

14. Ibid., 16.

15. Ibid., 33.

16. Ibid., 35.

17. See Staley, "Institute for Advanced Play," in *Alternative Universities*, 161–75.

18. Unger, *The Knowledge Economy*, 267.

19. Ibid., 36–37.

20. Ibid., 85.

21. Ibid., 93–94.

22. Ibid., 94–96.

23. John Mackey and Raj Sisodia, *Conscious Capitalism: Liberating the Heroic Spirit of Business* (Boston: Harvard Business Review Press, 2013), 54.

24. Ibid., 46.

25. Ibid., 49–50.

26. Ibid., 59.

27. Seattle Central College, "Humanities," https://seattlecentral.edu/programs /college-transfer/college-transfer-programs/arts-humanities-social-sciences /humanities.

28. "The Humanities Belong to Everyone," National Endowment for the Humanities (December 11, 2013), https://www.neh.gov/divisions/fedstate/resource /the-humanities-belong-everyone#:~:text=The%20humanities%20listen%20to%20 the,the%20record%20of%20human%20activity.

29. "Defining Community Engaged Learning at MSU," Michigan State University, Center for Community Engaged Learning, https://communityengagedlearning.msu .edu/about/defining-community-engaged-learning-at-msu.

30. "Humanities Institute and Institute for Urban Policy Research and Analysis Community Fellows Program," University of Texas at Austin Humanities Institute, https://liberalarts.utexas.edu/humanitiesinstitute/other-initiatives/internal -grants/community-sabbatical-apps.php.

31. Kim Willsher, "Paris Mayor Unveils '15-Minute City' Plan in Re-Election Campaign," *The Guardian* (February 7, 2020), https://www.theguardian.com/world /2020/feb/07/paris-mayor-unveils-15-minute-city-plan-in-re-election-campaign.

32. Andrés Duany and Robert Steuteville, "Defining the 15-Minute City," *Public Square* (February 8, 2021), https://www.cnu.org/publicsquare/2021/02/08/defining-15-minute-city.

33. Dan Luscher, "Introducing the 15-Minute City Project: Putting People at the Center of Urban Transformation," *15City* (June 16, 2021), https://www.15minutecity.com/blog/hello.

34. See Staley, "Microcollege," in *Alternative Universities*, 43–57.

35. Paul Downton, "Neighborhoods and Urban Fractals—The Building Blocks of Sustainable Cities," The Nature of Cities (October 17, 2012), https://www.thenatureofcities.com/2012/10/17/neighborhoods-and-urban-fractals-the-building-blocks-of-sustainable-cities/.

36. Jamie Merisotis, *Human Work in the Age of Smart Machines* (New York: Rosetta Books, 2020), viii–ix.

37. Judith K. Hellerstein and David Neumark, "Social Capital, Networks, and Economic Wellbeing," IZA Institute of Labor Economics (June 2020), https://docs.iza.org/dp13413.pdf.

38. Stuart M. Butler and Carmen Diaz, "'Third Places' as Community Builders," Brookings Institution (September 14, 2016), https://www.brookings.edu/blog/up-front/2016/09/14/third-places-as-community-builders/.

39. Nancy Cantor, "Academic Excellence and Civic Engagement: Constructing a Third Space for Higher Education" (2010), Office of the Chancellor, Syracuse University (2004-13), 3, https://surface.syr.edu/cgi/viewcontent.cgi?article=1001&context=chancellor.

40. Keith Smyth, "The University as a Third Space?," Ragged University (July 8, 2014), https://www.raggeduniversity.co.uk/2014/08/07/university-space-keith-smyth/.

41. KerryAnn O'Meara, "Meeting to Transgress," *Inside Higher Ed* (January 24, 2019), https://www.insidehighered.com/advice/2019/01/24/important-role-third-spaces-play-higher-education-opinion.

42. Sophie Benson, "The Third Space: Why Universities Need to Design for 'In-Between' Moments," iO, (May 9, 2019), https://io.education/inside-out/articles/the-third-space-why-universities-need-to-design-for-in-between-moments/.

43. Ibid.

44. Ray Fleming, "Australian Universities Need to Be Everybody's Future Third Place," LinkedIn (January 2, 2019), https://www.linkedin.com/pulse/australian-universities-need-everybodys-future-third-place-fleming/.

45. Lindsay Ellis, "The Rise of Remote Work May Reshape College Towns. Here's How These Campuses Are Wooing Transplants," *Chronicle of Higher Education* (June 1, 2021), https://www.chronicle.com/article/the-rise-of-remote-work-may-reshape-college-towns-heres-how-these-campuses-are-wooing-transplants.

46. Daniel F. Chambliss and Christopher G. Takacs, *How College Works* (Cambridge, MA: Harvard University Press, 2014), 5.

47. Ibid., 5.

48. Ibid., 53

49. Ibid., 54.

50. Ibid., 58.

51. See also Peter Felten and Leo M. Lambert, *Relationship-Rich Education: How Human Connections Drive Success in College* (Baltimore: Johns Hopkins University Press, 2020).

52. See Staley, *Alternative Universities*, 121–39.

53. Minouche Shafik, *What We Owe Each Other: A New Social Contract for a Better Society* (Princeton, NJ: Princeton University Press, 2021), 24.

54. Laurent Probst and Christian Scharff, "A Strategist's Guide to Upskilling," *strategy + business* (Autumn 2019), 96, https://www.strategy-business.com/feature /A-strategists-guide-to-upskilling?gko=obb8b.

55. Staley, *Alternative Universities*, 115–117.

56. Lasell Village: Senior Living at Lasell University, "Lifelong Learning," https://lasellvillage.com/lifestyle/.

57. See Alex Sayf Cummings, *Brain Magnet: Research Triangle Park and the Idea of the Idea Economy* (New York: Columbia University Press, 2020).

58. See Paul Basken, "US College's Student Inventors Gaining National Attention," *Times Higher Ed* (May 7, 2021), https://www.timeshighereducation.com/news /us-colleges-student-inventors-gaining-national-attention.

59. Barton Kunstler, *The Hothouse Effect* (New York: AMACON, 2004), 1.

60. Ibid., 7.

61. Charles Landry, *The Creative City: A Toolkit for Urban Innovators*, 2nd ed. (New York: Routledge, 2008), 133.

62. Ibid., 133.

63. David Edwards, *Artscience: Creativity in the Post-Google Generation* (Cambridge, MA: Harvard University Press, 2010), 8.

64. Ibid., 17.

65. David Edwards, *The Lab: Creativity and Culture* (Cambridge, MA: Harvard University Press, 2010), 8.

66. Ibid., 75.

67. Spirou, *Anchoring Innovation Districts*, 34.

68. James J. Farrell, *The Nature of College: How a New Understanding of Campus Life Can Change the World* (Minneapolis: Milkweed Editions, 2010), 251.

69. Ibid., xiii.

70. Ibid., xii.

71. Ibid., xii–xiii.

72. Ibid., 70, 69.

73. Ibid., 4–5.

74. David Orr, *Earth in Mind: On Education, Environment, and the Human Prospect* (Washington, DC: Island, 2004), 111.

75. Arnault Morisson, "A Typology of Places in the Knowledge Economy: Towards the Fourth Place," in Francesco Calabrò, Lucia Della Spina, and Carmelina Bevilacqua (eds.), *New Metropolitan Perspectives: Local Knowledge and Innovation Dynamics Towards Territory Attractiveness Through the Implementation of Horizon/ E2020/Agenda2030* 1 100:444–51 (Switzerland: Springer, 2019).

76. Ibid., 2–3.

77. Ibid., 4.

78. Hacker House, "Le Monde est ton nouveau lieu de travail," https://hackerhouse.world/.

79. Lassonde Entrepreneur Institue, https://lassonde.utah.edu/.

80. "Co-living means living with many other people in one space that encourages its residents to interact and work together. These spaces have popped up in response to the huge number of young people moving to expensive cities in search of work. Overall, co-living is a new kind of modern housing arrangement where residents with shared interests, intentions, and values share a living space where they're almost like a big family." See Bernhard Mehl, "The Rising Trend of Co-Living Spaces," Coworking Resources (March 28, 2021), https://www.coworkingresources .org/blog/coliving-spaces.

81. Morisson, "A Typology of Places," 5.

82. Ibid., 5.

83. Ibid., 5. See also Station F, "World's Largest Startup Campus in Paris," https://stationf.co/.

84. Morisson, "A Typology of Places," 5.

85. Ibid., 6.

86. Tanja Herdt, *The City and the Architecture of Change: The Work and Radical Visions of Cedric Price* (Switzerland: Park Books, 2017), 67.

87. Samantha Hardingham and Kester Rattenbury, *Supercrit #1: Cedric Price, Potteries Thinkbelt* (Oxford: Routledge, 2007), 17.

88. Ibid., 37.

89. Ibid., 17.

90. Ibid., 37.

91. Ibid., 20.

92. Ibid., 18.

93. Davarian L. Baldwin, *In the Shadow of the Ivory Tower: How Universities are Plundering Our Cities* (New York: Bold Type Books, 2021), 14.

94. Ibid., 36.

95. Ibid., 37.

96. David J. Staley, "The University as Public Utility," Ingenious blog (February 15, 2022), https://ingeniousu.org/2022/02/15/the-university-as-public-utility -by-david-j-staley/.

Chapter 3. Archetypes of a Talent Magnet/Knowledge Enterprise Strategy

1. Foundation for Intentional Community, https://www.ic.org/directory/.

2. "Number of Cities, Towns and Villages (Incorporated Places) in the United States in 2019, by Population Size," Statista, https://www.statista.com/statistics /241695/number-of-us-cities-towns-villages-by-population-size/.

3. *Federal Register*, "Census Designated Places (CDPs) for the 2020 Census-Final Criteria" (November 13, 2018), https://www.federalregister.gov/documents/2018/11 /13/2018-24571/census-designated-places-cdps-for-the-2020-census-final-criteria.

4. https://www2.census.gov/geo/pdfs/reference/GARM/Ch9GARM.pdf.

5. Calculation is 19,000 incorporated places + 4,000 unincorporated places + 13,000 "rural places" neither incorporated nor designated as CDPs = 36,000 unique places.

6. Database Company Simple maps offers information on up to 108,000 cities and towns: https://simplemaps.com/data/us-cities.

7. Elise Gould and Heidi Shierholz, "Not Everybody Can Work from Home: Black and Hispanic Workers Are Much Less Likely to Be Able to Telework," Economic Policy Institute (March 2020), https://www.epi.org/blog/black-and -hispanic-workers-are-much-less-likely-to-be-able-to-work-from-home/.

8. This implies $100K in household income per annum and $500K in household assets.

9. "National Highlight—Comparing Natural Lakes and Manmade Reservoirs," Environmental Protection Agency (EPA), https://www.epa.gov/national-aquatic -resource-surveys/national-highlight-comparing-natural-lakes-and-manmade -reservoirs.

10. David Sim, *Soft City: Building Density for Everyday Life* (Washington, DC: Island, August, 2019).

11. Based on buying 4,160 acres at an average price of $20K/acre (above US average of $3K per acre to factor lakefront premium—we assume 95% of land not on lakefront and costs $10K/acre and 5% is on lakefront, at $336K/acre).

12. This assumes a mix of infill, low-rise and single-family, with an average cost/unit of $200K https://www.fixr.com/costs/build-apartment#apartment -construction-costs-per-unit.

13. "CMS Issues New Roadmap for States to Address the Social Determinants of Health to Improve Outcomes, Lower Costs, Support State Value-Based Care Strategies," Centers for Medicare and Medicaid Services, https://www.cms.gov /newsroom/press-releases/cms-issues-new-roadmap-states-address-social -determinants-health-improve-outcomes-lower-costs.

14. Asher Lehrer-Small, "With DeVos Out, Movement for Private School Choice Shifts to State Legislatures," The 74 (January 27, 2021), https://www.the74million .org/article/with-devos-out-movement-for-private-school-choice-shifts-to-state -legislatures/.

15. Brian Ray, "Home Schooling: The Research," National Home Education Research Institute (September 9, 2021), https://www.nheri.org/research-facts-on -homeschooling/.

16. Jake Bryant, Emma Dorn, and Stephen Hall, "Reimagining a More Equitable and Resilient K-12 Education System," McKinsey and Company (September 8, 2020), https://www.mckinsey.com/industries/public-and-social-sector/our -insights/reimagining-a-more-equitable-and-resilient-k-12-education-system.

17. "What Is Montessori Education?," Montessori Northwest, https://montessori -nw.org/about-montessori-education.

18. The US ratio of college students to the total population is 20 million: 330 million, or 6%, which we apply to the "Laketown" population.

19. "Best Global Universities for Environment/Ecology in Switzerland," *US News and World Report*, https://www.usnews.com/education/best-global-universities /switzerland/environment-ecology.

20. "Zurich Population 2022," World Population Review, https://worldpopulation review.com/world-cities/zurich-population.

21. Michael Hengartner, "That Is Why Our Water Is So Clean," *Swiss Science Today* (November 2020), https://www.sciena.ch/research/That-s-why-our-water -is-so-clean.html.

22. "Climate Protection: Federal Council Adopts Switzerland's Long-Term Climate Strategy," Federal Council, Bern (January 28, 2021), https://www.admin.ch /gov/en/start/documentation/media-releases.msg-id-82140.html.

23. "3D Maps & Peaks Identification," PeakVisor, https://peakvisor.com; https://oceanservice.noaa.gov/facts/shorelength.html;NPM Online, "How Many Marinas Are There in the USA?," https://npmonline.com/how-many-marinas-in -usa/; Enchanted Learning, https://www.enchantedlearning.com/usa/rivers/.

24. Lauren Steele, "The Water That Couldn't Save," *Deseret News* (April 7, 2021), https://www.deseret.com/utah/2021/4/7/22370024/the-water-that-couldnt-save -great-salt-lake-utah-water-conservation-drought-crisis-california.

25. Deborah Perrone, "Water Wells Are at Risk of Going Dry in the US and Worldwide," *The Conversation* (May 10, 2021), https://theconversation.com/water -wells-are-at-risk-of-going-dry-in-the-us-and-worldwide-160147; World Bank, "Water in Agriculture," (November 2020), https://www.worldbank.org/en/topic /water-in-agriculture.

26. "Saline Agriculture: The Practical," Saline Agriculture Worldwide, https:// www.salineagricultureworldwide.com/saline-agriculture.

27. Katarzyna Negacz, Pier Vellinga, Edward Barrett-Lennard, Redouane Choukr-Allah, and Theo Elzenga, eds., *Future of Sustainable Agriculture in Saline Environments* (New York: CRC, 2022), https://library.oapen.org/handle/20.500.12657/48840.

28. Black Mountain College Museum and Arts Center, https://www .blackmountaincollege.org/history/.

29. "Black Mountain, North Carolina Population 2022," World Population Review, https://worldpopulationreview.com/us-cities/black-mountain-nc-population.

30. "Research Resources," Black Mountain College Museum and Arts Center, https://www.blackmountaincollege.org/resources/.

31. Christie Kafka, "Asheville Attracts Interest as an Enviable 'Zoom Town' Option," Mosaic Realty (October 28, 2020), https://mymosaicrealty.com/blog/posts /2020/10/28/asheville-attracts-interest-as-an-enviable-zoom-town-option/; "Asheville, NC Real Estate Market," realtor.com, https://www.realtor.com /realestateandhomes-search/Asheville_NC/overview; "Black Mountain, NC Real Estate Market," https://www.realtor.com/realestateandhomes-search/Black -Mountain_NC/overview.

32. "North Carolina: State of the Environment," North Carolina Conservation Network (2019), https://www.ncconservationnetwork.org/our-work/state-of-the -environment/.

33. "Best Global Universities for Environment/Ecology," *US News and World Report*, https://www.usnews.com/education/best-global-universities/environment -ecology.

34. Anne Wallace Allen, "Months of Covid-19 Could Undo Decades of Population Decline," *VT Digger* (August 9, 2020), https://vtdigger.org/2020/08/09/months-of -covid-19-could-undo-decades-of-population-decline/.

35. Vermont was a pioneer in "talent-attraction" strategies, funding a subsidy of up to $10K per person for people moving into the state, beginning in 2019. However, the program's value was challenged by the state auditor, and it only funded 140 workers in its first year. See Katie Jickling, "Lawmakers Vote to Extend Program to Reimburse Workers Who Move to Vermont," *VT Digger* (May 21, 2021), https://vtdigger.org/2021/05/21/lawmakers-vote-to-extend-program-to -reimburse-workers-who-move-to-vermont/.

36. Olivia Lyons, "Green Mountain College Sells at Auction Far below Asking Price," WCAX (August 18, 2020), https://www.wcax.com/2020/08/18/green -mountain-college-sells-at-auction-far-below-asking-price/.

37. "Remote Technical Writers: The Remote Zoom Town Boom," Essential Data Corporation, https://essentialdata.com/boom-of-the-remote-zoom-town/.

38. "Real Gross Domestic Product (GDP) of the Federal State of Vermont from 2000 to 2020," Statista, https://www.statista.com/statistics/188140/gdp-of-the-us -federal-state-of-vermont-since-1997.

39. Daniel Imhoff, "Make the Corn Belt a Carbon Belt," *Progressive* (December 10, 2020), https://progressive.org/op-eds/make-corn-belt-carbon-belt-imhoff-201210/.

40. "Resident Population in the Mid-West Census Region," Federal Reserve Economic Data, https://fred.stlouisfed.org/series/CMWRPOP; Shuai Zhang Feng, Michael Oppenheimer, and Wolfram Schlenker, "Weather Anomalies, Crop Yields, and Migration in the US Corn Belt," working paper, Columbia University (March 2015), http://www.columbia.edu/~ws2162/articles /FengOppenheimerSchlenker.pdf.

41. Evan A. Thaler, Isaac J. Larsen, and Qian Yu, "The Extent of Soil Loss across the US Corn Belt," *Proceedings of the National Academy of Sciences* 118(8) (February 15, 2021), https://www.pnas.org/doi/10.1073/pnas.1922375118.

42. "U.S. Farm Profit Projections Remain Mixed through 2030," *Hoosier Ag Today* (May 17, 2021), https://hoosieragtoday.com/u-s-farm-profit-projections-remain -mixed-through-2030/.

43. "Future of Food: Responsible Production," Deloitte (2020), https://www2 .deloitte.com/ch/en/pages/consumer-business/articles/future-of-food-responsible -production.html.

44. Lutz Goedde, Joshua Katz, Alexandre Ménard, and Julien Revellat, "Agriculture's Connected Future: How Technology Can Yield New Growth," McKinsey and Company (October 9, 2020), https://www.mckinsey.com/industries/agriculture/our -insights/agricultures-connected-future-how-technology-can-yield-new-growth.

45. "Growing Our Future: Scaling Regenerative Agriculture in the United States," Forum for the Future, 2020 https://www.forumforthefuture.org/scaling -regenerative-agriculture-in-the-us.

46. "Mississippi River Economic Impact Exceeds $400B, Twice as Much as Expected," *Agrimarketing* (September, 17, 201): 5, https://www.agrimarketing.com /ss.php?id=98737.

47. Peter Zeihan, *The Accidental Superpower: The Next Generation of American Preeminence and the Coming Global Disorder* (New York: Twelve, 2014).

48. Clayton M. Christensen and Michael B. Horn, "Perilous Times," *Inside Higher Ed* (April 1, 2019), https://www.insidehighered.com/views/2019/04/01 /many-private-colleges-remain-danger-opinion.

49. "The 2020 Mississippi River Watershed Report Card," America's Watershed Initiative, https://americaswatershed.org/reportcard/.

50. "Drinking Water Source Protection Plan for the City of Defiance" (April 2020), https://cityofdefiance.com/wp-content/uploads/SourceWater _ENDORSED_20.06.26.pdf.

51. Gary Wilson, "Overlooked: Small Streams Can Have a Big Impact on Great Lakes Water Quality," *Great Lakes Now* (November 4, 2020), https://www .greatlakesnow.org/2020/11/small-streams-impact-great-lakes-water-quality/.

52. "Defiance, OH Real Estate Market," realtor.com, https://www.realtor.com /realestateandhomes-search/Defiance_OH/overview; "Defiance, Ohio," Data USA, https://datausa.io/profile/geo/defiance-oh; "Defiance College," *US News and World Report*, https://www.usnews.com/best-colleges/defiance-college-3041.

53. Robert L. Fried and Eli O. Kramer, "Privileged Enclave or Village Commons? A Choice for Liberal Arts Colleges," *Inside Higher Ed* (January 21, 2021), https:// www.insidehighered.com/views/2021/01/21/struggling-liberal-arts-colleges -should-look-their-backyards-ensure-their-future.

54. See David J. Staley, "The Idea of the University as Incubator," *World Futures Review* 12(4) (2020): 363–68.

55. Phone interview with Aaron Bolzle, founding executive director of Tulsa Remote, by Dominic Endicott (September 2020).

56. James Martin, James E. Samels, and Associates, *The New American College Town: Designing Effective Campus and Community Partnerships* (Baltimore: Johns Hopkins University Press, 2019).

57. "Waterville, Maine Population 2022," World Population Review, https:// worldpopulationreview.com/us-cities/waterville-me-population.

58. Amy Calder, "Overseer of Colby Projects in Downtown Waterville Excited by All That Is Happening," centralmaine.com (February 6, 2020), https://www.central-maine.com/2020/02/06/overseer-of-colby-projects-in-downtown-waterville-updates -chamber-on-progress/.

59. "Waterville, Maine Population 2022," World Population Review, https:// worldpopulationreview.com/us-cities/waterville-me-population; "Waterville Home Values," Zillow (March 31, 2022), https://www.zillow.com/waterville-me /home-values/.

60. "Binghamton, New York Population 2022," World Population Review, https://worldpopulationreview.com/us-cities/binghamton-ny-population; "Binghamton Metro (Binghamton) Home Values," Zillow, https://www.zillow.com /binghamton-ny/home-values/.

61. Renee Cordes, "Central Maine Startup Stories: A Regional Roundup of 5 New Businesses," *Mainebiz* (July 12, 2021), https://www.mainebiz.biz/article/central -maine-startup-stories-a-regional-roundup-of-5-new-businesses.

62. "Endowment per Student at Selected Colleges (2021)," Reach High Scholars, https://reachhighscholars.org/college_endowments.html.

63. "Paula Volent Honored with CEE Visionary Award," *Bowdoin News* (June 10, 2021), https://www.bowdoin.edu/news/2021/06/paula-volent-honored-with-cee -visionary-award.html.

64. "Market Capitalization of Lockheed Martin (LMT)," https://companiesmarket cap.com/lockheed-martin/marketcap/; "UnitedHealth Group Incorporated (UNH)," Yahoo! Finance, https://finance.yahoo.com/quote/UNH/; "BAE Systems PLC (BAESY)," Yahoo! Finance, https://finance.yahoo.com/quote/baesy/.

65. Tracy Hadden-Loh and Hanna Love, "The Emerging Solidarity Economy: A Primer on Community Ownership of Real Estate," Brookings Institute (July 19, 2021), https://www.brookings.edu/essay/the-emerging-solidarity-economy-a -primer-on-community-ownership-of-real-estate/.

66. Richard Rudolph, "Maine Compass: Time to Extend Rail Service to Central Maine" (March 7, 2021), centralmaine.com, https://www.centralmaine.com/2021/03 /07/maine-compass-time-to-extend-rail-service-to-central-maine/.

67. "Brunswick Home Values," Zillow, https://www.zillow.com/brunswick-me /home-values/.

68. Vargha Moayed, "The Rise of Global Tech Entrepreneurship," *Forbes* (July 12, 2021), https://www.forbes.com/sites/forbesbusinessdevelopmentcouncil/2021/07 /12/the-rise-of-global-tech-entrepreneurship.

69. Hilary Burns, "The Interview: Colby College Doubles Down on Artificial Intelligence . . . and Its Hometown," *Business Journals* (February 8, 2021), https:// www.bizjournals.com/bizjournals/news/2021/02/08/colby-college-president -david-greene-interview.html.

70. "Silicon Valley Needs a Breath of Fresh Maine Air," Colby/Davis Institute for Artificial Intelligence," https://artificial-intelligence.colby.edu/.

71. "Your Future Is Powerful," University of Minnesota Rochester, https://r .umn.edu/.

72. See Stephen Lehmkuhle, *Campus with Purpose: Building a Mission-Driven Campus* (New Brunswick, NJ: Rutgers University Press, 2021).

73. "University of Minnesota Rochester Data & Information Overview," College Factual, https://www.collegefactual.com/colleges/university-of-minnesota -rochester/.

74. Visit Red Wing, https://redwing.org/.

75. Rick Seltzer, "Available City Seeks College," *Inside Higher Ed* (May 20, 2016), https://www.insidehighered.com/news/2016/05/20/minn-town-aims-attract -campus-competition-branches-heats.

76. Riley Sullivan, "College Towns and Covid 19: The Impact on New England," Federal Reserve Bank of Boston (June 25, 2020), https://www.bostonfed.org /publications/new-england-public-policy-center-regional-briefs/2020/college -towns-and-covid-19-the-impact-on-new-england.aspx.

77. "Minerva Project Closes $57 Million in Series C Funding," *Cision PR Newswire* (July 11, 2019), https://www.prnewswire.com/news-releases/minerva-project -closes-57-million-in-series-c-funding-300883338; "Student Achievement," Minerva University, https://www.minerva.kgi.edu/undergraduate-program /academics/student-achievement/.

78. Jessica Bryant, "How Many Colleges Are in the U.S.?" Best Colleges (May 25, 2021), https://www.bestcolleges.com/blog/how-many-colleges-in-us/.

79. Martin H. Stack, "A Concise History of America's Brewing Industry," Economic History Association, https://eh.net/encyclopedia/a-concise-history-of -americas-brewing-industry/.

80. "National Beer Sales & Production Data," Brewers Association for Small & Independent Craft Brewers, https://www.brewersassociation.org/statistics-and -data/national-beer-stats/.

81. "Capital Expenditures for Molson Coors Beverage Company," https://finbox .com/NYSE:TAP/explorer/capex; 2nd Kitchen, https://2ndkitchen.com/breweries /how-to-start-a-brewery.

82. "College Accreditation, Explained," Education Next, https://www.education next.org/college-accreditation-explained-ednext-guide-how-it-works-whos -responsible/.

83. Chris Woolston, "Huge Variations in US Postdoc Salaries Point to Under-valued Workforce," *Nature* (February 18, 2019), https://www.nature.com/articles /d41586-019-00587-y.

84. "Home Sharing: 44 Million Empty Bedrooms Await," John Burns Real Estate Consulting, https://www.realestateconsulting.com/home-sharing-44-million -empty-bedrooms-await.

85. US Census Bureau, March 25, 1952, https://www.census.gov/library /publications/1952/demo/p60-009.html.

86. "New Survey of Americans Examines Enduring Preference for Nondegree, Online Education and Training Programs," Strada Education Network, https:// stradaeducation.org/press-release/new-survey-of-americans-examines-enduring -preference-for-nondegree-online-education-and-training-programs/.

87. Chris Burt, "Parents, Students Leaning to Colleges Close to Home, Study Shows," *University Business* (November 19, 2020), https://universitybusiness.com /parents-students-lean-to-colleges-close-to-home-study-shows.

88. "Campuses," Pennsylvania State University, https://www.psu.edu/academics /campuses/.

89. "Penn State Expanded Its Branch Campuses Decades Ago," *Pittsburgh Post-Gazette*, https://www.post-gazette.com/news/education/2021/08/08/Penn -State-expanded-its-branch-campuses-decades-ago-Now-some-say-that-s-one -reason-state-universities-are-struggling/stories/202108020110.

90. "About Us," Prenda, https://www.prenda.com/about; "Mesa Edtech Firm Raises $19 Million amid Reported Attorney General Inquiry," *Phoenix Business Journal* (May 19, 2021), https://www.bizjournals.com/phoenix/news/2021/05/19 /mesa-tech-firm-raises-funds-amid-investigation.html.

91. Potential interest in forming a microcollege can be seen as part of a broader context, in which millions of Americans are starting new businesses. The hunger to start a new business can be seen in niches such as microbreweries as well as in the surge of people getting into farming or starting any kind of new firm. The total number of business start-ups in the United States was 2.5 million in 2010, passed 4.5 million in 2020, and is running at a rate of 6 million as of the second quarter of 2021, indicating a rapidly growing interest in company formation. See "How Many New Businesses Start Each Year," Oberlo, https://www.oberlo.com/statistics/how -many-new-businesses-start-each-year.

92. Andy Parker and Scott D. Anthony, "Digital Disruption in Australian Higher Education: A Dual Transformation Imperative Accelerated and Amplified by COVID-19," Innosight (May 2020), https://www.innosight.com/wp-content/uploads /2020/05/Innosight_Digital-Disruption-in-Australian-Higher-Education.pdf.

93. Note that Harvard generates over $5 billion/year in revenue, including grants, research, endowment contributions, and that student income is approximately 20% of total annual revenue.

94. Susan Adams, "Meet the English Professor Creating the Billion-Dollar College of the Future," *Forbes* (March 28, 2019), https://www.forbes.com/sites /susanadams/2019/03/28/meet-the-english-professor-creating-the-billion-dollar -college-of-the-future.

95. Harvard University, Annual Financial Reports, 2019/2020 https://finance .harvard.edu/annual-report.

96. "Financial Overview," Harvard University, https://finance.harvard.edu /files/fad/files/fy20_financial_overview.pdf.

97. Microcredentials are short, competency-based recognition, per the National Education Association (NEA).

98. "SNHU Acquires Kenzie Academy to Expand Access to In-Demand Micro-credentials," Southern New Hampshire University, https://www.snhu.edu/about -us/newsroom/2021/03/kenzie-academy.

99. SNHU Communications, "Southern New Hampshire University Sets Out to Reimagine Campus-Based Learning, Offers Full Tuition Scholarships for Incoming Freshmen," Southern New Hampshire University (April 22, 2020), https://www.snhu .edu/about-us/newsroom/2020/04/full-tuition-scholarships-for-incoming -freshmen; SNHU Communications, "Southern New Hampshire University Reinvents Campus Academic and Financial Models, Transforms Cost and Delivery of Higher Education," Southern New Hampshire University (December 16, 2020), https://www .snhu.edu/about-us/newsroom/2020/12/snhu-campus-transformation; "Academics," https://www.snhu.edu/about-us/partnerships/academics.

100. Andrew J. Magda, David Capranos, and Carol B. Aslanian, *Online College Students 2020: Comprehensive Data on Demands and Preferences* (Louisville, KY: Wiley Education Services, 2020), https://edservices.wiley.com/wp-content/uploads/2020 /06/OCS2020Report-ONLINE-FINAL.pdf. (Note that multiple answers are possible, and the percentages may total more than 100%.)

101. Phil Hill, "OPM Market Landscape and Dynamics: Fall 2020 Updates," Phil On Tech (October 28, 2020), https://philonedtech.com/opm-market-landscape -and-dynamics-fall-2020-updates/.

102. "Etsy Inc.," YCharts, https://ycharts.com/companies/ETSY/market_cap; "The Creator Economy Explained: How Companies Are Transforming the Self-Monetization Boom," CB Insights (June 15, 2021), https://www.cbinsights.com /research/report/what-is-the-creator-economy/.

103. National Center for Education Statistics, "Fast Facts," https://nces.ed.gov /fastfacts/display.asp?id=75.

104. "A US Workforce Training Plan for the Postpandemic Economy," Conference Board (April 2021), https://www.ced.org/solutions-briefs/a-us-workforce -training-plan-for-the-postPandemic-economy; Aaron O'Neill, "Employment in the United States 2022," Statista (November 23, 2021), https://www.statista.com /statistics/269959/employment-in-the-united-states.

105. Richard Fry, "The Pace of Boomer Retirements Has Accelerated in the Past Year," Pew Research Center (November 9, 2020), https://www.pewresearch.org /fact-tank/2020/11/09/the-pace-of-boomer-retirements-has-accelerated-in-the -past-year/.

106. Henrietta Fore, "5 Ways to Reset Education and How to Help," World Economic Forum (October 2020), https://www.weforum.org/agenda/2020/10/5 -ways-to-reset-education-and-how-to-help.

107. "Aggregate Ranking of Top Universities, 2021," University of New South Wales, http://research.unsw.edu.au/artu/.

108. "Best Universities in Boston 2022," *Student* (November 10, 2021), https:// www.timeshighereducation.com/student/best-universities/best-universities -boston.

109. Iman Ghosh, "3D Map: The U.S. Cities with the Highest Economic Output," *Visual Capitalist* (September 22, 2020), https://www.visualcapitalist.com/3d-map -the-u-s-cities-with-the-highest-economic-output/; Andrew Dehan, "10 Most Expensive Cities in the US," Rocket Mortgage (December 14, 2021), https://www .rocketmortgage.com/learn/most-expensive-cities-in-the-us.

110. Joe Robinson, "Where Are 15 Minute Cities Most Viable in the US?," Move Buddha (December 8, 2021), https://www.movebuddha.com/blog/15-minute-cities/.

111. Trevor Wheelwright, "America's Most Expensive Cities per Square Foot," move.org (October 26, 2020), https://www.move.org/ americas-most-expensive-cities-per-square-foot/.

112. Sarah Crump, Trevor Mattos, Jenny Schuetz, and Luc Schuster, "Fixing Greater Boston's Housing Crisis Starts with Legalizing Apartments Near Transit," Brookings Institution (October 14, 2020), https://www.brookings.edu/research /fixing-greater-bostons-housing-crisis-starts-with-legalizing-apartments-near -transit/.

113. "Greater Boston Housing Report Card: Housing Equity and Resilience in Greater Boston's Post-COVID Economy," Boston Foundation, https://www.tbf.org

/news-and-insights/reports/2020/september/greater-boston-housing-report-card
-equity-and-resilience-20200923.

114. "Massachusetts 2019 Air Quality Report," Massachusetts Department of Environmental Protection (March 2020), https://www.mass.gov/doc/2019-annual -air-quality-report/download; Michelle Samuels, "Air Pollution Inequality Growing in Massachusetts," Brink (January 12, 2018), https://www.bu.edu/articles /2018/air-pollution-inequality-growing-in-massachusetts/.

115. Sophie H. Goldman, "Harvard's Endowment Gains Are Not Something to Celebrate," *Harvard Crimson* (October 25, 2021), https://www.thecrimson.com /article/2021/10/25/goldman-harvard-endowment.

116. "Lakes and Rivers," Federal Council, https://www.eda.admin.ch/abouts witzerland/en/home/umwelt/geografie/seen-und-fluesse.html.

117. "Switzerland: Life Expectancy," World Health Rankings, https://www .worldlifeexpectancy.com/switzerland-life-expectancy; Environmental Perfor- mance Index, https://epi.yale.edu/epi-results/2020/component/epi; https://www .usnews.com/news/best-countries/rankings/social-purpose; America's Health Rankings, "2020 Annual Report: International Comparison," https://www .americashealthrankings.org/learn/reports/2020-annual-report/international -comparison; https://www.commonwealthfund.org/publications/issue-briefs /2020/jan/us-health-care-global-perspective-2019; "Switzerland—Gross Domestic Product per Capita in Current Prices," https://knoema.com/atlas/Switzerland /GDP-per-capita; based on US net worth of $137 trillion or 6.5x GDP, assuming New Hampshire net worth per capita is at US average. See Jeff Cox, "Household Net Worth Climbs to $136.9 trillion, Thanks to Big Stock Market Gains," CNBC (June 10, 2021), https://www.cnbc.com/2021/06/10/household-net-worth-climbs-to -136point9-trillion-thanks-to-big-stock-market-gains.html.

118. "New Hampshire State-Wide Analysis," Urban 3 (October 2020), https:// www.nhhfa.org/wp-content/uploads/2020/10/NH-Urban3-Report-10.2020.pdf.

119. Todd Litman, "Understanding Smart Growth Savings Evaluating Economic Savings and Benefits of Compact Development," Victoria Transport Policy Institute (March 3, 2022), https://www.vtpi.org/sg_save.pdf.

120. Jaison Abel, Ishita Dey, and Todd M. Gabe, "Productivity and the Density of Human Capital," Federal Reserve Bank of New York Staff Reports, Staff Report no. 440 (March 2010), 5–6, https://www.newyorkfed.org/medialibrary/media /research/staff_reports/sr440.pdf.

121. Duncan Lamont, "What 175 Years of Data Tell Us about House Price Afford- ability in the UK," Schroders (March 15, 2021), https://www.schroders.com/en /insights/economics/what-174-years-of-data-tell-us-about-house-price-affordability -in-the-uk/; Meghann Murdock, "London House Prices vs Salaries: How Affordabil- ity Has Changed since the Stamp Duty Holiday Began," *Evening Standard* (July 21, 2021), https://www.standard.co.uk/homesandproperty/property-news/london -house-prices-average-salaries-affordability-stamp-duty-holiday-b946785.html.

122. This would represent seven times the growth experienced in 2020. See Matthew J. Moury, "People Move to N.H. in Pandemic," *Concord Monitor* (March 29,

2021), https://www.concordmonitor.com/Pandemic-has-people-moving-to-New -Hampshire-39697738.

123. US net worth is $130 trillion and GDP is $21 trillion in 2020, implying a ratio of 6.2x. See "U.S. Households' Net Worth Hit $130 Trillion in 2020, and Two More Numbers to Know," *Barron's* (March 12, 2021), https://www.barrons.com/articles/u-s -households-net-worth-hit-130-trillion-in-2020-51615543202; "Gross Domestic Product, 4th Quarter and Year 2020 (Advance Estimate)," BEA, https://www.bea.gov /news/2021/gross-domestic-product-4th-quarter-and-year-2020-advance-estimate.

124. "Manchester Transit Oriented Development (TOD)," Southern New Hampshire Planning Commission, https://www.snhpc.org/transportation /multimodal/pages/manchester-transit-oriented-development-tod.

125. Lincoln Leong, "The 'Rail Plus Property' Model: Hong Kong's Successful Self-Financing Model," McKinsey and Company (June 2 2016), https://www .mckinsey.com/business-functions/operations/our-insights/the-rail-plus -property-model.

126. "Ticket to Ride: What's It Like to Commute to Boston on the Downeaster," *Ink Link*, https://manchesterinklink.com/ticket-to-ride-whats-it-like-to-commute -to-boston-on-the-downeaster/; "New Hampshire Railroad Map," New Hampshire Railroad Revitalization Association, http://www.nhrra.org/resources/map.htm; "Aeronautics, Rail and Transit," New Hampshire Department of Transportation, https://www.nh.gov/dot/org/aerorailtransit/railandtransit/rail.htm.

127. "VMT per Capita," Eno Center for Transportation (Eno) https://www .enotrans.org/wp-content/uploads/2019/06/VMT-per-capita-by-state-1981-2017-1 .pdf; "Transportation," International Comparisons, https://internationalcompari sons.org/environmental/transportation/.

Chapter 4. What Is to Be Done?

1. "Community Profile: Laramie, WY," Mainstreet America, 1–2, https:// higherlogicdownload.s3.amazonaws.com/NMSC/390e0055-2395-4d3b-af60 -81b53974430d/UploadedImages/Succcess_Stories/Laramie_profile.pdf.

2. "The Charitable Sector," Independent Sector, https://independentsector.org /about/the-charitable-sector.

3. Pete Davis, *Dedicated: The Case for Commitment in an Age of Infinite Browsing* (New York: Avid Reader Press/Simon and Schuster, 2021).

4. Cary Funk and Brian Kennedy, "For Earth Day 2020, How Americans See Climate Change and the Environment in 7 Charts," Pew Research Center (April 21, 2020), https://www.pewresearch.org/fact-tank/2020/04/21/how-americans-see -climate-change-and-the-environment-in-7-charts/.

5. Susan Gallagher, "What Can Hunter-Gatherers Teach Us about Staying Healthy," Global Health Institute, Duke University (April 21, 2019), https:// globalhealth.duke.edu/news/what-can-hunter-gatherers-teach-us-about-staying -healthy.

6. Paul Ronto, "Hiking in the US Has Never Been More Popular [Study]," RunRepeat (August 6, 2021), https://runrepeat.com/hiking-never-more-popular.

7. Lauren Thomas, "25% of US Malls Are Expected to Shut within 5 Years. Giving Them a New Life Won't Be Easy," CNBC (August 27, 2020), https://www.cnbc.com/2020/08/27/25percent-of-us-malls-are-set-to-shut-within-5-years-what-comes-next.html.

8. "Case Studies on Repurposing Vacant Retail Malls," National Association of Realtors (May 2020), https://www.nar.realtor/sites/default/files/documents/2020-case-studies-on-repurposing-vacant-retail-malls-05-08-2020.pdf.

9. Riley Sullivan, "Aging and Declining Populations in Northern New England: Is There a Role for Immigration," Federal Reserve Bank of Boston (2019), https://www.bostonfed.org/publications/new-england-public-policy-center-regional-briefs/2019/aging-and-declining-populations-in-northern-new-england.aspx.

10. "Rural America Has Been Slammed by Population Loss. In the Midwest, Small Towns Aren't Giving Up," *Quad-City Times* (September 28, 2019), https://qctimes.com/news/rural-america-has-been-slammed-by-population-loss-in-the-midwest-small-towns-aren-t/article_aba20037-9cad-5dab-bb63-59e82192b273.html.

11. "Middle America: Planning for Declining Mid-Western Cities," Smart Cities Dive, https://www.smartcitiesdive.com/ex/sustainablecitiescollective/outlook-middle-america-planning-declining-cities-midwest/133581/.

12. "Build Your Strong Town," *Strong Towns*, https://www.strongtowns.org/.

13. "Project Database," Congress for the New Urbanism, https://www.cnu.org/resources/project-database.

14. "Green Communities," American Planning Association, https://www.planning.org/nationalcenters/green/.

15. *Guide to Urban Planning Graduate Programs*, 6th ed., Planetizen, https://www.planetizen.com/topschools.

16. *Building Community Resilience with Nature-Based Solutions*, Federal Emergency Management Agency (June 2021), https://www.fema.gov/sites/default/files/documents/fema_riskmap-nature-based-solutions-guide_2021.pdf; "Greening America's Communities," Environmental Protection Agency (2020), https://www.epa.gov/smartgrowth/greening-americas-communities.

17. "The Best Green Colleges," *Best College Reviews* (October 22, 2021), https://www.bestcollegereviews.org/top/green-colleges/; Jessica King, "10 Colleges That Went Green before It Was Cool," Collegexpress (February 5, 2021), https://www.collegexpress.com/articles-and-advice/campus-visits/articles/evaluate-your-visit/green-campus-revolution/.

18. "Case Studies in Small Town Development," University of North Carolina School of Government, https://www.sog.unc.edu/resources/microsites/case-studies-small-town-development.

19. Ross DeVol and Jonas Crews, "Most Dynamic Micropolitans," Walton Family Foundation (February 19, 2019), https://www.waltonfamilyfoundation.org/learning/most-dynamic-micropolitans.

20. "Main Street Success Stories."

21. Enterprise Community Partners, https://www.enterprisecommunity.org/about.

22. Eileen Heisman, "The 2021 DAF Report," National Philanthropic Trust (2021), https://www.nptrust.org/reports/daf-report/; Michael Hartmann, "How Much Money Is in Non-Profit Endowments in America," *Philanthropy Daily* (July 27, 2020), https://www.philanthropydaily.com/how-much-money-is-in-nonprofit-endowments-in-america/.

23. Deborah Fallows and James Fallows, "Our Towns: A Journey into the Heart of America," *Atlantic*, https://www.theatlantic.com/our-towns/.

24. "Partners," National Alliance for Public Charter Schools, https://www.publiccharters.org/our-work/what-we-stand-for/partners; "Public Charter Startup Grants," Walton Family Foundation, https://www.waltonfamilyfoundation.org/grants/public-charter-startup-grants; "NH Gets Federal Grant to Open 27 New Charter Schools & Rebuild Authorization Process," *Reaching Higher New Hampshire* (September 6, 2019), https://reachinghighernh.org/2019/09/06/nh-gets-federal-grant-to-open-27-new-charter-schools-rebuild-authorization-process/.

25. Corey A. DeAngelis, Patrick J. Wolf, Larry D. Maloney, and Jay F. May, *Charter School Funding: Inequity Surges in the Cities*, School Choice Demonstration Project, Department of Education Reform, University of Arkansas (November 2020), https://files.eric.ed.gov/fulltext/ED612068.pdf; Sarah R. Cohodes and Katharine S. Parham, "Charter Schools' Effectiveness, Mechanisms, and Competitive Influence," National Bureau of Economic Research working paper (May 2021), https://www.nber.org/system/files/working_papers/w28477/w28477.pdf; State University of New York, Charter Schools Institute, https://www.newyorkcharters.org/.

26. Robert Berdahl and Terrence J. MacTaggart, "Charter Colleges: Balancing Freedom and Accountability," Pioneer Institute (January 1, 2000), https://pioneerinstitute.org/education/charter-colleges-balancing-freedom-and-accountability/.

27. "The Resilience of Manufacturing," Workforce Institute (May 2021), https://workforceinstitute.org/wp-content/uploads/2021/05/The-Resilience-of-Manufacturing.pdf.

28. Oleg Bestsennyy, "Telehealth: A Quarter-Trillion-Dollar Post-COVID-19 Reality?," McKinsey and Company (July 9, 2021), https://www.mckinsey.com/industries/healthcare-systems-and-services/our-insights/telehealth-a-quarter-trillion-dollar-post-covid-19-reality.

29. "Higher Ed Pulse Report: Future-proofing Institutions against the Demographic Cliff," Othot (2021), https://www.othot.com/2021-futureproof-institution-against-demographic-cliff-report.

30. Stephen Lehmkuhle, *Campus with Purpose: Building a Mission-Driven Campus* (New Brunswick, NJ: Rutgers University Press, 2020).

31. James Manyika et al., "Building a More Competitive US Manufacturing Sector," McKinsey and Company (April 15, 2021), https://www.mckinsey.com/us/our-insights/building-a-more-competitive-us-manufacturing-sector.

32. "US Manufacturing Skills Gap Could Leave as Many as 2.1 Million Jobs Unfilled by 2030, Deloitte and the Manufacturing Institute Study Finds," Deloitte/Manufacturing Institute (March 30, 2022), https://www2.deloitte.com/us

/en/pages/about-deloitte/articles/press-releases/deloitte-manufacturing-skills
-gap.html.

33. Industry 4.0, or the Fourth Industrial Revolution, refers to rapid change in technology, industry, and societal patterns.

34. "Donors Bet on Multifaceted Solutions to the World's Great Challenges," Fidelity Charitable (2020), https://www.fidelitycharitable.org/insights/2021 -future-of-philanthropy/worlds-greatest-challenges.html.

35. "Financial Capital's Versatility in Philanthropy," Milken Institute (September 23, 2020), https://milkeninstitute.org/article/financial-capitals-versatility -philanthropy.

36. "2020 Report on Sustainable and Impact Investing Trends," US/SIF (2020), https://www.ussif.org/files/Trends/2020_Trends_Highlights_OnePager.pdf.

37. "What Is a Community Foundation?," Fidelity Charitable, https://www .fidelitycharitable.org/guidance/philanthropy/community-foundations.html.

38. Tracy Abedon Filosa, Nita Patel, and Michael Pearce, "Community Foundations: The Power of Aggregated Capital," Cambridge Associates (November 2019), fhttps://www.cambridgeassociates.com/insight/community-foundations-the -power-of-aggregated-capital/.

39. Chris Nebenzahl and Paul Fiorilla, "The Growing Divergence between Gateway and Secondary Markets for Multifamily Performance," Real Assets Adviser (January 1, 2021), https://irei.com/publications/article/growing -divergence-gateway-secondary-markets-multifamily-performance/.

40. "Hi, Remote Workers! We'll Pay You to Work from Tulsa. You're Going to Love It Here," Tulsa Remote, https://tulsaremote.com/.

41. "Tulsa Remote Offers $10,000 for Buying a Home," Tulsa Remote, https:// tulsaremote.com/homeownership/.

42. "40 Facts about Habitat and Housing," Habitat for Humanity, https://www .habitat.org/stories/40-facts-about-habitat-humanity-and-housing; "Building Thriving Communities," Corporation for Supportive Housing, https://www.csh .org/; "Building a Future without Homelessness," HomeAid, https://www.homeaid .org/impact; "Who We Are," Keep America Beautiful, https://kab.org/about/; Madison Troyer, "Charities Working to Strengthen Homes and Communities across America," Stacker (October 15, 2019), https://stacker.com/stories/3587 /charities-working-strengthen-homes-and-communities-across-america.

43. "2021 NACUBO-TIAA Study of Endowments," Nacubo, https://www.nacubo .org/research/2021/nacubo-tiaa-study-of-endowments.

44. "Public NTSE Tables," Nacubo, https://www.nacubo.org/research/2021 /public-ntse-tables.

45. "Financial Overview," Harvard University, https://finance.harvard.edu/files /fad/files/fy20_financial_overview.pdf.

46. "Public NTSE Tables," Nacubo, https://www.nacubo.org/research/2021 /public-ntse-tables.

47. "Maine Economic Improvement Fund," University of Maine, https://umaine .edu/meif/.

48. "Research Center," *Commonfund*, https://www.commonfund.org/research -center.

49. A. Adam Schor, "Return for Good: A Model for Impact Investing for Endowments," Metropolitan Universities 31(1) (2020): 24-43, https://files.eric.ed .gov/fulltext/EJ1251626.pdf.

50. Jed Emerson, *The Purpose of Capital: Elements of Impact, Financial Flows, and Natural Being* (San Francisco: Blended Value Group, 2018).

51. "Commonfund Study of Responsible Investing," Council on Foundations (2016), https://www.cof.org/content/2016-council-foundations-commonfund -study-responsible-investing.

52. "Commonfund Survey Finds Nonprofit Investors Cautious, but Confident," *Commonfund*, https://www.commonfund.org/research-center/press-releases /commonfund-forum-2021-survey.

53. *Global Sustainable Investment Review 2020*, Global Sustainable Investment Alliance (2021), http://www.gsi-alliance.org/wp-content/uploads/2021/08/GSIR -20201.pdf.

54. "Larry Fink's 2022 Letter to CEOs: The Power of Capitalism," BlackRock, https://www.blackrock.com/corporate/investor-relations/larry-fink-ceo-letter.

55. Attracta Mooney, "Greenwashing in Finance: Europe's Push to Police ESG Investing," *Financial Times* (March 10, 2021), https://www.ft.com/content/74888921 -368d-42e1-91cd-c3c8ce64a05e.

56. Schor, "Return for Good," 37.

57. Niccolò Pisani, "How COVID-19 Will Change the Geography of Competition," *Sloan Management Review* (May 13, 2021). https://sloanreview.mit.edu/article/how -covid-19-will-change-the-geography-of-competition/.

58. Laura Meader, "Colby's Dare Northward Campaign Hits the $500-Million Mark on the Way to $750 Million," *Colby News* (November 21, 2019), https://www .colby.edu/news/2019/11/21/colbys-dare-northward-campaign-hits-the-500 -million-mark-on-the-way-to-750-million/.

59. Dwight R. Lee, "Thank You, Internal-Combustion Engine, for Cleaning Up the Environment," Foundation for Economic Education (October 1, 2007), https:// fee.org/articles/thank-you-internal-combustion-engine-for-cleaning-up-the -environment/.

60. "Digital Twin Market Size, Share & Trends Analysis Report by End Use (Manufacturing, Agriculture), by Solution (Component, Process, System), by Region (North America, APAC), and Segment Forecasts, 2022–2030," Grand View Research (April 20, 2021), https://www.grandviewresearch.com/industry-analysis /digital-twin-market.

Conclusion: History Does Not Repeat but It Does Rhyme

1. "Alma College," Alma College—Ohio History Central (accessed September 19, 2021), https://ohiohistorycentral.org/w/Alma_College.

2. See Jonathan Zimmerman, *Small Wonder: The Little Red Schoolhouse in History and Memory* (New Haven, CT: Yale University Press, 2009).

3. See Robert Zemsky, Susan Shaman, and Susan Campbell Baldridge, *The College Stress Test: Tracking Institutional Futures across a Crowded Market* (Baltimore: Johns Hopkins University Press, 2020).

4. Andrew McAfee, *More from Less: The Surprising Story of How We Learned to Prosper Using Fewer Resources—and What Happens* (New York: Scribner, 2019).

INDEX

academic leaders, 177-81

accreditation processes, 43, 147-49, 152-53

adaptability: in local initiatives, 19, 50, 52-53, 122, 155, 175; in placemaking, 119; of talent magnets, 13-14

agriculture: aquifer exhaustion and salt-water farming, 130; cloud tools in, 7; corn belt, 133-37; innovation clusters for, 105; regenerative agriculture versus, 19; reimagining Defiance College, 136-39; reimagining Green Mountain College, 132; rewilding and, 57-59

Amazon, 34-35, 56, 103, 154

American Prairie Reserve, 60

anchor institutions, 94, 110, 120-21

Arizona State University, 103

artificial intelligence (AI), 16, 38, 100-102, 144

arts and humanities, 6, 87-88, 165-66, 183, 184

Ascend West Virginia, 6

Baldwin, Davarian L., 120

Barcelona, Spain, 27, 29, 67

Bayh-Dole Act (1980), 105

Becker, Gary, 92

beer industry, 8, 147, 224n91

Benson, Sophie, 95, 96

Berdahl, Robert, 176

Berklee College of Music, 153

Berlin, New Hampshire, 69

Bezos, Jeff, 34-35

Bhakta, Raj and Danhee, 132

biking and bike infrastructure: art of placemaking and, 68; clean-air/slow-streets model for, 26-29; 15-minute city and, 90; gentle density and, 21; in green growth strategies, 20, 46, 63-64; growing downtown cores, 161, 208n18; health and

economic impacts of, 27-28; knowledge enterprises and, 90, 143; purposeful living and, 24; in town-gown regeneration, 137; transit-oriented development and, 161-62

Binghamton University and Binghamton, New York, 140-42

biochar carbon capture process, 44, 45, 210n55

bionic workers, 38-41, 80, 100-102, 128, 150

Black Mountain College, 130-31

Bolzle, Aaron, 36-37

Boston, Massachusetts, 56, 155-57, 185, 192

Boulder, Colorado, 20, 47, 60

broadband access. *See* information technology infrastructure

Brookings Institute, 94, 143, 156

Brown, Gabe, 58

Buffett, Warren, 10

business leaders, 177, 181-84. *See also* corporations

Cantor, Nancy, 94, 95

Capgemini, 39

car travel and infrastructure: clean-air/slow-streets model versus, 26-29; communities disrupted by, 30, 40; density and, 159-60; Detroit's decline and, 51-52; failures of, 49, 56-57, 201; mall repurposing and, 170; in modern society model, 25-26; motor society and, 18-19; placemaking versus, 66-68, 71-72; service models for, 60; transit-oriented development and, 161-62

Cellucci, Paul, 176

C40 (climate change group), 27, 68, 208n18

Chambliss, Daniel F., 98

Charlotte 2040 Plan, 171-72

charter schools, 44, 175-76

Christensen, Clayton, 135
cities and towns, 197; businesses downsizing in, 8; calculating number of "places" among, 123–25, 129, 218n5; clustering in, 10; college formation and, 145–51; marketing purpose of, 41; migration to, 5–7, 20; overcrowding and densification, 13–14; purposeful living as recruitment tool for, 33–34; real estate value in, 12–13; US demographics, 11–12, 123–25, 129, 203n3, 218n5. *See also* town-gown relations; *specific places*
citizen-based groups and civic organizations, 30–33, 36, 164–68, 197
clean-air/slow-streets model, 26–29, 71, 89–92, 137
climate change. *See* environment and environmentalism
cloud access and cloud-based economies. *See* information technology infrastructure; knowledge economy
Colby College, 77, 140–41, 144–45, 187, 188, 193–94
Colgate University, 76–77
colleges and universities, 196; business leaders and, 182–83; charter school movement and, 176; as civic organizations, 31, 120–21, 199; closure risks to, 178–79, 199; connection to place, 9–10; expanding demographic reach of, 81–82, 104, 179, 181; formation of, 145–51, 198–99; in innovation clusters, 50, 107–8; investment multiplier of, 146; knowledge enterprises compared to, 75, 79, 82, 119, 179; local reinvention through strength of, 139–45; of New England, 155–57; as relocation factor, 7–8; rewilding culture of, 111–13; service/utility model for, 82, 121, 177, 200; as talent magnets, 78–82, 139–45; as third places, 93–97. *See also* endowment funds; knowledge enterprises; microcolleges
commercial sector, 50–56, 76–78, 109–11, 170
communities and community-led growth: entrepreneurship and, 47–49; knowledge enterprises and, 80, 81, 92–97, 173; land trusts and cooperatives, 143; in place-based regeneration, 30–33, 173; senior living and, 64; service-learning

programs and, 88–89; in settlement archetype, 123–27, 129; town officials and, 173; university entrepreneurialism in, 76
Community Sabbatical Research Leave Program (UT Austin), 89
Congress for the New Urbanism, 66, 171
corn belt, 133–37
corporations, 197; business leaders in, 181–84; faculty entrepreneurship and, 109–10; innovation clusters and, 105; microcollege formation and, 148; in settlement archetype, 125; in strong college archetype, 142; town partnerships with, 175, 178; upskilling and, 103
Coursera, 41, 42
COVID-19 pandemic, 3–4; accelerated digital adoption during, 17, 38, 177; community-led growth and, 30, 31; decentralization and, 200; disrupting big-city concentration, 145; entrepreneurship during, 144; health inequality and, 73; New Hampshire and, 69; open streets initiatives during, 27; schooling during, 43, 127; social capital development and, 93; Zoom towns and, 5–7
coworking, comingling, and coliving spaces, 114–16, 180, 217n80
creative incubators and milieus, 84–85, 107–8, 131, 150, 174. *See also* innovation clusters and districts
Crow, Michael M., 3, 79
cultural programming, 80, 102–3

Dabars, William B., 3, 79
Daktronics, 109
data collection and data skills, 66, 68, 71
Davis, Pete, 168
decentralization: of academic institutions, 1, 117–19; of core services, 68; COVID-19 pandemic and, 200; of endowment funds, 192–93; of knowledge economy, 83, 214n10; of philanthropy, 186–87; of tech sector, 144; of work, 12–13
Deep Springs College, 91, 129–30
Defiance College and Defiance, Ohio, 135–39, 172
Deloitte, 134, 136, 182
density: balanced growth strategies for, 20–21, 25, 40, 47; environmental

sustainability and, 13–14, 159–60; gentle, 20, 28, 40, 67–68, 71, 125; in Midwest, 134–35; retail strategies for, 40

Detroit, Michigan, 51

digital tools. *See* artificial intelligence; bionic workers; remote work

digital twin models, 21, 183, 195

diversity, 35, 53, 63, 90, 126, 127, 166, 169

Downton, Paul, 91–92

Duany, Andrés, 90

Eastport, South Carolina, 52

ecological intentional communities (EICs), 170–72

ecotourism, 57, 177, 178

education: artificial intelligence and, 101–2; global, 154–55; as industrial undertaking, 117; purpose in, 87–89; reorienting to knowledge economy, 82–86; rewilding, 111–13; in settlement archetype, 127. *See also* colleges and universities; knowledge enterprises

Edwards, David, 108–9

EdX, 7–8, 41

endowment funds: colleges regenerating regions through, 139–42; community-oriented investment of, 157, 188, 190–97; historical patterns of, 187–88; knowledge enterprises and, 110; of philanthropies, 174, 185, 186–87; sustainability and, 188–90

enrollment management, 80, 97

environmental, social, and governance (ESG) principles, 185, 188–90

environment and environmentalism: balanced growth strategies for, 17, 20, 56–60, 158–59; in Boston, 156; of colleges and universities, 111–13; decentralization and, 201–2; degradation in, 13–14, 56–57; density and, 159–60; endowment funds and, 188–90; in innovation clusters, 47–49; intentional communities organizing around, 168–72; left and right interests combined in, 69; Midwest corn belt and water systems, 133–37; place-making and, 69–70; in reimagination archetype, 129–31; saline lakes and aquifers, 129–30; Swiss approach to, 128

European versus US universities, 9–10

faculty: commercializing work of, 109; entrepreneurship and, 80, 109–10; innovation clusters and, 105–9; recruiting and retention roles of, 98–100; rewilding and, 113; social capital development and, 93; wages, 148, 150

Fallows, James and Deborah, 52, 174

Farrell, James J., 111, 113

Feld, Brad, 47, 49

15-minute city or campus: academic leaders and, 179–80; Boston's potential to become, 156; business leaders and, 183; Charlotte 2040 Plan and, 171–72; features of, 90; for knowledge enterprises, 80–81, 90–92, 117; in placemaking, 68, 71, 81; Pottery Thinkbelt and, 117; rewilding and, 59

Fink, Larry, 190

Fleming, Ray, 96

Florida, Richard, 78

Forum for the Future, 134, 136

Foundation for Intentional Community, 123

fourth places, 114–15, 119, 137, 167, 179, 184

Franklin College, 198–99

Fraunhofer Institute, 183

gentle density, 20, 28, 40, 67–68, 71, 125

gentrification, 37–38, 56, 71

George Kaiser Foundation, 186

Gilbert, Dan, 52

Gilchrist, Ian, 49

Gompers, Paul, 53

Google, 43

Gratton, Lynda, 42

Great Lakes, 134–36

Greene, David A., 140, 193–94

green growth strategies. *See* environment and environmentalism

Green Mountain College, 132

Greenville, South Carolina, 52

Gyourko, Joseph, 61

HackerHouse startup, 114

Harvard University, 9, 23, 131, 151–53, 157, 187–88, 224n93

health and fitness: agriculture and, 58; clean-air / slow-streets model for, 26, 27, 125–26; community-led growth and, 32–33; purposeful living and, 87;